Solidarity of Strangers

Solidarity of Strangers

Feminism after Identity Politics

Jodi Dean

UNIVERSITY OF CALIFORNIA PRESS

Berkeley / Los Angeles / London

University of California Press
Berkeley and Los Angeles, California

University of California Press, Ltd.
London, England

© 1996 by
The Regents of the University of California

Library of Congress Cataloging-in-Publication Data

Dean, Jodi, 1962–
    Solidarity of strangers : feminism after identity politics / Jodi
Dean.
        p.   cm.
    Includes bibliographical references and index.
    ISBN 0-520-20230-9. — ISBN 0-520-20231-7 (pbk.)
    1. Feminism.   2. Feminist theory.   3. Identity (Psychology)
4. Community.   I. Title.
HQ1206.D357   1996
305.42 — dc20   95-13906
                                                                    CIP

Printed in the United States of America
9 8 7 6 5 4 3 2 1

In memory of my mother, Bette Jo Runnels Dean

Contents

Acknowledgments

The solidarity of many people supported me as I wrote this book. I am especially grateful to the following for their encouragement, their willingness to read draft after draft of various chapters, and their cheerfully relentless and reflective critiques: Mikael Carleheden, Jean Cohen, Carolin Emke, Karen Engle, Maureen Flynn, Rainer Forst, Raymond Geuss, Klaus Günther, Jürgen Habermas, Andrea Maihofer, Kate Mehuron, Frank Michelman, Herta Nagl-Docekal, Fran Olsen, Lee Quinby, and Lutz Wingert. I also wish to thank the participants in the Prague meetings of the Philosophy and Social Science course (May 1993 and April 1994), those in the working group on civil society at the Institut für Sozialforschung in Frankfurt, the members of the colloquia of Jürgen Habermas (winter 1992 and winter 1993) and Herta Nagl-Docekal (summer 1992), and my colleagues at Hobart and William Smith in the Not-Piss-Poor-Academy for their thoughtful comments on the early papers that became the basis for this book.

My editor, Will Murphy, showed infinite patience and provided great advice. My parents, David and BJ Dean, my sister, Dahn Dean, and my brother, David Dean, kept me going with their good-natured teasing and boundless love and enthusiasm. Finally, I want to thank my partner, Shane Kenyon, for coming with me to the cold of Geneva and keeping us warm.

Early drafts of several chapters have been previously published and appear here with permission. "Reflective Solidarity" appeared in *Constel-*

lations 2, no. 1 (April 1995). "Including Women: The Consequences and Side Effects of Feminist Critiques of Civil Society" appeared in *Philosophy and Social Criticism* 18, nos. 3/4 (1992). "Solidarity and Legal Indeterminancy" appeared as "From Sphere to Boundary: Sexual Harassment, Identity, and the Shift in Privacy" in *Yale Journal of Law and Feminism* 6, no. 2 (October 1994).

Introduction

The "We" of Identity Politics

Just as the eighties had been the "me" decade, early on it seemed as if the nineties were going to be the "we" decade. As it turned out, no one really knew who "we" were. At home, lesbians and gay men struggled to decide if "we queers" included bisexuals and the transgendered. Feminists worried that any notion of "we women" would end up essentialist, excluding lesbians, women of color, or the differently abled. The myriad groups classified as "Hispanic" grappled with the problem of finding any inclusionary identity category. Was the proper term "Latino," some compound form of American like "Puerto-Rican-American," or something more specific altogether, like "Chicano"? Situated at the borders and intersections of the "we," people with multiple identifications experimented with notions like "world-traveling," "hybridity," and "the new mestiza."[1] Academics fought over the terms "postmodern" and "poststructuralist," reluctant to claim an identity predefined by an opposing camp.[2] Even the Right and Left labels, which had apparently solidified during the Reagan era, were not immune. Republicans, despite their ability to capitalize on widespread public disillusionment with Clinton in the November 1994 elections, self-destructed in an effort to establish a core of family values, the espousal of which would separate "us"—the solid, untainted core of conservative Republicans—from "them"—the less-than-faithful whose alleged moderateness might conceal a latent "liberalism." Likewise distancing themselves from Jesse Jackson and much of the Rainbow Coalition important to Democrats in the seventies and eighties, the new voices of Clinton Democrats took up the themes of community and religion previously associated with conservatism.

Abroad, tribalism and nationalism came to the fore. As many of the boundaries constructed in the aftermath of World War II collapsed, migrations and immigrations resulted in confusing and exclusionary (re)assertions of identity. The phrase "we Germans" evoked the horrors of National Socialism. Serbs and Croats, and later Bosnian-Serbs and Bosnian-Muslims, rejected the idea of "we Yugoslavians" in favor of a pure identity that, for some, could only come from "ethnic cleansing." Finally, the dream of a European Community began to fray as the dissolution of internal borders seemed to come at the cost of strengthening external borders and ignoring the legacy of colonialism. For what would be the status of the guest workers, foreign nationals, and political and economic refugees in this new community? At the outset, then, the shift to the "we decade" floundered in the wake of the risks any articulation of identity seemed to entail.

Returning home, back to the more manageable microlevel of everyday life, I recently told my sister Dahn about the complicated identity politics dividing the lesbian/gay/bisexual student organization I sponsored at a Texas university. I described the debate over whether to include bisexuals in the group's name and constitution. I asked her how to handle the problem of racism—many Chicanas felt that their particular experiences were overlooked in such an Anglo setting and were considering breaking off to form their own group. Although sympathetic, Dahn was somewhat bored. "Labels are so eighties," she said. "We at Yale have moved beyond labels. We think people should just be people."

Dahn's response troubled me. The people-are-people line seemed defeatist in situations of continued exclusion and oppression. In fact, it reminded me of the response of one of the Anglo lesbians in my student group when she lost office to a Chicana. Deaf to the desire of many members to increase Chicano visibility and insure diversity, she argued that "race consciousness" was the term guilt-ridden white liberals used to mask their racism. In her view, the only proper response to "equal merit" was to flip a coin.

Such a laissez-faire approach to discrimination repeats the prevailing mentality of the "me" decade. While it may attempt to drape itself in a politically correct rejection of labels, the laissez-faire attitude nonetheless views social progress and change through the individualist lens of competitive self-assertion. Further, in so doing it fails to acknowledge the sense of community and responsibility underlying the hope for a "we." In place of solidarity, it offers only the possibility of the contingent integration of egocentric interests always on the verge of disruption.

Upon further reflection, I realized that my sister's response did not point in this direction, for at the very site of her rejection of labels she articulated an identity — "we at Yale." Clearly, identifying as a "Yalie" has its limits as a political option. But this is not the real insight contained in Dahn's remarks. She was saying that it's time to stop talking about ourselves and start thinking about and acting with others. Her simultaneous rejection of identity and assertion of community thus suggests the possibility of a "we" without labels, a way of conceiving social change through a politics that is neither the assertion and reassertion of identity nor the individualist resort to (un)free competition.

This book offers a way to conceive of a "we" without labels. Positioning reflective solidarity as the bridge between identity and universality, as the precondition of mutual recognition necessary for claims to universality under pluralist, postmodern conditions, it argues that a communicative understanding of "we" enables us to think of difference differently, to overcome the competing dualisms of us/them, male/female, white/black, straight/gay, public/private, general/particular. Further, it claims that the key to this overcoming can be found in the margins and spaces that mark the limits of our concepts, the boundaries of our discourses.

I define reflective solidarity as the mutual expectation of a responsible orientation to relationship. This conception of solidarity relies on the intuition that the risk of disagreement which accompanies diversity must be rationally transformed to provide a basis for our intersubjective ties and commitments. This means that the expression "we" must be interpreted not as given, but as "in process," as the discursive achievement of individuated "I's." Such an opening up of the notion of "we" makes possible a change in our attitude toward boundaries, a change which requires that each individual view group expectations from the perspective of a situated, hypothetical third.

Simply put, solidarity can be modeled as an interaction involving at least three persons: I ask you to stand by me over and against a third. But rather than presuming the exclusion and opposition of the third, the ideal of reflective solidarity thematizes the voice of the third to reconstruct solidarity as an inclusionary ideal for contemporary politics and societies. On the one hand, the third is always situated and particular, signifying the other who is excluded and marking the space of identity. On the other, including the third, seeing from her perspective, remains the precondition for any claim to universality and any appeal to solidarity. Conjoined with a discursively achieved "we," the perspective of a situated, hypothetical third articulates an ideal of solidarity attuned both to the vulnerability of contingent identities and to the universalist claims of democratic societies.

We can find a nascent conception of reflective solidarity at the interstices of the identity politics debate. Generally speaking, identity politics in the United States emerged over the past few decades in the struggle for rights. Frustrated with the failure of "equal" rights to secure equality amid the pervasive hierarchies of sex and race, racial and sexual minorities struggled for recognition by appealing to their identities. Although this appeal had the perverse effect of enabling the Right to score rhetorical points by coining the phrase "special rights," it nonetheless provided a focal point for collective action. Through affirmative action and juridical categories such as "suspect class," excluded and minority groups endeavored to gain access to the universal by articulating their particularity as groups with a history of discrimination.

This appeal to identity revealed the biases within the fiction of the subject of law. If claiming their status as legal subjects meant that women had to deny their femininity — that is, their biological potential for motherhood, or their position in the home as child rearer — then the legal subject itself was not universal, but particular — particularly masculine.[3] Similar experiences on the part of racial, ethnic, sexual, and disabled minorities exposed the legal subject as white, English-speaking, heterosexual, and able-bodied.[4]

In the course of articulating their differences, many members of minority groups felt empowered, taking pride in a self-identification denigrated in the larger society.[5] Submerged histories and traditions were uncovered that provided minority groups with a sense of self-in-community they had previously lacked and upon which they could now draw as a source of self-respect. As Todd Gitlin writes: "Identity politics is a form of self-understanding, an orientation toward the world, and a structure of feeling that is frequent in developed industrial societies. Identity politics presents itself as — and many young people experience it as — the most compelling remedy for anonymity in an impersonal world. This cluster of feelings seems to answer the questions, Who am I? Who is like me? Whom can I trust? Where do I belong?"[6] For many, finding answers to these questions within the comfort of a shared identity gave them reason to question the goals of their particular groups. If securing recognition as citizens required assimilation into the dominant culture, perhaps this goal should be abandoned in favor of the enhancement and celebration of their difference.[7] In place of the abstract identity of the citizen acting in a universal public sphere, many of the heretofore excluded have thus come to champion the situated and concrete identity offered in, to use Nancy Fraser's term, subaltern counterpublics.[8]

The articulation of particular identities has also led to the rigidification of these very identities. At the legislative level, this rigidification appears as the reinforcement of minority status with its negative connotations of inferiority. We see this in the critique of affirmative action and in the debate over pregnancy leave policies that explicitly recognize gender differences. Martha Minow highlights a similar dilemma with respect to the recognition of the needs and rights of disabled children: "Identifying a child as handicapped entitles her to individualized educational planning and special services but also labels the child as handicapped and may expose her to attributions of inferiority, risks of stigma, isolation, and reduced self-esteem."[9] At the level of the group, the assumption that a particular identity dictates a particular politics overlooks internal differences, stifling diversity and dissent. Voicing his frustration with gay politics, Ed Cohen writes:

Although the assumption that "we" constitute a "natural" community because we share a sexual identity might appear to offer a stable basis for group formations, my experience suggests that it can just as often interrupt the process of creating intellectual and political projects which can gather "us" together across time and space. By predicating "our" affinity upon the assertion of a common "sexuality," we tacitly agree to leave unexplored any "internal" contradictions which undermine the coherence we desire from the imagined certainty of an unassailable commonality or of incontestable sexuality.[10]

Indeed, the rigidification of identity concepts suggests that even "citizenship" in a subaltern counterpublic is suspect, encountering problems similar to the very ones it emerged to solve. Thus, in response to this rigidification, Cohen, like many critics of identity politics, urges the importance of inventing, multiplying, and negotiating the construction of the "we."[11]

The exposure of the particularity of the universal, the sense of community and empowerment, and the rigidification of identity categories have framed the identity politics debate. Supporters appeal to the already particular character of the universal and reassert their own particularity. Detractors point out the contingency of identity categories, the histories of otherness they risk reinstating, and their failure to live up to the promise of empowerment as they suppress internal differences.

But framing the debate as an opposition between solidarity and reflection prevents us from acknowledging the ideals shared by both sides. Supporters of identity politics are united by the ideals of inclusion and community. They struggle against exclusions enacted in the name of universality. They endeavor to establish a space of belonging, a community that strengthens its members and gives them a base from which they can say to others, "I am different, recognize me." Similarly, detractors and critics of identity politics also struggle against exclusion, this time that exclusion effected by the very sign of identity. Thus, they too strive to establish a space for the self, but one which *frees* the person to say within the group, "I am different, recognize me." They want to ensure that those aspects of the self that elude the boundaries established by any identity category will not remain silenced or neglected but will be allowed to appear and develop in all their difference and particularity.

Further, what each side fears from the other is the same: the loss of this space for difference, this "home" to which the self can retreat for sustenance, intimacy, reinvigoration, and play. For example, in their argument for a radical politics that comes directly out of their own identity, the Combahee River Collective maintains: "We realize that the only people who care enough about us to work consistently for our liberation is us. Our politics evolve from a healthy love for ourselves, our sisters and our community which allows us to continue our struggle and work."[12] On the other side, Diana Fuss writes: "The personal is political reprivatizes social experience, to the degree that one can be engaged in political praxis without ever leaving the bedroom. Sexual desire itself becomes invested with macropolitical significance."[13] Like the statement from the Combahee River Collective, Fuss's remark can be read as revealing a concern with care and intimacy. Once the personal is political we are left with the politics of the personal. There is no relationship that can serve as a retreat from politics; there is no space simply to *be* in one's difference. Thus, while the supporters' appeal to community seems to conflict with the detractors' desire for freedom, both sides share a longing for recognition, for a space in which they can explore, secure, and articulate the differences necessary for concrete individual identities. This book argues that reflective solidarity provides such a space.

A number of theorists have recently begun to explore the potential of solidarity. Although some have urged a concrete and historically specific understanding of solidarity, an understanding that would focus on pre-existing group identities,[14] others have sought to expand the category to encompass principles of egalitarian difference and to express more universal ideals of accountability.[15] Since the former fails to consider the gaps and contradictions that rupture any given identity, I contend that only the latter, universalistically conceived sense of solidarity can attend to the need for recognition in pluralist, democratic societies. Kathleen Jones writes: "If gender, race, class, and sexual preference are not to be used as mere "markers to describe the race [etc.] of the respondent" nor as disciplinary devices to police the borders of identity — either by keeping some "outside" or by insisting on the faithful being inside" — then we must abandon the search for sovereignty through any of them, or even all of them in combination, and work toward solidarity."[16] Indeed, her association of solidarity with "the responsibility to act combined with the responsibility to otherness" points toward precisely that ideal of universality which I seek to render more explicit through the concept of reflective solidarity.

To be sure, many writing today as feminists or poststructuralists reject even the ideal of universality as exclusionary, coercive, and totalizing. They worry that it necessarily precludes inquiries into our differences and the multiple configurations of power constructing them. They claim that universalist approaches to politics and ethics overlook the local, contextual, and everyday dimensions of our lives and struggles. What is striking to me is the way this line of argument mirrors the fragmentation, tribalization, and balkanization present on a global scale. Just as numerous ethnicities, nationalities, and nationalists are seeking to shore up their own boundaries and retreat from larger confederations and alliances, so contemporary theorists are involved in a politicization of the local that threatens to neglect larger interconnections.

The oddity of this move is that now, more than ever, boundaries have become so fluid as to reveal our myriad interconnections. As Chandra Monhanty points out, "One of the distinctive features of contemporary societies is the internationalization of economies and labor forces."[17] Transnational corporations link labor, production, and consumption markets across the globe. Widespread migration and immigration create new types of multiethnic communities. Communication networks and the media provide opportunities for nearly instantaneous cross-cultural dialogue and exchange. Given the extent and complexity of our interconnections, we cannot remain content with a focus on the local, for how can we even know what "local" means? More to the point, given the fact of our shared relationships, we have to reconceive solidarity so as to acknowledge our shared accountability for each other.

But, of course, as the critics of identity politics remind us, this accountability cannot deny our differences. Accordingly, in the first chapter of this book I argue that reflective solidarity provides spaces for difference because it upholds the possibility of a universal, communicative "we." Traditionally, solidarity has been conceived of oppositionally, on the model of "us vs. them." But this way of conceiving solidarity overlooks the fact that the term "we" does not require an opposing "they," "we" also denotes the relationship between "you" and "me." Once the term "we" is understood communicatively, difference can be respected as necessary to solidarity. Dissent, questioning, and disagreement no longer have to be seen as tearing us apart but instead can be viewed as characteristic of the bonds holding us together.

My emphasis on the importance of questioning and dissent for reflective solidarity overlaps with those poststructuralist arguments urging openness, multiplicity, conflict, and attention to difference. Skeptical of the notion of any "necessary opposition," I reject the idea that one must choose between poststructuralism and universalism. Indeed, recent theorists have begun exploring the intersections and commonalities among philosophers and philosophical positions previously assumed to be irreconcilable.[18] Some theorists have argued that the communicative ethics of Jürgen Habermas, far from providing some sort of closed and totalizing metanarrative, highlights a commitment to diversity, plurality, and contest that in many instances allows for fruitful dialogue and cooperation with the genealogical, deconstructive, and postmodern approaches of Michel Foucault, Jacques Derrida, and Jean-François Lyotard.[19] I want to extend this dialogue by bringing in feminist voices and exploring the ways in which these voices point toward and challenge us to rethink the relationship between difference and universality.

Thus, in the second chapter I show how the debate over identity politics leads us to reflective solidarity. As the recent work of queer theorists, critical race theorists, and feminists indicates, a set of exclusions confronts identity politics and prevents it from doing justice to the concerns of the excluded and marginalized. These theorists suggest a need for recognition that extends beyond the recognition of concrete particularities to account for the ways in which they are constructed. Contained within this insight, then, is a convergence between poststructuralist and universalist approaches to difference. For as they have developed notions of multiply situated and constructed subjectivities, recent theorists have drawn our attention to the relationships on which identities always depend. My intervention in this debate makes this convergence more explicit by emphasizing the ways these relationships require reflective solidarity if we are to respect and take responsibility for others in their difference.

The third chapter continues the engagement between feminist and universalist theories, this time situating it on the terrain of civil society. Feminists have long criticized those universalist approaches that locate justice in the public sphere while relegating women, particularity, and difference to the private sphere. Taking up these criticisms, I argue for an understanding of universality that rejects this opposition, suggesting a model of civil society based on the idea of multiple, interconnecting discursive spheres. Not only does such an understanding allow us to include women in civil society, but also it provides a conception of democracy no longer focused on the state. As it conceives of a variety of types and loci of action in terms of the participatory efforts of an engaged citizenry, this more open version of democracy shows us how reflective solidarity can be institutionalized as the mutual expectations of citizens in contemporary pluralist societies.

The fourth chapter also looks at the institutionalization of reflective solidarity, focusing on the role of law in transmitting solidarity. As it does so, it suggests a further convergence between poststructuralist and universalist approaches to difference by highlighting the democratic dimensions of the indeterminacy thesis developed by Critical Legal Studies theorists. In contemporary democracies, the indeterminacy of law enables it to serve as a transmitter of reflective solidarity. Its abstraction, its inability to lead to determinate outcomes, establishes a space and framework for interpretation, questioning, and critique. When law is embodied in a constitution, it provides a space of collected meanings upon which citizens draw in their debates regarding their shared histories, practices, and concerns. To the extent that they can enter this space and draw upon these meanings, citizens assert and reassert their connections with one another. Their relationship as consociates becomes strengthened and renewed as they contest the limits of this space and the various interpretations of its meaning. By focusing on shifting the notion of privacy from that of a sphere to that of a boundary, I show how identity-based defenses of privacy fail to keep this space open and indeterminate. In effect, they attempt to overdetermine privacy, failing to acknowledge the way in which it is always an aspect of legal persons' mutual and public recognition of each other.

Finally, in the fifth chapter I turn specifically to the theoretical encounter between feminism and universalism. Although many feminists writing today have rejected the ideal of universality as blind to women's concerns, I argue that, properly conceived, the discursive universalism of Jürgen Habermas both stands up to feminist critique and incorporates feminist ideals of inclusion and accountability. If we are to take seriously the insights and goals of identity politics while nonetheless moving beyond it, we have to find a way to conceive of shared connections and responsibilities that allows for freedom and difference. A universalist approach that anchors rightness or normative validity in the communicative agreement of real, embodied persons—in the solidary relationships of those who have turned away from violence and agreed to discuss and argue—thus presents itself as a promising ideal for a contemporary approach to difference. Accordingly, in this chapter I elaborate the philosophical presuppositions of reflective solidarity, asserting the priority of solidarity over justice in discourse ethics, replacing Habermas's "neutral observer" with the situated, hypothetical third, and stressing the fallibility, contextuality, and openness of the ideal of discursive universalism. My goal is to break through the opposition between difference and universality and to present an ideal of a universalism of difference—the ideal which infuses reflective solidarity.

Returning to my Texas students, I am reminded of their heated and often ugly debates over gun control, the death penalty, abortion, and gays in the military. Despite, and perhaps because of, the intense confrontations between competing sides, these students remain bound to each other. For as they return time and again to the Constitution upon which each side rests its claims, both proponents and opponents of the issue at hand strengthen their ties to each other through their confidence in the validity of the Constitution and the principles therein. Their acceptance of the possibility of universal principles and ideals and their shared efforts to find the meanings of these ideals within their own particular life contexts enable them to avoid fragmentation and division and to effect their own precarious and reflective solidarity. Of course, since their solidarity, like all reflective solidarities, remains unstable, they often fall back into identity politics, asserting that the other's inability to agree is the result of her inability to understand, a problem rooted in the absoluteness of her difference. Yet the difficulty of reflective solidarity does not belie its value or our need for it today. On the contrary, the very effort involved in achieving a solidarity that respects difference exposes our continued failure to include the voices of those others, those hypothetical thirds, who for so long have remained unheard.

I hope that the concept of reflective solidarity developed in this book can move us out of the "we" of identity politics and toward an inclusive and ultimately universal understanding of the "we" of discourse. Thus, as I shift from identity politics to discourse ethics, from Anita Hill to Lani Guinier, from an unnamed Somali woman to civil society, I endeavor to seek out and expand those spaces for difference in which the hypothetical third can appear. For breaking through boundaries is always the first step of reflection.

CHAPTER I

Reflective Solidarity

On 12 February 1992, the *Times* of London reported that a Somali woman had given birth on the side of an Italian road while members of the local community either passed by ignoring her or stood there laughing and jeering. "I will remember those faces as long as I live," the woman was quoted as saying. "They were passing by; they would stop and linger as if they were at the cinema, careful not to miss any of the show." Like a number of countries, Italy in recent years has witnessed a rise in racism and antipathy toward immigrants. Still, accounts of the incident in Italian newspapers "prompted telephone calls of solidarity and job offers." Television broadcasts led to calls "expressing solidarity" phoned in to the hospital where she was taken. The *Times* cited a semiofficial Vatican newspaper's condemnation of the bystanders as "not worthy of the word man." This paper noted that "now there are many statements of solidarity from every region to try to make her forget and to convince her that humanity has not been extinguished in the hearts of the Italians."

Let's leave aside the voices of the journalists and take the story at face value. What were the callers seeking to get across with their expressions of solidarity? Why did they call at all? I'd like to suggest two related interpretations, one oriented toward the woman, the other toward the Italians' own self-understanding of themselves as a community.

The interpretation oriented toward the woman focuses on recognition, affirmation, and inclusion. This interpretation tells us that we can understand the expression of solidarity as a sort of recognition. Those who called were recognizing the woman in her vulnerability and suffering, trying to let her know that they saw her as a person who had experienced a particularly human form of personal degradation and injury. She had been humiliated and abandoned. Part of a "show," she was seen only as an actor to be watched, not as an embodied person with dignity worthy of recognition and response. The solidarity expressed by the callers was also a form of affirmation. Aware of the damage that the bystanders and passersby had caused to her sense of self, the callers were reaffirming the Somali through their concern for her welfare. They were telling her that what happened to her matters because she is a person whose integrity, like that of us all, depends on her relationships with others. In their very act of "telling," the callers were disrupting the "show," breaking through the barrier of the theater to interact with her as a concrete and vulnerable person. The callers, then, were assuring her that she was not alone, that others were standing with her. They were including her as someone with whom they experienced a shared life context. While acknowledging her as different, as not Italian, by including her within the group of those to whom solidarity is owed, they were taking accountability for her.

The interpretation oriented toward the Italians focuses on the callers' own understanding of their community. Their indignation at the behavior of the bystanders reflects their conviction that these bystanders violated the Italians' shared understanding of their responsibility toward others: all Italians are not like these bystanders who were not even worthy of the word "man." By treating the woman as an object of consumption, something to be watched like a piece of theater and then forgotten, the bystanders indicated that they could think of themselves as persons and as Italians without attending to the needs of the Somali woman. But the callers vehemently rejected this way of thinking. Stressing that "humanity was not extinguished in the hearts of the Italians," they claimed that a concern for the welfare of another, an "other" who is not Italian, was a constitutive part of their conception of themselves as a group. The callers, then, can be understood as trying to reestablish their own sense of the meaning of their life context. They were asserting the importance of taking responsibility for whatever other might come into contact with their community. The bystanders had abnegated this responsibility. They broke a bond within their own community by refusing to attend to the needs of someone they saw as an outsider.

What can we learn from these interpretations of this story? What can they tell us about solidarity today? The interpretation focused on the

Somali woman suggests that we now understand expressions of solidarity as signs of inclusion and affirmation, as ways of reassuring another that we will stand with her, that we will not leave her abandoned and alone. The interpretation centered on the Italians indicates that solidarity today involves a set of shared expectations that constitute a context of meaning central to a group's self-understanding.

Although this story helps to point out what is involved in an *expression* of solidarity, it is less helpful in explaining *appeals* to solidarity. Thinking about how it could elucidate such appeals, we might want to say that the Somali woman appealed to the Italians to stand by her in her need. Or we might want to think that the Italians who spoke out were appealing to the solidarity of the other members of their community. But this does not tell us to *to what* any of them would be appealing.

This distinction between *expressions of* and *appeals to* solidarity is important because, despite my emphasis on what the story of the Somali woman tells us about solidarity today, a number of participants in the current debate over identity politics write as if appeals to solidarity are no longer meaningful. They often think of appeals to solidarity as ways that people with power compel the allegiance of those without it, as if solidarity automatically excluded difference and forced people to sacrifice their sense of self for the sake of the group.[1] While they may accept the idea of an expression of solidarity as a particular response to local issues and concerns, these critics of solidarity might well challenge from the outset any effort to look more deeply into appeals to solidarity.

Underlying this challenge to solidarity is the suspicion that solidarity operates with a notion of membership that is both exclusionary and repressive. For example, bell hooks has successfully exposed the "victim" identity at the heart of the notion of sisterhood espoused by white women's liberationists.[2] She explains that when white women's liberationists appealed to the "sisterhood" of all women, they predetermined who women are and can be, denied differences among women, and refused to acknowledge women's own accountability for their oppression of each other. The white women's liberationists constructed a sisterhood that necessarily precluded the acknowledgment and investigation of women's differences. Although hooks does not dismiss the worth of solidarity, suggesting instead the need for a new understanding of it, other feminists have urged that we reject or "overcome" it. Thus, for Judith Butler, solidarity is an "exclusionary norm" that must be challenged.[3] Appeals to solidarity seek to shore up the unity of a group in advance, foreclosing any attempt to challenge and critique preexisting identity concepts. These brief examples illustrate the way the identity politics debate has exposed the problems of essentialism and exclusion, problems which have been misinterpreted as caused by the very goal of solidarity. Consequently, for recent thinkers solidarity has seemed to ask more of us than we can give. It has been assumed to require that we repress our differences and give up our identities for the sake of a larger group.

Although it may *seem* as if solidarity requires us to sacrifice difference, the critics of solidarity are, to use one of my favorite clichés, throwing out the baby with the bathwater. There *is* something still compelling in appeals to solidarity, as the story of the Somali woman makes clear. The question thus remains: When we appeal to solidarity, to what, exactly, are we appealing? Are we appealing to a set of feelings; to our shared values or histories; to our mutual vulnerability to isolation, denigration, and neglect and our common need for recognition? Further, since we do continue to appeal to solidarity, I want to know how these appeals can still be meaningful in pluralist, multicultural societies when traditional values have been exposed as biased and exclusionary. At issue is whether the collapse of traditional values requires us to forfeit solidarity in the interests of freedom and diversity or whether we can have a conception of solidarity based on a respect for difference. Caught up in the problems of identity politics, critics of solidarity equate solidarity with identity, presuming that it will always exclude difference. They are thus in the position of having to dismiss appeals to solidarity out of hand. But what if these appeals were anchored in our respect for each other's differences? What if they are meaningful precisely because they draw upon our capacity to engage communicatively with another?

Based on the idea that the ties we create through our discussions and questions engender shared expectations of recognition and response, reflective solidarity finds the meaning of appeals to solidarity rests in our awareness of and regard for those multiple interconnections in which differences emerge. The story of the Somali woman escapes the confines of identity politics — the solidarity expressed by the Italians was to someone whose identity differed from their own. Were we to try to twist the story to make it fit, we would ignore the way accountability for another extends beyond given identities. We would be establishing points of closure and finality where the Italian callers were creating openness, an openness to difference. In contemporary multicultural societies, closure is no longer an option. It leads to rigidification, violence, and exclusion. It prevents us from acknowledging our accountability for others. Thus,

I present reflective solidarity as that openness to difference which lets our disagreements provide the basis for connection.

Feelings and Values

My writing on solidarity grew out of a paper I presented in Frankfurt in December 1992. Underprepared when I arrived, I stayed up all night trying to finish the draft I would present the following evening. I finished my paper at about six o'clock in the morning, ready to hand it over for photocopying at nine. Unfortunately, as I attempted to print it, I confronted computer problems: neither the printer I had brought with me nor the one in the office where I was struggling would work. In a panic, I called my friend Carolin. She came, calmed me down, and drove me to her apartment to try her printer. As we walked up her stairs, she jokingly said that this was real solidarity. Who else would get up so early on a cold, miserable morning (after almost no sleep, since she was busy with her own writing)? I thought about what she said. When I called her at the crack of dawn, I *was* appealing to her sense of solidarity. Yet this appeal doesn't mesh with the story of the Somali woman. I was appealing to Carolin's feelings, to her affection for me as a friend. Although she is an exceptionally nice woman, I doubt Carolin would do the same for a complete stranger. No, the solidarity she expressed was a sign and result of our friendship.

This story provides an example of *affectional solidarity,* the kind of solidarity that grows out of intimate relationships of love and friendship.[4] In these associations of emotional affirmation, the bond uniting each to the other is a feeling of mutual care and concern. As Seyla Benhabib notes, here each "assumes from the other forms of behavior through which the other feels recognized and confirmed as a concrete, individual being with specific needs, talents and capacities."[5] Each expects from the other a willingness to put aside self-interest and attend to the other's psychical, emotional, and physical needs. Necessarily, then, affectional solidarities are both primary and particular. They are primary insofar as the child's early experiences of love and connection provide the basis for the development of a sense of self-trust and of an ability to engage with and respond to the needs of the other. These solidarities are particular in that responding to and validating the other as the "person she is"[6] demands a depth of attention to the uniqueness of the other that cannot be extended to a limitless variety of others. Affectional solidarity thus has a universal dimension: recognizing the other as the person she is requires that we remain attuned to the myriad differences comprising her individuality. We acknowledge universality on the microlevel as the "yet-to-be-expressed" dimension of the other's identity. Indeed, part of the "we feeling" of affectional solidarity stems from the immediacy of our tie to another, the awareness of the specialness and exclusivity of a relationship attuned to complexities of individual specificity.[7]

Conventional solidarity grows out of common interests and concerns. On the one hand, conventional solidarity arises out of the shared traditions and values uniting a group or community. In this inward-oriented type of conventional solidarity, members raise their claims and concerns to each other. For example, we might think of the expectations that the adherents of particular religious beliefs have of one another or of the kinds of loyalties expected of party members. In each case, being a member of a group means that other members are entitled to expect certain forms of behavior. On the other hand, conventional solidarity refers to the sense of "we-ness" of groups involved in a common struggle or endeavor. This outward-oriented type of solidarity extends the circle of addressees, raising claims on behalf of its members to the "community at large" or humanity as a whole. Thus, the evangelical thrust of various Christian denominations seeks the conversion and salvation of those outside the group. And in marxist political parties, for example, the effort of the group is made on behalf of the working class, whose emancipation will be that of us all.

For both inward- and outward-oriented conventional solidarities, the expectations of members are given, whether rooted in traditional values or engendered by a situation that constructs various individuals as members of a group (as in the way racism in the United States constructs people of varying skin colors and backgrounds as black). Conventional solidarities take their form from a shared adherence to common beliefs or goals that unite people in membership. These goals and beliefs serve as mediations surpassing the actual interconnections among members. As they bind the group together, these mediations delimit the self-understanding of the group. They provide boundaries beyond which one *as a member* cannot go. The expectation that one will adhere to the norms of the group is the primary attribute of membership, of being validated as one of "us." Those evangelicals who fail to proselytize or who indulge in "sins of the flesh," or those party members who veer from the party line or question the commands of the leadership risk ostracism. They have challenged the boundary distinguishing the saved and the damned; they have crossed party lines. For outward-oriented conventional solidarities, then, the limitations on the behavior and attitudes of members can be understood as closing off internal or microlevel universality in the interest of external or macrolevel universality. So, while they raise universal claims in what George Herbert Mead has referred to as the "conversation of humanity," they do not extend universality within the group through the recognition of individual difference.

Limited Solidarities I:
Immediate Feelings

Both affectional and conventional solidarities have built-in limits that prevent their extension beyond a particular group. Supporters of these types of solidarity often view these limits as intrinsic to solidarity. They think that solidarity must be understood as "us" in contrast to "them." Even those few who want to extend solidarity tend to accept the basic assumptions underlying each type and thus remain unable to conceive of a universal solidarity. In turn, this makes them all the more vulnerable to solidarity's critics since supporters as well as critics presume that solidarity limits communication. While supporters see these limits as necessary for cohesion, critics read them as leading to the isolation of the group against an outside other or as imposing homogeneity within the solidary group itself.

We recall that my story about Carolin was based on the opposition between "we friends" and "those strangers" for whom she wouldn't venture out at dawn in the cold. Supporters of solidarity would emphasize the importance of our feelings of friendship, stressing that such feelings are the result of experiences that cannot be communicated to a larger group. That our friendship is the result of such experiences would be viewed as crucial to my ability to appeal to her for help. Were they to urge us to universalize and extend our affectional solidarity, these supporters would tell us to try to feel the same way toward strangers. Critics of solidarity would look at the opposition between friends and strangers as foundational, essential to any appeal to solidarity. Perhaps attuned to the potential for coercion in my phone call, in my appeal to Carolin for help, critics might worry about a friendship that requires a friend to get up at dawn. They would question not only the limited and exclusionary nature of our solidarity, but also its potential to eliminate discussion and dissent.

What, then, are the assumptions underlying affectional and conventional solidarity, which I have claimed are shared by both supporters and critics? Affectional solidarity is based on two assumptions: that solidarity is somehow the same as the conditions under which it is learned, and that it is a particular sort of feeling. Though they rarely mention solidarity per se, the work of feminist care theorists such as Carol Gilligan and Nel Noddings illustrates the first assumption. Whether grounded in women's capacity to bear children, the nurturing qualities of mothering, or the emotional bond between mother and child, these writings take primary family relations to be the sources of an ethic that can be potentially extended to all through our capacity for sympathy, for taking the role of the other.[8] One of the strengths of this conception is an intersubjective approach that conceives of the ties between self and other in terms of mutual recognition. Yet since the relational tie connecting the "one caring" and the "one cared for" gains its strength from the immediacy of direct, interpersonal relationships, care theorists confront the limits of affectional solidarity. They can only resolve the dilemma of how to respond to those beyond the original circle with an injunction, "Care, because caring is good," or a hypothetical imperative, "If you want a relationship with the other, care for her."[9] This lends an unsettling ambiguity to the word "care," blurring the distinctions among the different ways care is felt and expressed. It also cannot help us when we have no desire for a relationship with the other. Our care or solidarity remains confined to those "concrete others" to whom we can see ourselves related. Because solidarity is viewed as a feeling that cannot be communicated abstractly (for most care theorists abstraction itself is seen as endangering feeling-based ties), it cannot extend beyond the conditions under which it is learned. The solidarity of intimate ties thus results in the isolation of those within the circle of care from those who remain outside it.

Although Richard Rorty tends to view solidarity as based in the historical contingency of a shared final vocabulary, he sometimes writes as if he assumes that solidarity is a particular sort of feeling. Because he has offered solidarity as an alternative to universalist understandings of the ties connecting "humanity," it is important to remember that for him the bonds connecting us as "we twentieth-century intellectuals" are affective: "My position entails that feelings of solidarity are necessarily a matter of which similarities and dissimilarities strike us as salient."[10] Of course, Rorty is not completely wrong here. Feelings are like that. Feelings of, say, outrage or indignation are responses to violations of the norms and cultural interpretations structuring our understanding of the world. Similarly, feelings of affection or compassion emerge out of social contexts that establish certain others as worthy of our affection or deserving of our compassion. Nonetheless, when Rorty says that he is against the claim that we have a moral obligation to feel solidarity with all other human beings, he steps onto much shakier ground.[11] He suggests that "we" are constituted through our feelings of regard for each other and disregard for outsiders. This corresponds to his view that "the force of 'us' is typically contrastive in the sense that it contrasts with a 'they' which is also made up of human beings—the wrong sort of human beings."[12] Because the ties connecting "us" are affective, they cannot be extended to those for whom we have no strong feelings of regard. But feelings are not things one can be obligated to have. By assuming that solidarity can be reduced to a feeling, Rorty misstates the issue. Of course, we can't be obliged to *feel* a particular way toward others. Indeed, I claim that we cannot even be obliged to *act* solidarily.

In part, my claim here is formal. Solidarity refers to a generalized observance of norms, a stable degree of norm compliance. The "ought quality" of moral norms means that valid norms are obligatory. To say that we are obliged to follow norms, obligated to observe our obligations, then, is redundant—the idea of obligation is already built into the concept of a norm. Yet the idea that we cannot be obliged to act out of solidarity tells us something important about solidarity, namely, that it cannot be demanded. The demand itself reveals the lack of solidarity, a member's failure to stand with and take responsibility for an other. We don't *demand* solidarity; we *appeal* to solidarity. We call upon others to maintain their connection with us. As consociates, we can be obligated to act in ways that renew our intersubjective ties, protect the integrity of our relationship, and affirm the irreplaceable individuality of one another. In so doing, we strengthen the solidarity of our association. So Rorty misstates the issue by neglecting to ask whether there are connections extending potentially to all of us, where "us" is a group potentially as large or larger than the human race, strong enough to provide a solidarity to which any one could appeal. And, again, he misstates the issue because feelings cannot be communicated abstractly enough to break out of the isolation of the primary group.

Limited Solidarities II:
Mediating Values and the Crisis of Solidarity

I've already mentioned that the "we-ness" of groups united by shared values or in common struggle is not immediate, but mediated by something standing beyond the actual relationships among group members. This tells us that the assumptions underlying conventional solidarity differ significantly from those underlying affectional solidarity. In conventional solidarity ties between members are not conceived strictly in terms of feelings. Bonds connecting people may be the result of habit or training, the product of education or consciousness-raising, or the shared perception of common needs and suffering.

The insertion of a cognitive dimension into our relationship allows solidarity to be understood more abstractly. It now extends beyond those to whom we are immediately connected through our mutual feelings to include those to whom we are mediately connected through all of our common ties to that something standing beyond us which constructs us as a group. In place of the mutual recognition of each as "the person she is," members are recognized *as members* — as Americans, as women, as African Americans.[13] This "recognized-as" characteristic of membership restricts the scope of available identity concepts and need interpretations to those corresponding to the overall group. Not only is who "we" are defined behind the backs of members, but who "I" am and can be is determined by the requirements of membership. How I show my solidarity, the expectations I must uphold if I am to fulfill my role in the group and sustain the interconnections among us, is given in advance. Replacing the recognition of persons with the recognition of members, conventional solidarities extend the range of our intersubjective ties at the cost of the "concrete other," setting limits on what she can do and how she can be seen. Thus, they tend to reinforce the homogeneity of the solidary group.

The racialized sexual or sexualized racial politics of the Clarence Thomas hearings provide a clear example of the crisis facing not only the solidarity of the African American community but also conventional solidarities in general. Conventional solidarities respond to the value pluralism of contemporary multicultural societies by increasing the demands made on group members, by rigidifying identity categories. To this end, they compel members to make a choice: Are you for us or against us? If solidarity necessarily requires this sort of choice, as various voices in the identity politics debate presume it does, many of us will understandably want to discard solidarity. After all, what do we do when we can't choose? What do we do when we both agree and disagree with our group? What do we do when we are both included and excluded from the group? Understanding what is at work in the heightened rigidity of conventional solidarity is thus crucial if we are to take seriously the fears of solidarity's critics.

Even before the civil rights movement, black progress toward social and economic justice had been thought to require blacks fighting and working together. bell hooks notes that "when black people collectively experienced racist oppression in similar ways, there was greater group solidarity."[14] But in recent years class differences and the emergence of multiple black experiences have caused many African Americans "seriously to doubt the point of solidarity for themselves and its value for their race."[15] Manning Marable explains:

During the period of Jim Crow, the oppressive external constraints of legal discrimination imposed norms of racial conformity and solidarity. Despite an individual's educational attainments, capital formation, or excellence on the athletic field, for example, a person could never entirely escape the oppressive reality of segregation. The very definition of "race" was a social category defined by the presumed and very real hierarchies within the socioeconomic and political system, preserving and perpetuating black subordination. . . . But in the post–civil rights period, in the absence of legal structures of formal discrimination, the bonds of cultural kinship, social familiarity, and human responsibility that had once linked the most affluent and upwardly mobile African Americans with their economically marginalized sisters and brothers were severely weakened.[16]

With the rise of more conservative and anti–affirmative action voices among the African American elite, often as far removed from the more oppressed segments of the black community as the white middle class, the meaning and place of black solidarity are no longer clear — "there is no longer a consensus about what blacks anxious to help their race as well as themselves should do or support."[17]

Clarence Thomas himself signifies this aspect of the current crisis of black solidarity. A rejector of affirmative action, Thomas called on blacks to stand by him in the interest of having a black on the Supreme Court. As one of "us," where us is understood as "we African Americans," Thomas asked for black support. Yet he had rejected traditional African American identifications, persistently denouncing "any effort to link the history of racism to ongoing racial inequalities."[18] He had sought to distance himself from the black community, but when he needed African Americans to stand by him and support his nomination to the Supreme Court, his past policies and pronouncements were no longer those of a Republican "sell-out." Now they were signs of the diversity among African Americans. African Americans were thus asked to choose between having a black on the Court, an option which required them to accept political and economic diversity, or potentially giving up Thurgood Marshall's seat to a white nominee.

At the heart of Thomas's appeal to black solidarity was his evocation of the "lynching" trope. This evocation erased Anita Hill as a black woman, signifying another dimension of the crisis in black solidarity — the oppression of black women and exclusion of their needs and sufferings in the interest of securing better conditions for the "race" (read: black men).[19] The lynching trope constructed Thomas as a victim of white aggression, making Hill's racial identity either irrelevant or white. Failing to heed Thomas's call for solidarity would place blacks in the same camp as the white mobs that had oppressed blacks in the past. As Kendall Thomas points out, historically lynching has been associated with black men's contact with white women: "No African-American man was ever lynched on the word of an aggrieved black woman. This was because black women had no honor that a white lynch mob felt bound to respect."[20] Clarence Thomas thus appealed to a solidarity constructed to keep hidden the sufferings endured by black women. The "we" of conventional black solidarity was determined by a set of racist practices setting up an opposition between black and white such that to be one of "us" meant to be a black man. Black women (and men) were asked to choose between "blackness" and "white womanhood."

The lynching trope enabled Thomas to present himself as "authentically black," thereby turning Hill into a "race traitor." If he was "being lynched" (an awkward phrase given his ability to evoke the term in speech), then she, because of her accusations, was part of the lynch mob. Her words themselves constituted the noose around Thomas's throat. Kimberlé Crenshaw describes the "code of silence" long understood by African Americans as "a self-imposed gesture of racial solidarity" with coercive dimensions.[21] Condemned in the black press as a traitor to her race who compromised the integrity of a black man and embarrassed the African American community, Anita Hill violated a cardinal norm of conventional black solidarity. In raising her own voice, not only did she fail to subordinate her experiences as a black woman to the advancement of a black man, but also she called into question the very code of silence deemed essential for black solidarity. Her speech was an effort to hang Thomas. African Americans were asked to choose between speech and silence.

This fear of speech and emphasis on silence indicate how dissent in the African American community has been quieted in the interest of presenting a solid front. Despite credentials sorely inadequate for a Supreme Court nominee, Thomas was shielded from serious criticism and scrutiny because of his race. For many liberal whites as well as for African American leaders, the importance of securing Thurgood Marshall's vacated seat as a site of black representation on the Court overrode any interest in finding a competent judge concerned with protecting the established interests of the black community. Crenshaw writes:

Our failure to readily criticize African Americans, based on a belief that our interests are served whenever a black rises through the ranks of power, will increasingly be used to undermine and dismantle policies that have been responsible for the moderate successes that group politics have brought about. Already, African-American individuals have played key roles in attacking minority scholarships, cutting back on available remedies for civil rights injuries, and lifting sanctions against South Africa.[22]

By silencing questions and criticism, conventional black solidarity is starting to subvert its very purpose and further its own demise. The rigidity of the norms on which this solidarity is based is coming up against the ends of black solidarity itself. The choice has become one between criticism and solidarity.

The crisis of solidarity in the African American community exemplified by the Thomas hearings tells us that conventional solidarities confront serious problems. It reminds us that we are often forced into a choice which threatens the solidarity of our groups and communities. Conventional solidarities confront a problem of time. Beliefs and values of generations standing outside of those periods of history central to the political culture of their group may not resonate with the group's traditional goals and concerns. At a time of increased questioning and value pluralism, previously accepted norms lose their legitimizing force as components of a shared experience because precisely this experience is no longer shared. That norms grew out of a specific historical context is not enough to guarantee their binding capacity once times have changed. In fact, the tension and space that arise between the norms and the contexts in which they originated make them vulnerable to cynical manipulation—the evocative power of historically charged symbols may be used to obscure the meanings of the norms themselves.

Conventional solidarities face problems of exclusion. Because they are limited by their construction in terms of "us" and "them," by their placement over and against an outside other in reference to which the group is defined, conventional solidarities offer a restricted range of available identity concepts. Thus, their dominant tropes acquire an organizing power through a simplified presentation of who "we" are and what "we" have endured. When persons seek simultaneously to realize themselves as individuals and to be one of "us," they are presented with a choice between a self-understanding consonant with the requirements of the group and either exile or ostracism. The differences among members, their individual needs and experiences, thus elude expression. Silenced, these differences loom outside the group's symbolic space, always threatening to disrupt its solidarity.

Conventional solidarities face a problem of accountability. The norms and values constituting the expectations that group members have of each other so tightly confine the range of acceptable action that one confronts the dilemma of conformity or betrayal, of complicity or personal integrity.[23] In their neglect of needs and experiences different from those captured by the dominant tropes and their compulsion of a choice between honor and loyalty, conventional solidarities often result in an impoverished sense of responsibility. There is a failure to take account of the potential for injustice and the ever present reality of exclusion within the group.

This failure is closely connected to the problem of the place of criticism. Conventional solidarities are threatened by questioning. Because the ties connecting members are mediated by histories and values beyond the group itself, a reflective attitude toward these very histories and values brings with it the risk of disintegration. But, by shielding themselves from dissent and demanding support at any cost, conventional solidarities present themselves as almost otherworldly utopias, all the while falling into the dystopian trap of the unquestioning acceptance of and mindless adherence to already given norms.[24] As conventional solidarities both presume and reinforce a homogeneous group identity, they restrict communication, requiring members to confine themselves and their discussion within the range of acceptable tropes.

These problems of time, exclusion, accountability, and critique have met with different sorts of responses: the reassertion of values, group fragmentation, and tactical solidarities. None of these, however, is capable of solving the problem of solidarity. Because none opens up communication within the group or among differing groups, none escapes the problems of isolation and homogenization.

We cannot blind ourselves to the plurality of competing traditions and beliefs. Whether it takes the form of a conservative retrenchment (as in the "family values" plank in the Republican party platform during the 1992 presidential election or in the growing strains of nationalism in Europe) or the communitarian search for "constitutive" or "higher-order" goods, the reassertion of values ignores the way in which value indeterminacy itself is part of the crisis of solidarity. Rather than questioning the basic terms of conventional solidarity, this reassertion-of-values solution merely seeks to replace one set of mediations with another.

Fragmentation, or the splintering off of subgroups defined in terms of their relevant differences, has appeared as a solution designed to offset the denigration experienced by marginalized others in need of support and affirmation. We see this in the chain of hyphens familiar to identity politics: black-feminist-lesbian-working-class-disabled-senior-citizen-mother. Yet this, too, fails to solve the crisis of solidarity; indeed, it hastens solidarity's demise. When solidarity requires that members be "recognized as," their concrete particularities will always be excluded. Because flight is preferred to dialogue and critique, fragmentation tends to leave the basic assumptions of the dominant group intact. Sequestered in the security of shared identity, these splinter groups forfeit responsibility for the historical and interpretative contexts in which identities are constructed and valued, focusing instead on the "difference of the day."

Finally, the tactical solidarity of coalition politics relies on the contingent meeting of disparate interests. Solidarity is reduced to a means, subject to the calculations of success of those seeking to benefit from it. Interests and needs are conceived statically as well as strategically: taken as given, they remain unquestioningly accepted and immune from critique, ready to be used when the proper moment arises. Relationships become chance associations ready to be consumed. Contributing to the renewal of the shared sense of "we" or maintaining the welfare of those concerned is set aside as solidarity becomes the currency used to purchase other ends. Tactical solidarity thus repeats the "us-them" logic of conventional solidarities, filling in the place previously occupied by one conception of "them" with a series of ever-changing "them's."

Despite the inadequacy of these responses to the crisis of conventional solidarity, they share a commitment to the ideal of solidarity. They do not dismiss the worth of solidarity or neglect the fact that solidarity is something to which people continue to appeal. The reassertion-of-values response asserts the continued importance of our shared under-standings and commitments. As this response answers the question "to what do we appeal when we appeal to solidarity?" with the word "tradi-tion," it implicitly calls attention to the sense of meaning which group membership provides. For example, communitarians acknowledge that the self is always dependent on other selves for its realization.[25] Al-though they fail to account for the plurality of possible relationships and values in their attempt to designate a set of higher goods, communitari-ans nonetheless recognize that the simultaneity of individuation and so-cialization means that we are always dependent on and accountable to others.

Fragmentation responds to the pain and anguish experienced by those whose sufferings are ignored and degradations neglected. It an-swers the question of our appeal to solidarity by saying that we appeal to the same experiences of those who are like us. Again, while this response neglects the way we can and do respond to those who are different, it, too, contains an insight into our need for recognition and affirmation as particular identities. Finally, despite its tendency to instrumentalize solidarity, the response of coalition politics exhibits a commitment to the universalist promise of outward-oriented solidarity.

Underlying solidarity as a tactic is the goal of challenging the bound-aries of community that have rendered many outsiders. This response views an appeal to solidarity as a call for action, an appeal to those of us who recognize the injustices inflicted by "them" to put aside our differ-ences and fight for our rightful place. Yet precisely because it puts our differences aside, tactical solidarity neglects the way freedom and equal-ity, say, are not simply goals to be achieved through solidary action but require for their very sustenance solidary relationships. In other words, it recognizes the importance of solidarity for democracy, but instead of seeing solidarity as a precondition for democratic discourse, tactical solidarity reduces it to a means of entering the debate. It is as if tactical solidarities reject identity politics by focusing on politics and throwing out identity.

Toward Reflective Solidarity

If solidarity is not to be discarded as yet another exclu-sionary ideal, it will have to be conceived so as to take seriously the historical conditions of value pluralism, the ever present potential for exclusion, the demands of accountability, and the importance of critique. This suggests that the permanent risk of disagreement must itself provide a basis for solidarity. In contrast to conventional solidarity in which dissent always carries with it the potential for disruption, *reflective solidarity* builds from ties created by dissent.

In a short essay in *Making Face, Making Soul: Haciendo Caras,* Lynet Uttal gives an account of her experiences in Anglo feminist groups and Women of Color feminist groups that illustrates the differences between conventional and reflective solidarity and suggests the potential of a solidarity based on disagreement and dissent.[26] Describing her feelings of distance and disconnection from the smooth, efficient, and orderly discussions among Anglo women, Uttal worries about the way their emphasis on agreement, support, and commonality ended up replacing dialogue with polite nods and silent, blank-faced, acquiescence. "If this is all that feminist sisterhood is about — protecting ourselves from any differences, maintaining at all costs an illusion of solidarity," she writes, "it's a fruitless practice that leaves us at a standstill."[27] But, for Uttal, this is not all that feminist sisterhood is about. She describes a solidarity that is more than an illusion, a solidarity that arises out of disagreement and difference. In groups of Women of Color she found confusion, conflict, questioning, and laughter. Far from threatening the solidarity among group participants, differences brought them together: "Our shared efforts to figure out the differences make us feel closer to women whom we initially perceived as 'others'."[28] Thus, the solution Uttal offers to the problem of solidarity is that "we have to be allowed to get messy."

Although Uttal's own account isn't very messy at all, relying in fact on a neat opposition between an Anglo feminist group and a Women of Color feminist group, her idea that solidarity requires us to "get messy" is an important one. I want to use it to think about how conflicts and disagreements might bring us together as a "we." Reflective solidarity refers to *a mutual expectation of a responsible orientation to relationship. Mutual expectation* involves the different uses of the term "we." I emphasize how a "we" is constituted through the communicative efforts of different "I's." *Responsibility* stresses our accountability for exclusion. It relies on what I call the perspective of the situated, hypothetical third. Finally, an *orientation to relationship* recognizes that we can acknowledge our mutual expectations without hypostatizing them into a restrictive set of norms. To explain how this kind of orientation is possible, I reinterpret George Herbert Mead's concept of the generalized other.

The universalist underpinnings of reflective solidarity both enable and require us to rethink the boundaries of community, the demarcation between "us" and "them." That is, because reflective solidarity is attuned to the universality within concrete identities as well as to an ideal community of us all, it highlights two dimensions of exclusion, those of criteria and those of range. By elaborating on the concept of reflective solidarity, I endeavor to show how it provides a form of consideration of the other where the other is considered a member despite, indeed because of, her difference. Reflective solidarity conceives the ties connecting us as communicative and open. This openness creates a space for accountability, enabling us to grasp the ways this notion of solidarity no longer blocks us from difference, but instead provides a bridge between identity and universality.

MUTUAL EXPECTATION:
THE COMMUNICATIVE "WE"

In her discussion of the Anglo and Women of Color feminist groups, Uttal suggests that the difference between them results from each group's understanding of itself as a group. The Anglo feminists understood themselves as a "we" in opposition to others — to men, explicitly, and to women of color, implicitly. Their knowledge of who they were depended on their exclusion of somebody else. For the Anglo feminists, then, the term "we" was contrastive and externally established, always dependent on a "they." Through their conflict, questioning, and laughter, the feminists of color, however, recognized and confirmed each other as part of their "we." Their "we" did not rely primarily on the exclusion of some "outside other." The "we" used by the feminists of color was communicative and internally established, referring to the relationship among the various women.[29]

Uttal also suggests how the feminists of color were able to establish their "we" when she writes, "Instead of a patronizing nod, I prefer the query which makes my comments a building block in the discussion."[30] The "query" constructs the "we." Unlike the Anglo feminists who presumed that they all shared the same experience of oppression, the feminists of color used language and communication to construct a new experience of belonging. What created this communicative sense of "we" was not simply a shared experience but the expression of the experience in language.[31]

Uttal acknowledges that these communicative expressions are, of course, rarely peaceful or neutral. In the discussions among the feminists of color, goal-oriented participants often wanted to take control and prevent the group from wasting time. Some women were aggressive, siding against others. Feelings got hurt. But because the communicative efforts of the feminists of color were a means of reaching understanding, "putting ideas in order and creating a shared picture which all can see,"[32] the "query" often enabled them to challenge attempts to control, to take sides, and to hurt feelings. Questioning and disagreement enabled each woman to take part in the construction of the group's "we." Those who sought to push through their own agendas were challenged to defend their views. They had to explain, to give reasons for their opinions. The "query" is thus at the heart of the binding capacity of communication, of the communicative "we."[33] Faced with a "query," a participant in the discussions of the feminists of color was expected to engage in the messy process of thinking things through.

Uttal's account of her experiences in Women of Color feminist groups is important for reflective solidarity because it tells us that the term "we" is a form of communication. We don't have to understand ourselves as "us" against "them"; we can recognize each other as belonging to "us." Through language we establish a relationship, creating a common, social space. With our "queries" we challenge each other, letting our space, for a time, be one of negotiation. Neither ontological nor teleological, this internally designated, communicative "we" does not deny that the term "we" often refers to a relationship among a limited number of members. Instead, it stresses the possibility of an inclusive understanding of "we" whereby the strength of the bond connecting us stems from our mutual recognition of each other instead of from our exclusion of someone else. Most importantly, because it is created through communicative utterances, this "we" cannot remain fixed. It is constantly recreated and renewed by the "query" as members confront and challenge, accept and reject, the claims raised by each and all.

We should not overlook the oppositional place of "we" found in Uttal's account of the Anglo feminists. This contrastive and externally established "we" is also crucial to the activist dimension of discussions among feminists of color—solidarity is always connected with action. This tells us that reflective solidarity has to attend to the contexts in which appeals to solidarity are raised. Generally, we call on another to stand by us over and against an "other" who seeks to oppress us or who fails to recognize and include us. So here reflective solidarity refers to the exclusion of exclusion: we are connected through our struggle against those who threaten, denigrate, and silence us. Additionally, if we are to move doubt to the foundations of our notion of solidarity, we must always be aware of the limits of any given understanding of "we."

Changing the criteria for what it means to be one of "us" requires that we take seriously the ever present fact of exclusion. We can never be sure who "we" are in any final or ultimate sense. Thus, we have to acknowledge the distinction between actual and potential members, the way we may always exclude another.

The communicative "we" enables reflective solidarity to overcome the problems of exclusion and critique characteristic of conventional solidarity. Because this "we" provides an inclusive understanding of solidarity, it avoids the exclusion of individual difference. With the realization that uttering "we" does not presuppose the existence of a "they," we can move away from rigid identity categories, the limits of which are established by the dualities of any opposition. This makes possible an inward opening-up of the criteria for membership. Unlike the Anglo feminists, the feminists of color whom Uttal describes did not presume that women should avoid conflict. Because these feminists did not presuppose the sisterhood of women in opposition to the patriarchal oppression of men, they were able to accept the differences among the members of their group. Aggression and confrontation did not make these women of color "less womanly." The communicative understanding of "we" also fights exclusion by challenging us to oppose those who try to exclude others and by reminding us of our own failures to include. It thus provides an outward opening-up of the concept of membership. In order to extend the range of our responsibility we have to acknowledge that any given conception of "we" may articulate a set of categories delimiting membership in advance. Recognizing another as a member despite her difference means that we must remain attuned to the possibility of omission.

Reflective solidarity is able to use criticism as a basis for our interconnection because it is rooted in the communicative "we." Through our arguments with each other we establish a mutual expectation that each will be able to accept or reject the claims of the other on the basis of good reasons. So rather than viewing criticism as potentially disruptive, reflective solidarity sees it as furthering the intersubjective recognition characteristic of solidarily bound members.

RESPONSIBILITY: THE SITUATED, HYPOTHETICAL THIRD

Part of Uttal's dissatisfaction with Anglo feminist groups can be traced to their failure to look carefully at what brought them together as women. The Anglo feminists took for granted the idea that all women *just are* sisters. They assumed that all women are united because they are all oppressed by patriarchy. These Anglo feminists thus ascribed an identity to women, whereas the feminists of color were working toward achieving new identities. Although less manipulative, the Anglo feminists' reliance on ascribed identity resembles Clarence Thomas's assumption of a common black identity. His efforts, too, were rooted in the idea that insofar as "blackness" is ascribed to African Americans, they all share a common identity; they are all solidarily bound.

What my critique of conventional solidarity and Uttal's discussion of feminists of color indicate, however, is that a solidarity based on ascribed identities is inadequate. It can account neither for difference nor for the way our goals and values change. When the norms and expectations of members are simply given, the differences constituting our individual identities remain suppressed and unseen. How I understand myself, how I can interpret and express my needs, is overlooked in favor of already existing notions of what it means to be one of "us." The problem of time confronting conventional solidarities shows us that solidarity today can no longer be viewed as fixed or given. Achieving solidarity requires that we open up notions of membership to communicative reflection. Solidarity itself has to be understood as an accomplishment requiring a self-reflective understanding of who "we" are on the part of those making up "us."

For this self-reflection to be possible, group members have to be able to adopt a hypothetical attitude toward the norms and expectations of their group. Although she doesn't say this, Uttal *does* this as she moves back and forth between the Anglo feminist group and the Women of Color feminist group. Her experience in one enables her to reflect on the norms and expectations of the other. Trinh T. Minh-ha describes such movement as an intervention which undercuts the inside/outside opposition. It creates an "inappropriate other or same who moves about with always at least two gestures: that of affirming 'I am like you' while persisting in her difference and that of reminding 'I am different' while unsettling every definition of otherness arrived at."[34]

As I read her, Trinh is not only elaborating a new concept of subjectivity, but also telling us how we acquire or develop the capacity for reflection. As we take over the norms and expectations of a group, as we are socialized as insiders, we acquire a particular self-understanding. Once we step "outside" this group and "into" another one, we acquire a greater sense of our individual specificity. We have distanced ourselves from the first group and acquired the capacity to reflect on our identity as a member of this group. Our movement, moreover, is communica tively marked: we "affirm" and "remind." This communication thus tells us that our capacity for reflection depends on the recognition we receive from others, from those making up the various groups into and out of which we step.

While Trinh designates the subjectivity produced by the movement into and out of groups as that of an "inappropriate other," because I am interested in the conditions necessary for reflective solidarity I prefer to think about what kind of perspective this movement enables us to take. I refer to this perspective as that of a situated, hypothetical third. The stress on "situatedness" tells us that the person who moves is embodied and concrete. Her physical movement into and out of groups gives her a perspective from which to evaluate group norms and expectations. Adopting the perspective of a situated third enables solidarily bound members to discard the elements of homogeneity and isolation from other groups characteristic of conventional solidarities as they bridge the gap between insider and outsider. The emphasis on the "hypothetical" nature of this perspective reminds us of our limits. Our solidary reflection may never enable us fully to include the voices and experiences we exclude. Nonetheless, as we adopt this perspective, we take accountability for our exclusions, attempting to include excluded others in our "we." The designation of this perspective as that of a "third" thus supplements the mutual "I-you" composition of the communicative "we" by bringing in a "they" or a "she" or "he." When we take this perspective, we are able to expose the omissions and blind spots within the narratives of our shared identity. We acquire the capacity to criticize and question the expectations of our group.

The perspective of the situated, hypothetical third is central to the ability of reflective solidarity to conceive of a "we" that moves beyond the "we" of conventional solidarity. In conventional solidarities members are expected to sacrifice their own identities, desires, and opinions for the good of the group. They are expected to nod in silent acquiescence. Reflective solidarity, however, recognizes that members and participants are always insiders and outsiders. It acknowledges that we are always situated in a variety of differing groups all of which play a role in the development of our individual identities. As the perspective of the situated, hypothetical third incorporates our movement into and out of these groups in an understanding of our capacity for reflection, it enables us to take responsibility for others as well as for ourselves. So rather than remaining trapped within merely given identities, groups, and communities, reflective solidarity evokes the potential of a community of us all.

ORIENTATION TOWARD RELATIONSHIP:
THE GENERALIZED OTHER

But we must not let this emphasis on queries, criticism, and movement overshadow connection and relationship. Reflection should not subvert solidarity. Those who do not participate in a variety of activist or discussion groups might be tempted to throw this book aside, dismayed that they may never acquire the capacity to take the perspective of the situated, hypothetical third. And even those who do participate may think that my version of solidarity is only about discord and disruption, a rather unappealing substitute for the close-knit community promised by identity politics. To ward off resistance and show what is appealing about reflective solidarity, I now need to explain more generally how developing the capacity for reflection is possible and how this reflection can be combined with an orientation toward relationship.

Once again, Uttal's experience in Anglo feminist groups is helpful. She writes: "Every time I try to visualize my thoughts, I think over and over again in my head how to state my thoughts diplomatically. Yet even with this careful attention to words, after I speak I always end up feeling that I have breached a code of conduct."[35] Despite the conflict and anguish expressed in Uttal's words, she is telling us that, at least for a time, she had internalized the norms and expectations of the Anglo feminists. Although these norms conflicted with her own sense of self, by internalizing them, by taking the perspective of the Anglo feminists, by identifying with them, she was acknowledging a relationship to them. She was adopting the shared expectations of this "we," a particular understanding of the meaning of membership. For a while, this was part of her identity.

George Herbert Mead's concept of the generalized other explains what is involved in taking the perspective of relationship. The generalized other refers to the organized set of expectations of a social group. When we adopt this perspective, we are seeing from the standpoint of relationship, taking account of the shared expectations members have of one another and our common understanding of what it means to identify as a member of a group. By looking more closely at the generalized other, we can understand how it is possible to combine the notion of reflection with a concept of relationship.

Mead's examples of the generalized other are the shared expectations institutionalized in the police officer or the state's attorney.[36] What is interesting about these examples is their openness — there are different ways of interpreting the indeterminate expectations organized in these generalized others. Thus, middle-class whites might assume that the expectations organized in the "police officer" include enforcing law and order, protecting property, and securing the peace. Yet for poor urban blacks, say, these same expectations may have a radically different meaning. Law and order might represent a system that keeps us in our place, reinforcing our inequality. Protecting property might involve making sure that we don't venture into white neighborhoods. Securing the peace might evoke images of being beaten into submission—even after we have the strength to do nothing but submit.

Similarly, the expectations of the Anglo feminist group carried a meaning for Uttal that differed from their meaning for white feminists. What the latter saw as norms important for moving beyond the competition and silencing they encountered in interactions with men, Uttal experienced as a repressive code of conduct. Again, the point here is that we can take the perspective of relationship without presuming that this perspective is fixed. We can identify with or as a group without having to fix this identity in a set of pregiven assumptions.

Uttal's internalization of the norms and expectations of the feminists of color tells us further that there is not merely one generalized other, but a number of different generalized others. We internalize the expectations of more than one group. Socialization itself, especially in pluralist societies, entails the internalization of a variety of conflicting expectations. This, I think, is one of the key insights recent feminist theorists have expressed through concepts such as "positionality," "intersectionality," and "multiple-voiced subjectivity."[37] They all refer to the multiple, and often contradictory, feelings, experiences, and expectations internalized in and as our identities. Thus, Gloria Anzaldúa describes the contradictory consciousness of the new *mestiza:* "She learns to be an Indian in Mexican culture, to be Mexican from an Anglo point of view. She learns to juggle cultures."[38] Although this juggling is difficult and painful, we learn from Uttal's experience that the recognition and reinforcement we receive through one set of connections can provide us with a standpoint for interpreting, and often combating and rejecting, the distorted recognition or even lack of recognition we experience in other groups. Because there are many generalized others, we are able to develop our juggling skills; we are able to adopt different perspectives.

Once we understand that the norms and expectations organized in the generalized other are varied and interpretable, and once we realize that there are actually a number of different generalized others, we can grasp the openness present in Mead's notion of the perspective of relationship. We can never "be" *an* identity; we can never completely assume the perspective of *the* generalized other. Instead, we adopt an interpretation of it, an interpretation which arises out of our understanding of identity in the context of the relationships in which we are situated. In turn, this interpretability points toward yet another open space in the generalized other — we can argue about our interpretations. "We are not simply bound by the community," Mead writes. "We are engaged in a conversation in which what we say is listened to by the community and its response is one which is affected by what we have to say." [39] This suggests that reflective solidarity has to be understood dialogically — the expectations organized within the generalized other can always be brought up for questioning. Rather than viewing criticism and dissent as threats to solidarity, Mead points out that the ties connecting us with one another can be strengthened through our shared engagement in dialogue. As members of a universal community that includes the voices of past and future, our solidarity requires us to take responsibility by holding up merely given interpretations of the generalized other to the more demanding standards of "the universe of discourse."

Mead's concept of the generalized other organizes the voices of past and future into a dynamic understanding of the perspective of relationship. The voices of the past speak of our traditional criteria for membership. They call on us to heed the values and concerns implicit in how we have formed an identity as "one of us." The voices of the future challenge us to be aware of the criteria we use for membership and to be ready to change them. This challenge in and of itself is a prerequisite for the internal presence of revision which constitutes reflective solidarity. Because it acknowledges and respects the openness and indeterminacy of identity, reflective solidarity provides the bridge to universality.

By stressing that the orientation toward relationship refers to the set of common responses organized in the generalized other and extended through reflection to the community of universal discourse, I have sought to reverse the understanding of the concrete and generalized other offered by Seyla Benhabib. [40] Given the influence of Benhabib's conception, especially on feminist writing, I want now to make this point more explicit.

Benhabib claims that taking the perspective of the generalized other requires viewing each and every individual as a rational being entitled to the same rights that we would ascribe to ourselves. As embodied in the norms of *formal equality* and the *reciprocity* of rights and duties, the perspective of the generalized other is supposed to require that we abstract from the concrete identity of the other. The norms governing our interactions with the generalized other, then, are the public norms of justice. In contrast, Benhabib depicts the concrete other as affective and emotional, with a particular life history and identity. In taking this perspective, we abstract from the commonality of the other to recognize her difference. Here "our relation to the other is governed by the norms of *equity* and *complementary reciprocity:* each is entitled to respect and to assume from the other forms of behavior through which the other feels recognized and confirmed as a concrete, individual being with specific needs, talents and capacities."[41] Arguing that these norms are the private ones of friendship, love, and care, Benhabib views solidarity as one of the moral feelings required when the moral domain is seen from the perspective of the concrete other.[42]

Benhabib raises this distinction to point out the gendered and "ideological" limits of the concept of the self in the idea of taking the standpoint of the other as formulated by John Rawls and Lawrence Kohlberg. Although her critique is pointed and insightful, it overly polarizes the concepts of the generalized and the concrete other and overlooks the usefulness of Mead's vision of the perspective of relationship. Benhabib links the generalized other to the public sphere and the concrete other to the private sphere. This prevents us from seeing how generalized conceptions of role identity influence our domestic and intimate interactions. In other words, Benhabib neglects the fact that norms are always generalized sets of expectations no matter where they come into play. She also overly simplifies the notions of "general" and "concrete." For example, when we think about the reciprocity of justice in order to "treat like as like and unlike as unlike" we can choose from among a dizzying array of standards and levels of detail. Finally, Benhabib's use of the generalized other prevents her from attending to the relationships in which the concrete other is situated. She argues that the generalized other is a way of looking at persons. For Mead, the concept refers to a way of considering relationships: "The attitude of the generalized other is the attitude of the whole community."[43] It is the perspective of relationship essential to reflective solidarity.

Evaluating Reflective Solidarity

The concept of reflective solidarity is formal enough to avoid the problems confronting affectional and conventional solidarities. But this formality does not deny that our experience of these types of solidarity helps anchor our shared expectation that we will take a responsible orientation to our relationships. As we have seen, in affective solidarity we appeal to another to stand with us on the basis of our mutual feelings of care and concern. In conventional solidarity our appeal is based on our common interests, concerns, and struggles. With reflective solidarity we appeal to others to include and support us because our communicative engagement allows us to expect another to take responsibility for our relationship. Here we recognize the other in a way that is neither immediate nor restrictively mediated. We recognize her in her difference, yet understand this difference as part of the very basis of what it means to be one of "us." In other words, we take the attitude of the group, but we take it reflectively, attuned to the standpoint of the situated, hypothetical third.

Because reflection is tied to a responsible orientation to relationships, it does not eliminate the affective moment present in the other two types of solidarity. Indeed, expectations are particular sorts of feelings. So rather than push our feelings aside in order to achieve universality, reflective solidarity transforms the risk of permanent disagreement into a type of feeling, an expectation that we will responsibly attend to each other. By anchoring responsibility in the perspective of the third, reflective solidarity bridges the gap between identity and universality. It thus opens up universality internally, as the recognition of the inalienable individuality of each, and externally, as the willingness to view all as members of the conversation of humanity.

These internal and external dimensions of universality tell us how we can evaluate reflective solidarity. Our failure to acknowledge and respect the other's affirmation of her individual identity indicates a lack of solidarity. It reflects an individualistic attitude toward self insofar as one prioritizes one's own interpretation over an awareness of mutuality.[44] While this emphasis on the recognition of concrete particularity resembles the universality of affective solidarity, it does not require that we completely recognize the other as the "person she is." Instead, reflective solidarity entails that we give the other *the space to be* the person she is. Thus, we don't try to make her a feminist *or* an African American; we don't ask her to be a lesbian *or* an anticolonialist. We respect the depth of her difference and trust her enough to stand with her.

We can also evaluate reflective solidarity by looking at the readiness of members to take responsibility for their shared relationships. We exhibit a responsibility toward relationship when we engage in discussion and critique, when we recognize that cooperation depends on our willingness "to talk things through." We also exhibit responsibility through our awareness of the variety of forms that consideration for the other can take. We adapt to circumstances, realizing that our differences may mean that what strikes me as rude and offensive might be a playful joke to you. We look for compromises, moving beyond the alternatives "either/or." A lack of solidarity here appears as a "consumerist" orientation toward relationships, an orientation which treats association with the other merely as a means to one's own ends. bell hooks seems to have this "consumerist" problem in mind when she criticizes "trendy cultural criticism": "When white critics write about black culture 'cause it's the 'in' subject without interrogating their work to see whether or not it helps perpetuate and maintain racist domination, they participate in the commodification of blackness that is so peculiar to postmodern strategies of colonization."[45] One thus "consumes" a relationship when one fails to contribute to the maintenance of the welfare of those involved and the ongoing renewal of the shared sense of "we."

Contexts of Solidarity

Once solidarity becomes reflective, we can no longer establish once and for all the expectations of solidary groups. How we understand ourselves as a "we," the expectations we have of ourselves and others, changes over time, varying with respect to our needs, circumstances, and understanding of what is necessary to secure the integrity of our relationships. What it means to stand by and take responsibility for another differs according to the context. Admittedly, this could render solidarity so formal as to empty it completely. To avoid this problem, I fill out the concept by suggesting four different ways in which we share in another's life context. Rather than empirical or logical categories, these levels are conceptual "courts of appeal," increasingly larger groups to which we appeal for solidarity. They remind us that we can never establish once and for all who is included in any given "we"; the criteria for inclusion always vary with respect to our context and circumstances.

The solidarity of the "we" of intimate relationships with family, friends, and lovers relies on emotional affirmation. As in affectional solidarity, the expectations of those bound by intimate ties are the strongest and most particular of any social bond. They appear as expectations of physical and emotional fulfillment and nurturance, of mutual willing-ness to overcome self-interest, and of a readiness to put aside one's own concerns to tend to the needs of the others. Because these relationships provide the basis for members' sense of self-trust and security, their in-tegrity requires that each member pay special attention to the changing needs and circumstances of the other, exhibiting responsiveness and un-derstanding.

In groups united by sexuality, ethnicity, and interest, what is expected is commitment. Unlike conventional loyalties, reflectively solidary com-mitments acknowledge the dignity of personal choice. Rejecting the as-sumption that a particular identity necessitates a particular politics, those who reflect on their solidary ties seek to use their differences to come to a communicative agreement on their political goals. They no longer seek to shore up and consolidate identity categories, urging in-stead our attention to and accountability toward the ways in which differences are constructed. So while we understand the importance of ties based on gender and ethnicity, we do not assume that everyone is committed in the same way, or even shoulders the same commitment. We trust each other enough to allow for different perspectives regarding each person's relationship to the group of which we are all a part. We replace narrow, oppositional assessments with ethical assessments, mak-ing democratic dialogue a fundamental component of our group identity.

Cornel West makes a similar point when he urges African Americans to reject cathartic appeals to black authenticity, a closing-ranks mentality, and black cultural conservatism and to adopt a black prophetic framework:

A black prophetic framework encourages *moral* assessment of the variety of perspectives held by black people and selects those views based on black dignity and decency that eschew putting any group of people or culture on a pedestal or in the gutter. Instead, blackness is understood to be either the perennial possibility of white-supremacist abuse or the distinct styles and dominant modes of expression found in black cultures and communities. These styles and modes are diverse — yet they do stand apart from those of other groups (even as they are shaped by and shape those of other groups). And all such styles and modes stand in need of ethical evaluation.[46]

In stressing that blackness contains an element of "standing apart" and in reminding us of the continued presence of white-supremacist abuse,

West's black prophetic framework includes the oppositional moment of the externally designated "we." This reminds us that the importance of the "exclusion of exclusion" appears at the level of sexuality, ethnicity, and interest more strongly than at any other: identity politics has been motivated in part by a struggle against those persons and practices excluding us because of our differences, a motivation which has called into question those exclusions operating within identity groups themselves. When differences are self-affirmed rather than results of labeling or traditional spatial and cultural boundaries, they provide "a standpoint from which to criticize prevailing institutions and norms,"[47] helping to anchor a sense of involvement with the plurality of others in our communities, societies, and the world. Unlike ascribed identities, achieved identities provide us with a critical strength. We have rejected merely given labels and claimed for ourselves a position of resistance.

The expectations of solidarily bound members of states and societies, of citizens, center on legal and material enablement. As embodiments of the expectations of social members, the law and legal institutions represent a basic form of the generalized other. When we think of ourselves and others as citizens we are adopting the perspective of our shared understanding of the rights and duties of participants in our community. Once we take a reflective attitude toward this shared understanding, we realize that citizenship in a pluralist society requires support for the other in her difference. We must allow her the freedom to remain a stranger.[48] To be sure, the concept of rights embodies an appreciation of the concreteness and individuality of each. But, as Julia Kristeva argues, what is important is that instead of seeing the stranger as the other of the citizen, citizens must recognize themselves as "strange."[49]

This means that we need to jettison the abstract concept of the citizen with all its traditionalistic trappings of masculinity and whiteness. Freed from such a restrictive norm, we can acknowledge the diverse forms of action and participation already present in the institutions, associations, and movements in civil society. We can recognize the multiplicity of our interpretations of the meaning of citizenship. Just as progressive women long ago reinterpreted motherhood as the fundamental activity of the feminine citizen, so can we today reconceive our cultural interventions and critical dialogues as themselves the actions of citizens. Acting as citizens, then, does not mean that we must focus our efforts on the state. Our participation extends beyond efforts to change legislation. While this is of course important, once we grasp the variety among citizens, we can think of our work in rape crisis centers, our involvement in religious communities, and our marching in Gay Pride parades as the efforts of an engaged citizenry.

Recognizing ourselves as strange enables us to grasp the way in which we are all already different. We recognize that our individuality, our strangeness, is inextricably tied to those many others constituting our community. No line marks some as normal, as citizens, and others as strange. Although another may strike us as strange, we are nonetheless accountable to and for her. Thus, I agree with Chantal Mouffe's radical democratic emphasis on the variety of ways in which citizenship is exercised, but reject her claim that "to construct a 'we' it must be distinguished from the 'them' and that means establishing a frontier, defining an 'enemy'."[50] Because she presumes that a "we" must always be externally constituted, she neglects the way a "constitutive outside" can be understood as already part of and within each citizen. This presumption, moreover, enables her to neglect our responsibility toward those who might be our "enemies" and reify "outsiders" as *the* "them." So reified, this "them" never threatens or challenges our own understanding of the meaning of citizenship. Mouffe is correct to note that each "we" in a contemporary democratic society is constructed in a context of diversity and conflict. She is right when she claims that there is no "final unity." But neither of these claims requires us to relinquish the effort to include the excluded and acknowledge our accountability for our failures.

Even if another communicates in ways we do not understand, we cannot simply dismiss her as "the enemy." We are obliged to hear her and, when necessary, to alter our discourse so as to allow her voice to emerge. In part, altering our discourse entails that we abandon rhetorical gestures which reinscribe alienness. I'm thinking here of terms like "welfare *queen*," "AIDS *victim*," and, the totalizing expression, "*the* homeless." Additionally, altering our discourse requires us to attend to the histories and metaphors in which we embed our arguments. Although I disagree with parts of their analysis, I am struck by Elizabeth Mensch and Alan Freeman's observation of the way in which Nazism and civil rights frame the abortion discussion. They show how both the pro-choice and the pro-life movements cloak themselves in the language of civil rights while using Nazi images to describe their opponents.[51]

Civic solidarity thus views legal rights and norms as enabling citizens to carry out their lives and projects. Consequently, rights should not provide barriers to the safety of some while securing the advantages of others. To ensure that rights are enabling, reflective solidarity entails an explicit commitment to democratic processes.[52] While this commitment involves the championing of participatory rights that have long been part of the democratic tradition, in reflective solidarity the commitment goes further. Enablement itself projects a vision of equality and reciprocity — our responsibility as citizens to recognize, fight against, and overcome those racist, sexist, and homophobic hatreds that have turned many among us into strangers.

Moreover, given the impact of material conditions on the ability of citizens to exercise their rights, the shared expectation of legal enablement always presumes a commitment to material enablement. As the debates surrounding the welfare state attest, exactly what this means and how it is to be secured is unclear.[53] But the lack of clarity in these debates should not obscure the fact that an underlying expectation of civic solidarity is a commitment to the material needs of fellow citizens. Indeed, the current tragedy of American health care is its violation of our expectation that we must attend to the suffering of those requiring medical attention. It betrays our lack of solidarity as we fail to recognize the call of the sick and injured and affirm our relationship with them. Do "we Americans" really understand ourselves as those who turn away each other at the emergency room door?

The democratic thrust of the reflective solidarity of citizens reminds us that democracy itself is an achieved form of social integration. Its achievement relies on universal ideals capable of securing the integrity of individual identities, ideals embodied in the concepts of rights, liberty, and equality. Such ideals have been the mainstay of the connection between individuality and solidarity underlying the democratic tradition. Ideals of community, as in the evocation "We, the People," rely on the promise of guarantees to individuality. Liberty and equality are conjoined with fraternity, that dimension of solidarity and collective responsibility necessary for the realization of freedom. Autonomy itself, as Kant conceives it, presupposes *membership* in a kingdom of ends. Yet what has been lacking is an emphasis on communication as a primary vehicle of social integration. In the liberal tradition, achieving a "we" has been conceived as taking place in a founding moment, behind the backs of members. For classical republicans, the "we" is merely given, viewed in terms of a preexisting ethical consensus. In contrast, the communicative notion of "we" conceives the achievement of solidarity as an ongoing process of engagement and critique. This thus allows reflective solidarity to embrace the universal ideals necessary for democracy as it urges us to strive communicatively to engage with and recognize each and all as part of our "we."

At the universal level, "we" refers to "we all" as solidarily bound members of an ideal communication community. What is expected is the recognition of our interdependency and shared vulnerability, the acknowledgment of our relationship to one another. At a time of increasing globalization, (im)migration and individualization, we have both the opportunity and the need to see the differences of others as contributions to and aspects of the community of all of us. Our economies are interconnected as workers throughout the world participate in the production of common consumer items. Our cultures are mixing and blending (could anyone clearly explain what American cuisine might be?). Our communication extends throughout the world in increasingly complicated information nets. Thus, in pluralist societies the limitation of solidarity to those in our *ethnos* — even if we could draw such a line — threatens the very possibility of democratic discourse.[54]

To be sure, exactly how we express this universal solidarity remains open. Solidarity with earlier generations manifests itself through the recognition of their struggles, pains, and sacrifices.[55] We have to remember and acknowledge the violence and betrayals in our pasts. We have to recover the histories that have been silenced and forgotten. Solidarity toward future generations calls on us to see more than the present. We must accept our responsibility for the environment. We must institutionalize processes of greater inclusion and communication. We must avoid saddling those who come after us with debts, pains, and obligations that will simply repeat hierarchies of domination and subordination benefiting the few. Finally, solidarity toward present generations is expressed in our willingness to recognize and strengthen the ties connecting all of us, to let others know that they are neither forgotten nor alone. Here solidarity requires us to speak out against oppression and exclusion. Recently, German soccer fans exhibited such reflective solidarity.[56] The Frankfurt team was playing a match in Austria. Each time their star black player entered the field, the Austrians made monkey noises. The German fans responded by shouting "Nazis get out!" They took out full-page ads and had banners made proclaiming "We don't have anything against Austrians. Just racists." This is the universal dimension of reflective solidarity.

Jürgen Habermas writes that solidarity "is rooted in the realization that each person must take responsibility for the other because as consociates all must have an interest in the integrity of their shared life context in the same way."[57] We are interested in "the same way" not simply because of our mutual interdependence, though this is important, but also because each of us wants to be acknowledged as an individual, with unique perspectives and contributions that give shape and are *allowed* to give shape to the collectivities of which we are a part. Reflective solidarity relies on this fundamental reciprocity. More abstract than affectional and conventional notions of solidarity, reflective solidarity's commitment to reciprocity reminds us that solidarity in postmodern conditions has to be achieved. Unlike the ascribed identity which secures even as it undermines identity politics, reflective solidarity is never easy and always at risk. Yet given that the risk is either abandonment and isolation or coercion and conformity, reflective solidarity offers the possibility of community among those who respect and take accountability for their differences.

CHAPTER 2

Struggling for Recognition

Identity Politics and Democracy

My brother David was an undergraduate minoring in women's studies at Denison University when he joined his first lesbian, gay, and friends coalition. An outspoken feminist oriented sexually toward women, he joined the group out of solidarity with a closeted member of his fraternity. He didn't "advertise" his membership as trendy, chic, or "lefter than thou." He didn't try to persuade his closeted friend to accompany him to meetings. His solidarity was quieter, his own way of affirming his friend, of showing his support for him if and when he chose to come out. Later, as a graduate student at Union Theological Seminary, David spoke to me of his frustration with his classes' often heated arguments surrounding race and ethnicity, sexuality and gender. His very presence as a straight, white man was, for some, offensive. David's frustration was not the whining of some "uppity white boy" upset by "reverse discrimination" or by the deconstruction of the academy by "tenured radicals" and "political correctness." He recognized and detested his sexual, racial, and class privilege. So, he was joking when he said that he was "insufficiently marginalized." (I've since wondered if his numerous tatoos and piercings were efforts to become more marginalized.)

For me, David's joke symbolizes the fundamental problem with identity politics. Because of his privilege as a straight, upper-middle-class, white male, he could have no "real" politics. Were he to root a politics in his identity, he would risk rearticulating precisely those structures of power, privilege, and domination that he has spent most of his life fighting. Just as he rejected the racisms of Alabama and Texas as a child and adolescent, his graduate work as an adult has focused on investigating and destabilizing contemporary notions of masculinity. So even a nonessentialist identity politics, an identity politics that urges us to transform and reconstruct our identities, fails to account for David's politics. Although rooted in who he is, his politics cannot be reduced to or equated with his identity. More complex than the statement "the personal is political" can acknowledge, his politics have led him to try to enter the margins and place sexual and racial "others" at the center. He has sought to take the perspective of situated, hypothetical thirds. His is a politics of reflective solidarity.

Despite the fact that identity politics cannot account for my brother's politics, it is important to it. Without the struggles for recognition of women and men of differing ethnicities and sexualities, David may have remained unaware of his privilege, a privilege which itself explains why identity politics for straight, white men strikes us as absurdly, if not maliciously, reactionary. Without identity politics, we could not understand even the possibility of a perspective of the situated, hypothetical third. Indeed, a number of critics of identity politics, although convinced of the need to eschew essentialist conceptions of identity, have been reluctant to discard the concept altogether. Aware of the critical and transformational potential of a politics deeply rooted in our sense of who we are, they are actively thinking through the impact and repercussions of identity politics on contemporary democratic praxis. For, as Henry Giroux writes, "A critical perspective on identity politics should be seen as fundamental to any discourse and social movement that believes in the radical renewal of democratic society."[1]

Over the past few decades identity politics has presented itself as a radical form of political agency. Indeed, identity politics has, for many, replaced an emphasis on class to emerge as the quintessential form of the struggle for recognition and inclusion. It has seemed to provide precisely that combination of community and contest, of security and change, capable of addressing the concerns of those who have been excluded in contemporary democratic societies. Most importantly, to its adherents, identity politics offers an assurance of safety and community.

Identity politics makes this offer, however, at the cost of difference and reflection: those aspects of our identities that differ from those designated by our identity categories, those aspects that remain unique and particular to us as individuals, have to be suppressed or denied. Put somewhat differently, the identities offered by identity politics are generalized others; they are the organized expectations of group members. After all, the identity within identity politics designates a relationship. But what has happened is that these generalized others have been interpreted as already given. There has not been a space for members to question and criticize *as members* the group's conception of its identity. There has not been a space for hypothetical thirds. I want to look at the impact of identity politics on struggles for recognition in contemporary democracies to see where we might find spaces for difference, for queries and thirds, capable of sustaining the reflective solidarity of groups and movements actively engaged in social and political change.

Wendy Brown and Kirstie McClure have recently provided interesting and important analyses of the relationship between identity politics and contemporary democracy.[2] Keenly attuned to the ways in which power and exclusion have produced the "subjects" of identity politics, Brown and McClure suggest alternative visions of identity and the political rooted in desire and agency. My own account of identity politics supplements rather than strictly opposes Brown and McClure's analyses. It takes the perspective of those struggling for recognition to show how reflective solidarity emerges out of the problems of recognition exposed in the course of this struggle. Reflective solidarity seeks to retain a sense of community while also providing a space for questioning and critique. Based on the communicative ties between the "you" and "I" that are always part of "we," it makes contestation the basis for connection. To this end, it presents itself as the activist ideal of a post–identity politics. So while I find much that is convincing in arguments that stress the "disciplinary production" of politicized identities, I am interested in the meaning of identity politics for those who have used it to fight against exclusion. Accordingly, I offer a brief sketch of the movements of lesbians and gay men, African Americans, and women as they have struggled for different sorts of recognition. Although each movement confronts a particular problem — visibility, memory, and experience — they all follow a common pattern as they move from assimilation, through accommodation, to accountability.

As I offer this sketch, I do not mean to imply that each phase of identity politics is separate, confined to a particular historical moment. On the contrary, each phase represents a current position in a hotly contested debate. As will become clear, my reading of the third phase in terms of accountability and solidarity is an intervention in this debate. Further, the distinctions I draw among these groups are artificial, as artificial as the identity categories of identity politics themselves. These groups overlap in innumerable significant ways, as we see in the impact of black lesbian writing on all these three fields of identity politics. Finally, in drawing attention to the similarities among the groups, I risk of course overlooking their differences and encountering the same problems I criticize in identity politics. But, again, I am offering a sketch, not a detailed or comprehensive reading of the variety of positions and texts that have come to constitute the identity politics debate. Caveats aside, by focusing on the struggles for recognition in which identity politics engages, I show how different demands for recognition are responses to differing experiences of exclusion; how the shift from one phase or strategy to the next is occasioned by the problem of the speaking subject; how identity politics affects our understanding of contemporary democracy; and how identity politics leads to a reflective notion of solidarity.

The Three Phases of Identity Politics

In the United States, identity politics has evolved through three distinct phases: assimilation, accommodation, and accountability. Each phase is characterized by a particular notion of the subject, the sort of recognition demanded, the type of appeal raised in making this demand, a vision of society or culture, and a corresponding political theory or conception of the state and legal system. To introduce these phases, I reconstruct them by taking the perspective of the situated, hypothetical third. That is, I situate myself as one of those struggling for recognition, rather than beginning as one of "us."

ASSIMILATION

The self at phase one is the modern subject. When I speak, I am the same as any other "I." I am rational and autonomous. Although I have feelings and needs, what authorizes my ability to speak, what stands behind me as an "I" is my capacity to reason. In raising my voice, in claiming my right to speak at all, I am asking to be recognized as like you. I am asking for those rights that will guarantee that you will hear me, that my voice will not be ignored and dismissed as unworthy, but will instead at least be tolerated and included as a voice equal to your own. As I speak, I am shedding my second-class status and, again, attempting to "be" like you, rational and autonomous. Thus, I appeal to the reason that unites us. Although it may seem as if in asking for toleration I am asking you to include me despite my differences, my request is premised on the underlying reason that unites us and on my tacit acceptance of you as an arbiter, for you are the one who should tolerate me. I want to assimilate into your society, that melting pot of equal opportunity. Law will help me. Neutral and liberal, it will protect me just as it does you. It will secure our equality. I therefore target my efforts on the state, striving to secure legal recognition of my rights as a free and equal citizen.

ACCOMMODATION

At the accommodation phase, the self is viewed as essentially different. "I am" a race, sex, class, sexual orientation, age, and ability. These identifications "authorize" my capacity to speak. They establish the legitimacy of my words, experiences, and claims. As they connect me with those beyond myself, with those others who are like me, my identifications reinforce my authority, allowing me to speak. When I speak to you, I want you to recognize me in my difference: I want you to see who I am in my need and particularity. Moreover, I want you to recognize not only my needs but also my culture, those values, attributes, and contributions that you have ignored for so long. I thus appeal to those experiences that both unite me with others like me and set me apart from you. While I may emphasize my oppression, more often than not when I appeal to my experience, I am doing so triumphantly, taking pride in my ability to survive and create without your recognition.

Of course, it is difficult for me to speak. I must recover both the past that connects me to those who authorize my voice and my own sense of self-worth and self-respect. I seek authenticity, trying to find the authentic histories and experiences that give content to who I am. I am less interested in your society than in my own culture. Your society is hierarchical and exclusionary. You exert power in myriad ways that attempt to stifle my voice. Since you and your values determine what counts and who can be heard, your law can neither help nor hear me. Its rulings and decisions are value judgments, embedded in those traditions and particularities so important to communitarians. At best, I can take this law and change it in my own image. My interest in the state is thus ambiguous. That it excludes me determines who I am, giving significance and import to my difference, but I prefer to concentrate my efforts more on building and developing this identity than on challenging the state.

ACCOUNTABILITY

At the accountability phase, the self is viewed as constructed, formed through multiple interconnections with others. When I speak to you, our context and relationship affect how you hear me; they affect who "I" am and can be. But I am always more than the "I" speaking to you. I am involved in myriad conversations in which who I am shifts and changes. My demand for recognition, then, calls upon you to address the context and relationships in which "we" are formed. I am asking you to take responsibility for your complicity in the ways in which I am excluded and devalued. You must be accountable, admitting your privilege and the costs at which it has been bought. When I speak to you, I am establishing a connection with you, trying to get you to recognize that we are all in this together. I am appealing to solidarity, to our collective responsibilities toward each other and our life context.

Of course, like our identities, these responsibilities remain open and in need of interpretation. Neither fixed nor given, they necessitate that we adopt a reflective attitude toward them. When we participate in making the laws that will govern our relationship, we recognize their limits and their inadequacies. We accept responsibility for those we have excluded, seeking to find new ways to include by constantly challenging restrictive interpretations and representations. Within our already multicultural society, we can together question and critique, accept and celebrate those parts of our traditions which are meaningful for us. So I participate in democratic practices and institutions, while also seeking to disrupt and challenge them. I accept a variety of terrains as fora for our conflict and debate. Everyday social practices, cultural representations, performances and exhibitions, the variety of intersections of public and private — all constitute the field of my politics.

Lesbians and Gay Men: The Problem of Visibility

The "homophile" phase of the struggle by lesbians and gay men for recognition lasted from the early fifties until the 1969

Stonewall Rebellion.[3] During this period, homosexual thought described same-sex love as a fundamental character trait. The publications of the Daughters of Bilitis and the Mattachine Society often accepted early sexologists' diagnoses of homosexuality or "inversion" as abnormal or even degenerate. Nonetheless, they argued for an end to discrimination against lesbians and gay men on the grounds of "the underlying shared humanity of homosexuals and heterosexuals."[4] Thus focused on the similarities between homo- and heterosexuals, those in the homophile movement urged assimilation. Describing the Mattachine Society's strategy for attaining equality, Barry Adam writes that "it was an approach founded on an implicit contract with the larger society wherein gay identity, culture, and values would be disavowed (or at least concealed) in return for the *promise* of equal treatment."[5] Looking at the politics of the Daughters of Bilitis (DOB), Vera Whisman explains that "the DOB saw its mission as educating the public, participating in research and assisting 'the adjustment of the variant to society.' That program of adjustment discouraged the embrace of butch-femme styles, seeking to teach butches, in particular, 'a mode of behavior and dress acceptable to society.'"[6] The DOB wanted recognition for lesbians as visible members of the community, but not as visible lesbians.

For lesbians as well as gay men the politics of assimilation had a fundamental drawback: it rendered them invisible, reinforcing their deviant and excluded status. If rights were to be predicated on similarity, the very differences marking their exclusion disappeared. What, exactly, was left to be protected? Toleration as a goal accepted the heterosexism of the dominant society because it allowed that which was to be tolerated to escape from view. Put somewhat differently, the emphasis on the fundamental sameness of homo- and heterosexuals created a problem for the subject seeking to assimilate. If her right and capacity to speak were premised on commonality, if the "I" seeking recognition is authorized by an already given understanding of the meaning of subjectivity, then the difference that prompts the need to voice the demand for inclusion can neither be part of the concept of the subject nor be recognized. Inessential and unworthy of protection or recognition, difference is forced into secrecy.

The next phase of the lesbian and gay struggle for recognition focused on difference and visibility. Marked by the Stonewall Rebellion and the rise of lesbian feminism, this phase could be summed up by the slogan "Gay is Good." However, the simplicity of the slogan belies the complexity of the identity politics at phase two. As they responded to the tensions that the goal of assimilation created for the speaking subject, lesbians and gay men turned from society to culture. They endeavored to recover and solidify their identities by taking pride in and building up their communities. In part, this effort involved an attack on the structures of heterosexism, institutional as well as representational and symbolic, that had excluded them in the first place. Recognizing that assimilation left heterosexism intact, lesbians and gay men shifted to an emphasis on difference that would challenge the exclusionary nature of the dominant society. However, as they moved toward a politics of accommodation, of difference, they retained a focus on similarity that, even as it buttressed their cultural critique, undermined their ability to solve the problem of the speaking subject.

Lesbian and gay theory at phase two, though it sought to challenge the sexism and heterosexism of mainstream society, split along gender lines. Separating from gay men and stressing their similarity to straight women, lesbian feminists argued that lesbianism was a political choice available to all women. No longer primarily a sexual or character trait, lesbianism was theorized both as "the rage of all women condensed to the point of explosion" and a continuum of bonding and identification with women.[7] Lesbians were the feminist vanguard. Lesbianism itself was a vehicle for women's liberation, an act of resistance, an attack "on male right of access to women."[8] Paradoxically, this view of lesbianism as uniting all women was seen as enabling women to achieve the autonomy necessary for equality with men.[9] As Cheryl Clarke writes: "For a woman to be a lesbian in a male-supremacist, capitalist, misogynist, homophobic, imperialist culture, such as that of North America, is an act of resistance. . . . No matter how a woman lives out her lesbianism—in the closet, in the state legislature, in the bedroom—she has rebelled against becoming the slave master's concubine, viz. the male-dependent female, the female heterosexual."[10] Choosing lesbianism would enable a woman to escape her connection with a man and become equal to him.

The emphasis on difference characteristic of phase two is thus mitigated by an underlying current of sameness. For just as lesbian feminists stressed the connections between lesbian and straight women, so did gay male theorists rely on a core concept of the self as innately bisexual. Again challenging heterosexist presumptions, gay liberation theorists such as Dennis Altman and Allen Young viewed homosexuals as the vanguard of a movement against sexism wherein sexism is defined as "a belief or practice that the sex or sexual orientation of human beings gives to some the right to certain privileges, powers, or roles, while denying to others their potential."[11] The gay liberation phase thus exhibits the outward orientation characteristic of conventional solidarities. Adams explains that "gay liberation never thought of itself as a civil rights movement for a particular minority, but as a revolutionary struggle to free the homosexuality in everyone."[12] As the vanguard, homosexuals were said to be better able to build equitable relationships because they had escaped the confines of a rigid sex/gender system.

But despite (or because of?) the undercurrent of sameness, the vanguardism of lesbian and gay theory was at the center of lesbians' and gay men's celebration of difference. Vanguardism provided an identity around which to base claims for inclusion: homosexuality was the way out, for all of us, of the restrictions of normalized heterosexuality. Consequently, a vision not only of the repressive monotony of straight life but also of the new life to come was necessary. Lesbians developed the womanculture of Lesbian Nation with an eye to ending gender and hierarchy altogether — an effort that led to close scrutiny of dress, food, and sexual behavior. Gay men turned to community building, focusing on lifestyle and personal identity. In short, as they developed common identities and communities, lesbians and gay men were actively engaged in constructing a generalized other — a "Lesbian," a "Gay Man" — who differed from the dominant heterosexual society and embodied the expectations of their own groups.

With the growing stress on community and the expectations it embodied, the vanguard idea came to be equated with, and superseded by, the idea of "coming out." If homosexuality was a way out, what was it out of? The answer was the closet, that symbol of heterosexual oppression and forced denial of one's identity and experience as a gay man or a lesbian.[13] Being homosexual was not in itself liberating or liberatory; one had to choose and proclaim one's identity. This act of claiming and taking pride in a previously stigmatized identity would challenge the heterosexism of the dominant society by making visible what had for so long remained secret and unseen. The coming-out story thus became the key narrative of gay and lesbian identity.

As Judith Butler asks, however, what were lesbians and gay men coming in to?[14] As it became the marker of gay identity and the vanguardism of homosexuality, the notion of coming out embodied the tension of the speaking subject that was already disrupting identity politics at phase two. What had been, and for many still is, a profoundly meaningful experience of personal pain and understanding was not enough to guarantee community. If "we" are all already gay, or have the possibility for gay and bisexual identifications, what could it mean to come out? We are all already there. (Lesbian feminism, with its emphasis on lesbianism as a political choice available to all women, is interesting here because of its lack of a coming-out narrative.) By focusing on a unifying experience, gay and lesbian theorists subverted the premise of sameness on which the vanguard theory rested. Clearly, not everyone wanted to or felt safe enough to claim a gay identity.

As gay and lesbian subcultures solidified, voices of dissent emerged criticizing the dominant norms of these communities. "Coming out" could not in itself replace the differences of where people were "coming from." Issues involving race and class, bisexuality, butch-femme, S/M, the transgendered, and pedophilia challenged the stability of gay and lesbian identity. Steven Seidman explains that for many of the excluded "the very discourse of liberation, with its notion of a gay subject unified by common interests, was viewed as a disciplining social force oppressive to large segments of the community in whose name it spoke."[15] Asserting an identity could not guarantee a "politics"; it could not in and of itself anchor a specific course of action. Identities already were political, themselves positions in and products of contestation. The emphasis on coming out thus began to overshadow the importance of politics. Instead of a first step, coming out acquired the connotations of the ultimate step, leaving the hard work of organizing, protesting, and coalition building undone.

The coming-out story establishes a premature closure that subverts the position of the speaking subject.[16] As it marks the entrée into gay community, this story narrates "the revisionist history of our lives in which we recount all the events leading to the magic moment when— ah—it finally all made sense. Identity and interpretation come together in one compact tale."[17] This finality of meaning has its costs: it presupposes a commonality of experience over and against which differences have no claim. Would those parts of my story left out of the dominant narrative no longer be part of "me" after I claimed a lesbian or gay identity? Into what space or under what sign would I place these differences? All of us who have told the same story are through this telling assumed to be in agreement, but our differences nonetheless remain, themselves constituted as differences through our very telling of "the same story."

If the telling of the coming-out story is what renders the narrative "I" coherent, it isn't clear what sort of response is expected or required from those outside the gay community. Although the coming-out story challenges heterosexual society through its demand to be heard, to the extent that it rests on an oppositional and experiential notion of identity (for identity is constructed through telling the story of its difference), it cannot serve as a bridge between communities. If your experiences are not mine, what is left for you to say upon hearing my story? At best, you can accept my sincerity with no thought as to the potential normative consequences of my speech. At worst you can say, "I knew it all along," reducing my performative assertion of my identity to pure description.[18] Indeed, we have seen this "worst" as the Right has been able to avoid dealing with AIDS by reducing it to an identity issue for "homosexual, minority, and drug-addicted others" and creating for itself a false image of a "pure, healthy, safe, white, normal we."

Attuned to the dilemma that the politics of accommodation poses for the speaking subject, gay and lesbian theorists of the third phase — more precisely, queer theorists — have moved away from the rigid identity politics of phase two.[19] Although some still speak the language of identity, they reconceive it as multiple, overlapping, and in process. Lisa Kahaleole Chang Hall writes: "Our identities never become final because new experiences continue to affect the way we see ourselves, and these new identifications in turn affect the kinds of experience we can have and the kinds of communities we can create."[20] Her appreciation of the openness and change within identities thus reminds us of the way that generalized others can never be fixed — they are always open for revision and reinterpretation. Numerous writers, moreover, focus on possibilities of community and coalition, attuned to the exclusionary as well as the liberatory impact of representations, discourses, and institutions. Dan Danielson has looked at how the courts have treated homosexuality as both central to identity and separate from it, in effect exhibiting the contradictions and complexity already present in lived experiences of gay identity.[21] In the indeterminacy of law, Danielson finds the radical possibility of ongoing interpretative struggles. Lauren Berlant and Elizabeth Freeman have examined the boundary-crossing tactics of Queer Nation. They note how it operates on a variety of terrains, from the national to the local, from the representational to the consumerist.[22]

The very word "queer" signifies the change between the second and third phases. In his discussion of debates in San Francisco over the word, David Thomas points out that, rather than focusing on genes or desire, the "q-word" challenges "the social construction that created queer confinement."[23] This word seeks to provide an inclusive category of election and coalition while simultaneously confronting the problem of public hostility. Indeed, the tensions "queer" invokes disrupt the possibility and meaning of recognition. Claiming "queer" as a label "is an aggressive demand for recognition which simultaneously calls into question that which is to be recognized and denies the recognizer use of the term of what is to be recognized."[24] By destabilizing the position of the one who recognizes, "queer" asserts from the outset its own public visibility; by disrupting the notion of what is recognized, it transforms the debate over recognition into a discussion of accountability. The issue is less one of asserting an identity to be recognized than of acknowledging the ways in which our spaces, discourses, representations, and bodies are already connected.

At phase three, the tensions of the speaking subject are not so much solved as they are revealed as the problematic repercussions of static conceptions of identity. By replacing the modern subject of phase one and the identified subject of phase two with the subject of discourse in phase three, queer theorists restructure the problem of speaking as an issue of what is spoken and the conditions for and of speech itself. They are now concerned with the ways in which particular discourses and relations of power create and structure the categories of homosexual and heterosexual, gay and straight.[25] Far from eliminating the capacity for speech, this new concern challenges us to develop an awareness of the impact of languages on us, as well as "our" impact on them. It creates a space in which the concrete differences signified by the situated, hypothetical third can be acknowledged. The third phase, then, is one of accountability. Appeals are implicitly raised to our solidarity, to our material and discursive interconnections, and to our capacity to reflect upon the meaning of and expectations within our relations as consociates in a multicultural democracy.

African Americans: The Problem of Memory

For many African Americans the first phase of the civil rights movement was a time of promise and potential. Inspired by Martin Luther King, Jr., and others, blacks in the United States sought to secure their dignity and equality by ending segregation and overturning restrictions that had prevented them from exercising their right to vote. Yet, as Cornel West explains, early civil rights activists

uncritically accepted nonblack conventions and standards in two ways. First, they proceeded in an *assimilationist manner* that set out to show that black people were really like white people—thereby eliding differences (in history, culture) between whites and blacks. Black specificity and particularity was thus banished in order to gain white acceptance and approval. Second, these black responses rested on a *homogenizing impulse* that assumed that all black people were really alike—hence obliterating differences (class, gender, region, sexual orientation) between black peoples.[26]

Compounding the problem of the assimilationist strategy, the entrenched racism of white America proved for many blacks that achieving freedom and equality would take more than civil rights. In the face of racism, blacks remained different and other in ways in which rights alone could not address. Rights alone could not erase the memory of slavery for blacks or whites. Indeed, more often than not, the granting of civil rights had the unhappy result of absolving whites from their complicity in the continuation of black oppression. Content that blacks now had "their rights," white people could forget the costs at which white privilege had been bought.

Part of the mistake of assimilation was its forgetting of the meaning of historically constructed and entrenched differences. Discussing the disillusionment she and other African Americans felt *after the success* of the civil rights movement, Jean Smith observes:

The crux of the matter is that they believed there was a link between representation in government and making that government work for you. What they—and I—discovered was that for some people, this link does not exist. For most black people, voting has not much more benefit than the exercise of walking to the polls. Why is this the case? Because the link between voting and partaking of the benefits of society exists at the pleasure of society. The society must be willing to respond to the legitimate needs of the people; only then can the channels for the expression of these needs, such channels as voting, be meaningfully exploited.[27]

Consequently, Smith, like others around her, rejected the politics of assimilation, a politics rooted in an emphasis on sameness and equality, to become consciously black. This meant recovering the memory of the black experience.

The second phase of the African American struggle for inclusion and recognition was based on reclaiming black identity, an identity rooted in the powerful symbol of "Africa." "Black is beautiful," proclaimed the popular slogan. Recovering the origins of that beauty in the preslavery homeland provided a space for the construction of a black subjectivity that was much more than that allotted by assimilation. So as black nationalism rose to the fore, "the veneration of 'black' symbols, rituals, styles, hairdos, values, sensibilities and flag escalated."[28] Taking pride in black culture and achievements supplanted the previous phase's emphasis on sameness. Integration was now condemned as an affirmation of whiteness and a denigration of blackness.[29] Thus, Stokely Carmichael and others argued for a black power stemming from the common experience of and pride in being black. This common experience and pride were thought to enable black power to solve the problem of speech and representation present in phase one: only those who could find their roots in this experience could speak to black needs.

But the ability of a memory to provide a stable basis from which one could speak was problematic. Cornel West describes the tension as one of leadership—which leaders could claim to speak for the community depended on the interpretation of *the* black experience.[30] Since this experience legitimated black leadership, "getting it right" became crucial—as we saw in the construction and reconstruction of Clarence Thomas's personal history as "black." For Glenn Loury, the orthodoxy of *the* black experience created an internal conflict that led him to question his own identity:

As my evolving understanding of our history began to clash with the black consensus, and my definition of the struggle took on a different, more conservative form from that popular among other black intellectuals, I found myself cut off from the group, my racial bona fides in question. I was therefore forced to choose between my intellectual integrity and my access to that collective consciousness of racial violation and shared experience of struggle which I saw as essential to my black identity.[31]

Black nationalism endeavored to force racial unity through homogenization. It sought to solidify the variety of experiences and expectations within the black community into one generalized other. But this generalized other was not general but specific, specifically masculine and specifically straight. As bell hooks and others have argued, black nationalism was profoundly sexist—that is, misogynist and homophobic—in its efforts to buttress an ideal of black manhood. These critics challenge the ability of the black nationalist subject to speak for women and gays.

Additionally, far from overcoming the duality of black and white, the second phase solidified it in oppositional "us vs. them" terms: what was one to make of the presence of mulattos and "light-skinned blacks," of the sometimes tense relations between African nationals and African Americans, of interracial relationships and their offspring? Finally, the idea of *the* black experience covered up the differences of class and privilege already dividing African Americans among themselves. Were those with wealth, opportunity, and relative prestige, or those who had grown up in more integrated contexts, somehow "less black"?

Consequently, the third phase of the African American struggle for inclusion and recognition "re-members" differently. Rather than employing a unifying account of *the* black experience, theorists of this phase work on uncovering and clarifying the different meanings and constructions of terms such as "black" and "white," examining how the very concept of race has been deployed.[32] A number of theorists, moreover, explicitly link this work to the project of rebuilding African American community and solidarity. For example, bell hooks argues:

We cannot respond to the emergence of multiple black experiences by advocating a return to narrow cultural nationalism. Contemporary critiques of essentialism (the assumption that there is a black essence shaping all African-American experience, expressed traditionally by the concept of "soul") challenge the idea that there is only "one" legitimate black experience. Facing the reality of multiple black experiences enables us to develop diverse agendas for unification, taking into account the specificity and diversity of who we are.[33]

In fact, hooks argues that a "critical consciousness" that emphasizes "airing diverse perspectives" is crucial to transformative politics: "Engaging in intellectual exchange where people hear a diversity of viewpoints enables them to witness first hand a solidarity that grows stronger in a context of productive critical exchange and confrontation."[34]

With an understanding of "black" as a social and political construction, Cornel West appeals to accountability.[35] He rejects the second phase's emphasis on sameness: "As we go forward as black progressives, we must remember that community is not about homogeneity. Homogeneity is dogmatic imposition, pushing your way of life, your way of doing things onto somebody else. That is not what we mean by community."[36] As it refuses to respect the irreplaceable uniqueness of each, homogeneity provides a false sense of community, one that urges the accommodation of a pregiven set of differences rather than our shared accountability in the face of multiplicity. Also rejecting homogenizing and truncated understandings of authentic racial identity, Michael Eric Dyson offers the aspiration of an "enabling solidarity" that will "only appeal to the richly varied meanings of cultural practices, the diversity of authentic roles one may express within the repertoire of black cultural identities, and the ever-expanding context of historical experience in supporting its vision of racial cooperation."[37]

The emphasis on community and solidarity through diversity found in the third phase corresponds to a renewed emphasis on struggles for rights. But unlike the focus in phase one on state-centered rights, third-phase theorists retain and expand the emphasis on culture found in the black power phase. This means that democratic contestation itself is viewed as a central aspect of African American history. Urging the importance of rights in the context of contemporary democracy, West argues that "work within the existing legal system helps keep alive a memory of the social traces left by past progressive movements of resistance — a memory requisite for future movements."[38] Democracy is itself a repository of memory pointing toward the future. The rights that have been won are reasserted, reinterpreted, and expanded through the contestation and engagement that they guarantee.

As she argues for a jurisprudence of generosity, Patricia Williams seeks to provide a more nuanced understanding of legal and social responsibility by exposing the ways in which the so-called objectivity of legal authority is "in fact mired in hidden subjectivities and unexamined claims."[39] She exposes them through various acts of remembering, urging a collective responsibility not to forget the legacy of the past, a past that remains embodied in the law. After all, blacks were included in the Constitution — as three-fifths of a person. And, as racism and bigotry persist, there is no accountability: "Laws become described and enforced in the spirit of our prejudices."[40] Nonetheless, Williams remains committed to the potential of law. Williams remembers both the white lawyer who was her great-great-grandfather and the slave, Sophie, her great-great-grandmother, reinterpreting the rights of the white lawyer as her own. As she claims those rights denied to Sophie, Williams embraces the spirit and the ideal of law. She sees law as the embodiment of collective responsibility, a responsibility that requires us to become "multilingual in the semantics of evaluating rights."[41] Thus, Williams accepts the indeterminacy of rights while changing and challenging the context of meaning that has limited and distorted their application. For her, reinterpreting rights means extending the power of rights to the disempowered, manipulating the images of power within rights through this extension: "In principle, therefore, the more dizzyingly diverse the images that are propagated, the more empowered we will be as a society."[42]

As are queer theorists, so are a number of African American writers rejecting the rigid identity politics of the second phase to urge a broader solidarity that breaks with and questions the confines of race. To be sure, they use racial categories, aware of the histories of discrimination in which race-blindness hides accountability for racism. Yet unlike the re-emerging voices of separatism and nationalism, they reject the "us/them" mentality that reduces solutions to racism to issues of taking sides — solutions that over the last few years have erupted in violence. Confronting the barely submerged warfare raging through America's inner cities, these theorists of the third phase reassert the importance of democratic contestation, aware that although the reflective solidarity offered therein is fallible, fragile, and often illusory, it nonetheless provides the possibility of remembering and overcoming exclusion.

Women: The Problem of Experience

What is generally known as first-wave feminism centered around women's struggle for the rights to acquire an education, own property, and vote. Emphasizing their capacity to reason, they appealed to rational men to recognize them as human beings. Although some women stressed women's role as the mothers of future citizens and evoked the importance of feminine qualities of care and nurturance as remedies to early problems of industrialization and urbanization, to the extent that they sought to insert feminine experience into a public sphere, first-wave feminists relied on a universal notion of participatory citizenship and accepted the importance of rights as the vehicle for entry.

Having won these rights, however, women remained subordinate to men. Consequently, they encountered the problem of voice: "If I am a rational, autonomous subject like you, why am I still different? Why is my voice still not heard?" In trying to answer this question, second-wave feminists began critiquing the notion of the modern subject, arguing that the "I" itself was already masculine. Understood from the outset as separate, autonomous, and independent, this "I" signified masculinity, the male experience of detachment from others.[43] In contrast, women's experiences were said to be those of deep connection, both physical and emotional, to the people and world around them. For them, to utter "I" would be to deny the fundamental character of their femininity. Thus, second-wave feminists explained the limits of recognition possible at the assimilation phase as a failure of the politics of rights and equality and turned to a celebration of feminine specificity. Replacing the universal "I" with a particular one, they fought for recognition of women's distinct moral voice, feminine cultural achievements, and those bodily needs specific to women. For many, recovering the feminine was viewed as essential for the survival of the species and the planet. Critical of the instrumental reason that has led to environmental destruction and the possibility of nuclear annihilation, their struggle to recover feminine and maternal values was thus profoundly outward oriented.

Underlying this struggle was an appeal to those experiences differentiating women from men. On the one hand, the emphasis on experience was an epistemological strategy. As Susan Sherwin writes:

Feminists do not assume that the truth is readily accessible if only we concentrate hard enough. Recognizing that what has been claimed to be objective and universal is in reality the male point of view, feminists seek to concentrate on women's own experience and explicitly avoid any claims of being "objective, abstract or universal."[44]

On the other hand, it was an effort to give content and validity to the category "Woman"; that is, it was an attempt to solve the problem of the speaking subject by reauthorizing women's voices.[45] For example, Catharine MacKinnon draws from the experiences voiced in consciousness raising as grounds not only for a new epistemology, but also for female subjectivity: "This process gives both content and form to women's point of view."[46] In *Only Words* MacKinnon takes one set of experiences to be synonymous with Woman's point of view, asking the reader to adopt this perspective: "Imagine that for hundreds of years your most formative traumas, your daily suffering and pain, the abuse you live through, the terror you live, are unspeakable. . . . You grow up with your father holding you down and covering your mouth so another man can make a horrible searing pain between your legs."[47]

Precisely this effort to ground the concept of Woman in women's experiences remained exclusionary. Rooted in an essentialist and reductive presumption that the experiences of white women—be they as mothers, heterosexuals, middle-class wives, white-collar employees, or victims—could stand for the experiences of all women, attempts to define the meaning and content of women's voices ended up alienating large numbers of women. Someone was already left out, as women of color, lesbians, and others explained.

The critique of essentialism led to an awareness of the myriad meanings and interpretations of experience. Women began to explore and write from their differences, emphasizing their particular experiences of racism, homophobia, ageism, ableism, and "lookism" as well as their desires, longings, fantasies, and dreams. Numerous anthologies and collections issued as texts for women's studies courses sought to include difference by publishing firsthand narratives of the experiences of Anglo lesbians and lesbians of color, straight women of differing abilities and classes, and women whose ethnic and sexual identities escaped easy categorization. At the same time, white feminists sought to overcome their own essentialism by broadening notions of feminine experience and Woman's standpoint to include multiple experiences and standpoints.

Simply adding an "s," however, failed to challenge the primacy of the white woman and her experiences. Class, race, and sexual orientation were presumed secondary to gender. As Norma Alarćon explains in her discussion of Anglo-American feminists' reception of the anthology *This Bridge Called My Back*, "Anglo feminist readers of *Bridge* tend to appropriate it, cite it as instance of difference between women, and proceed to negate that difference by subsuming women of color into the unitary category of woman/women. The latter is often viewed as the 'common denominator' in an oppositional (counter-identifying) discourse with some white men, that leaves us unable to explore relationships with white women."[48]

But for some Anglo feminists the common-denominator approach seemed the only way to avoid excessive fragmentation. By emphasizing the relationships and expectations organized under a general category "Woman," they hoped to defend even as they created a common identity capable of uniting women. Fearing the demise of feminism in the face of a variety of hyphenated, identity-based movements, they adopted a just-add-it-on strategy to deal with difference: "Woman" was a generalized other to be concretized—later. Further, and perhaps more importantly, white feminists were reluctant to abandon either the category of experience just as it was becoming crucial to the writings of lesbians and women of color or the ideal of a feminist politics capable of uniting diverse women.

The awareness of the various meanings and interpretations of experience next appeared as a critical engagement with the concept of experience itself.[49] By stressing the ways in which experiences are constructed and produced, and the connection between these experiences and a less singular and immobile conception of identity, recent feminists have sought to overcome the oppositions between essentialism and fragmentation, political agency and exclusion. Judith Butler criticizes the perceived need to base feminist action on women's identities, arguing that this perception has impeded investigation into the "multiplicity of cultural, social, and political intersections in which the concrete array of 'women' are constructed."[50] Leaving the category "women" open as a site of contested meanings will better facilitate coalition politics and allow for new identity concepts to emerge through engaged political action: "Without the compulsory expectation that feminist actions must be instituted from some stable, unified, and agreed upon identity, those actions might well get a quicker start and seem more congenial to a number of 'women' for whom the meaning of the category is permanently moot."[51]

Until now, my argument has been that in its third phase identity politics shifts toward something like reflective solidarity. Although third-phase feminist work has involved itself in the close examination of the discourses, practices, and structures of power within which identities, sexualities, and genders are constructed and performed, I have to confess that finding within this work anything resembling an emphasis on solidarity is rather difficult. The ethical insights of third-phase feminism are sometimes overshadowed by vehement debates over notions of subjectivity and the regulatory production of the subject. The very investigation into relations between discourse and domination, the exposure of the workings of power in every aspect of our lives, seems to have supplanted the possibility of speaking about goals of freedom and equality for women. It isn't exactly correct to say that "power is everywhere; everything is coerced and constrained" because much of this work uncovers micropossibilities for disruption, agency, and transformation in the very workings of and reiterations produced in and through power. Nonetheless, this attention to power has itself produced a vision of the world that cannot account for the positive and communicative dimensions of our lives.[52] Not only are microdisruptions and performative reiterations hardly enough to challenge the continued brutalization of women in their homes, the reinvigorated homophobia of the Right, and the continued economic exploitation of women across the globe, but such disruptions and reiterations themselves, as their theorists admit, can backfire, either manipulated by their opponents or coopted into new practices of violence. More importantly, once every possible position and move is reduced to a strategy, we are left asking, "But to what end?" Once communities and solidarities are replaced by networks of coercion and control, we are left wondering, "So why bother?"

But, of course, deep down, we know to what end and why we should bother — women face continual violence, degradation, harassment, rape, unwanted pregnancies, and inadequate health care; the United States and numerous countries throughout Europe are witnessing a renewed nationalism that expresses itself in racism, anti-Semitism, and organized acts of violence against women. All over the world women's bodies and labor are exploited and abused. What isn't clear to me is whether third-phase feminist theory has lost the outward orientation of the second phase or whether everything is outward oriented to the extent that there is no longer an inward orientation. On the one hand, the emphasis on microresistances seems to have replaced larger goals like "saving the world" with saving one's self — or at least securing for oneself a small scope of freedom. On the other hand, the ostensibly universal presence of violence and coercion in our everyday values, commitments, and relationships has fostered the perception of "enemies everywhere," which in turn fuels suspicions even of the connections "among us."

Of course, once one moves away from third-phase feminist writing and looks at feminist actions, the possibility of solidarity reemerges. And, fortunately, there are important exceptions within feminist writing itself. I am thinking here of work done by feminists like Gloria Anzaldúa, Susan Bordo, Nancy Fraser, bell hooks, Martha Minow, and Iris Marion Young. The problem, then, is the increased distance between debates in feminist theory and "real life." The dismay expressed by women students new to feminism, the anguish voiced by feminists of color at the exclusionary and orthodox world of theory, and the increased disregard of feminist colleagues in other, more practical, disciplines remind us of the need for a reflective solidarity among women, of the need for accountability within our theories. If we forget or disregard the importance of solidarity and responsibility, we risk allowing investigations into localized configurations of power to replace our awareness of and complicity in larger relationships and interconnections.

So while I agree with and respect Butler's contention that coalitions have to acknowledge their contradictions and that the conditions and limits of dialogue must be interrogated, I disagree with her claim that the effort to establish an ideal form for coalitions is a reinsertion of sovereignty. In fact, I find Habermas's account of the conditions for agreement in moral argumentation extremely helpful for imagining an *ideal* form for coalitions. Generally speaking, the conditions of practical discourse require that the participants respect one another as competent and truthful speakers, recognize the worthiness of each other to raise issues and claims, and understand each other as a responsible agent.[53] With these sorts of requirements, coalitions can move beyond competing identity claims and achieve a reflective solidarity. Participants would have to respect the identities of each other while acknowledging the right of each to question and challenge the claims made on the basis of these identities. Identities are respected without remaining fixed, thus allowing for both the transformation of existing identity categories and the possibility of coalitional agreement and action.

Returning to my discussion of third-phase feminism and the problem of women's experience, although I accept the importance of what Teresa de Lauretis has referred to as the "erotic drive" of feminist theory, one that "enhances images of feminism as difference, rebellion, daring, excess, subversion," I nonetheless emphasize the "ethical drive" that works toward community and accountability as it appears in some recent critiques of experience.[54] Whereas many have focused on Donna Haraway's perverse and ironic myth of the cyborg, I look to the appeal to accountability in her investigation of experience. According to Haraway:

It is crucial to be accountable for the politics of experience in the *institution* of women's studies. Such accountability is not easy, nor is it obvious what forms it might take, nor how struggles over different articulations of experience and different positionings for making these articulations should be addressed. Nor can experience be allowed simply to appear as endlessly plural and unchallengeable, as if self-evident, readily available when we look "inside" ourselves, and only one's own, or only one's group's. . . . Feminism is collective; and difference is political, that is, about power, accountability, and hope. Experience, like difference, is about contradictory and necessary connections.[55]

Similarly, I see in Biddy Martin and Chandra Talpade Mohanty's reading of Minnie Bruce Pratt's autobiographical essay not only a new notion of multiple and shifting subjectivity but also the possibility of a reflective solidarity. Their reading seeks to challenge the simple "conflation of experience, identity, and political perspective."[56] As they look at the shifts and displacements, the exclusions and contradictions, in Pratt's narrative of the relationship between home, community, and her own identity as a white, Southern lesbian, they expose the multiple and overlapping systems of power and relations of oppression in which identities are constructed and experienced. They conclude that community "is the product of work, of struggle; it is inherently unstable, contextual; it has to be constantly reevaluated in relation to critical political priorities; and it is the product of interpretation, interpretation based on an attention to history."[57] The community they envision is thus reflectively solidary. Its members engage in questioning and interpretation, reevaluating the expectations members have of one another in light of their contexts, histories, and political priorities.

What Martin and Mohanty's essay shares with Haraway's is an emphasis on the local and specific that does not hesitate to extend to and evoke the global—both challenge the colonialist prioritizing of the West. Martin and Mohanty deliberately chose Pratt's Western feminist text because it "attempts to expose the bases and supports of privileges even as it renegotiates political and personal alliances."[58] Haraway continues her discussion of experience with a reading of Nigerian author Buchi Emechta. "Inclusions and exclusions," Haraway concludes, "are not determined in advance by fixed categories of race, gender, sexuality, or nationality. 'We' are accountable for the inclusions and exclusions, identifications and separations, produced in the highly political practices called reading fiction."[59] As each writer moves from local to global, then, each implicitly suggests the possibility of a universal solidarity, a reflective solidarity that posits the possibility of a community of all us by evoking our responsibility for each other.

Democracy: The Problem of Identity Politics

We have seen how the demands for recognition in identity politics are responses to differing experiences of exclusion and how these differing experiences create a tension in the speaking subject. When the speaking subject cannot speak, cannot be heard as a speaker, it is because of the contradictions between the conditions that make speech possible and those that make speech necessary. Each movement begins as a response to exclusion on the universal level, exclusion from the category of citizen or rights-bearing subject worthy of inclusion. At the first phase of assimilation, the subject is the reasoning subject, like all other subjects. This presents a problem because precisely those differences that marked the group as other, as less worthy, are denied: lesbians and gay men are forced to deny or hide their sexuality; African Americans are supposed to forget their historical roots in Africa and the impact of slavery; women are required to ignore those experiences not shared by men.

This conflict leads to the second phase where differences are to be accommodated. For each group, those differences that separate them from the dominant society are now revalued and explored. Lesbians and gay men come out, making themselves visible. African Americans recover their history. Women focus on their experiences as mothers, nurturers, and caregivers. But, again, accommodation presents a problem for the speaking subject. If speaking requires a unitary identity, those aspects of the self that subvert this unity remain hidden. And, perhaps more fundamentally, if all of us are characterized by these unitary identities, it is not clear what speaking from one's identity can accomplish. Speaking from an identity often takes on the character of an excuse: I cannot/will not be accountable to or for those who do not share my identity. It is as if the proper formulation of identity will somehow make hard political questions go away.

These problems of the limits of rights and the limits of identity, as the latter designate what is to be seen, remembered, and experienced, set the stage for the third phase, that of accountability. Aware that even the revaluation of a heretofore denigrated identity can fail to disrupt those hierarchical and oppositional structures that lead to denigration, third-phase theorists now challenge the structures themselves. They subvert the very categories of straight/gay, black/white, male/female, opening up generalized others by recognizing that the identities and expectations embodied therein can never be fixed but are themselves multiple and open to interpretation. And this move, far from leading to the demise of the speaking subject, resituates the speaker as one who is always already part of a multiplicity of dialogues. This constructed, situated subject remains in process, changing through each discursive engagement and intervention. Rather than appealing to what it has in common with us all, or what makes it different, it appeals to our reflective solidarity, our ability to connect through our questioning, debate, and conflict.

Not only do demands for recognition change from one phase to the next, but also the need for recognition changes. Each phase of identity politics is about this change. Aspects of our identities that had previously remained invisible, forgotten, or suppressed now need to be recognized. The accountability toward each other that was either taken for granted by traditional, pregiven values and forms of life or denied in a mythological assertion of independence and autonomy now has to be recognized. Now the need for recognition has changed so as to necessitate reflection. We must always ask "But recognized as what?"—and in asking we must be attuned to our histories of categorization and exclusion, accountable for those situated, hypothetical thirds whom we risk overlooking. Gay men and lesbians, African Americans, and women need recognition — of their rights, differences, and of all of our accountability — and meeting this need entails changing what we understand by recognition. The issue is not simply about being recognized as equal or as having worth. It is about what and how we see, remember, and interpret. Ultimately, it is about whether we can recognize our responsibility to each other to take a reflective attitude toward what and how we see, remember, and interpret. The simple need for recognition has splintered to become a set of needs for different sorts of recognition, needs that demand reflection.

What, then, do the changes in the politics of and need for recognition tell us about the impact and role of identity politics in contemporary democracies?

Identity politics play a critical role in contemporary democracy, indicating its failures and gaps. The struggles for recognition that we see in identity politics will not be settled simply by coming up with the right set of juridical procedures and categories. Securing recognition at the universal level as a rational subject is not enough when cultural norms and traditions predetermine what it can mean to be a rational subject. As a response to exclusion at the universal level, identity politics reminds us that the subject of law is always already determined. This entails a shift away from liberal democracy with its claims of neutrality and objectivity, and, correspondingly, away from the goal of toleration. Since law is anchored in already given cultural formations, we have to acknowledge that "it" is never fully neutral; it will always be our product, related to the fallible and contingent outcomes of our politics. Because of the embeddedness and interpretability of right and law, toleration remains too limited a goal. Leaving our interpretations and understandings of who we are intact, toleration fails to respond to our complicity in exclusion. Instead of demanding reflection, it accepts complacency.

Identity politics plays a transformational role in contemporary democracy. If we take seriously the idea of a decentered state, accepting that political action is neither directed strictly to the state nor confined to a privatized realm of power, we have to acknowledge the ways in which the process of appealing to and contesting identity categories is itself an aspect of democratic praxis. I tend to agree with Shane Phelan: "Identity politics must be based, not only on identity, but on an appreciation for politics as the art of living together. Politics that ignores our identities, that makes them 'private,' is useless; but nonnegotiable identities will enslave us whether they are imposed from within or without."[60] While I am less optimistic about the continued use of identity politics, her insight that politics should not ignore identity is valuable. As long as rights remain attached to persons, transforming these rights will depend on the ability of groups to transform themselves, from invisible to visible, forgotten to remembered, denied to embraced. As both groups and rights are transformed, so will our understanding of democracy also be transformed from a conversation among those who are already part of "us" to include those who are potentially part of "us." We will no longer accept pregiven descriptions of who "we" are, attempting either to exclude or mold those who don't fit these descriptions. Rather we will acknowledge that accountability means transforming these descriptions themselves.

Identity politics plays a limiting role in contemporary democracy. It reminds us that the very rights, the very legal codes, that make recognition possible at one level are inadequate at other levels. Given identity politics' consistent focus on the level of culture, we have to acknowledge the limits of rights. Identity politics exposes the inability of rights to secure those relationships necessary for our identities—as the gay need for and stress on visibility shows us, as we learn from the African American endeavor to construct and remember a meaningful history, and as feminists have shown by their attention to women's experiences. Although rights are of course important preconditions for democratic participation, as long as the possible meaning and content of rights stem from cultural understandings and representations, the rights we have will remain particular and this particularity will shape the ways in which we are able to conceive our public life and interaction. In other words, identity politics responds to and exposes preinscribed particularity. It exposes the intersection between cultural representations and societal ideals. In so doing, it has shifted the terrain of rights discussion to include issues of content heretofore deemed secondary. If the battle of democracy is fought on this terrain, the terrain of culture, rights are in a paradoxical situation: Precisely those conditions that necessitate claims to rights are beyond the scope of rights. Indeed, more often than not rights claims are left open to be determined by the market and the economy. The problem is this: How can we understand ourselves as the authors of law, as the source of rights, when rights are embedded in a culture that distorts who we are and what we can be?

In part, the third phase of identity politics moves us toward an answer. It reminds us that we have to think about the ways in which rights attach to persons, to identities. We generally think of persons as "rights-bearers." They not only carry rights with them, but also produce them, give birth to them, usually through contestation and struggle. Yet rights are never completely produced. They remain in production, continually reasserted and reinterpreted. As they are "in production," they reattach to persons, bringing with them new understandings of the meaning of personality and identity in different contexts. Thus, rights are also "person-bearers." They both carry persons with them and produce and reproduce particular sorts of persons. By intervening in the struggle for rights with an investigation into the productive dimensions of rights, the third phase of identity politics enables us to reflect on and challenge the meanings and interpretations underlying rights. And once these meanings are exposed, we acquire a renewed capacity for democracy and solidarity.

Identity politics directs us toward reflection, toward the permanent questioning and contestation of traditions, rights, law, and the cultural representations giving meaning and body to our experiences of all these. If we attempt to bracket this reflection, we risk reifying a particular practice and understanding of democracy; in effect, we risk democracy itself. This reflection, then, has to extend to identity itself.

So while we may recognize the critical, transformational, and limiting potential of identity politics, we cannot remain in its second phase. As third-phase critics have shown, our identities are not fixed and given. They are the products of constructs and relationships that themselves must be questioned. Indeed, when we fail to question them, we recreate precisely those differences that have subordinated us, presuming that they are somehow natural to and given by the world.[61] Because we, and our politics, always exceed our identities, we can no longer hold on to a politics so insistently rooted in identity. Trying to do so keeps us within the philosophy of the subject — that philosophy of isolated, rationalistic subjectivity of which so many are critical because it sets a limit to discourse and dialogue. When our politics are anchored in our identities, we can no longer argue; whatever is contentious is sequestered in the sacred realm of the self. It is no accident that identity politics frequently dissolves into struggle and fragmentation. It forfeits relation for the sake of identity, all the while doing violence to the ties necessary for identity.

Not every political issue is a matter of identity. I sometimes wonder what would happen if animal rights activists fought on the terrain of identity politics. Would they have to argue that we all need to uncover the beast within? A further problem with identity politics is thus the way it has prevented us from looking at problems beyond identity, problems such as health care, nuclear waste, and, in fact, class. For although class is often one of the chain of identifications listed with identity categories, it is remarkably difficult to develop a coherent identity politics rooted in a class analysis. If one is working class, one must value that class while challenging the conditions and structure that created it. Describing her conflicting feelings of pride and shame toward her family's poverty, Dorothy Allison remarks:

I have felt a powerful temptation to write about my family as a kind of morality tale, with us as the heroes and middle and upper classes as the villains. It would be within the romantic myth, for example, to pretend that we were the kind of noble Southern whites portrayed in the movies, mill workers for generations until driven out by alcoholism and a family propensity for rebellion and union talk. But that would be a lie. The truth is that no one in my family ever joined a union.[62]

Additionally, the issues posed by the Clarence Thomas hearings cannot be resolved in terms of identity politics. Such an attempt ends up subordinating race to sex or sex to race, obscuring the question of Thomas's competency and the problem of sexual harassment.

Without certain foundations or traditions capable of bringing us together, reflection itself has to become the basis of our shared connection. Because political contestation in contemporary democracies includes cultural representations as well as social obligations, there is no solution or final answer to the proper configuration of identity and democracy. All we have left is reflective solidarity — a solidarity rooted in our ability to connect with each other through contestation and critique. We have to accept our interconnections even as we question them.

CHAPTER 3

Including Women

The Consequences and Side Effects of Feminist
Critiques of Civil Society

The ideal of reflective solidarity and the struggles for recognition key to identity politics direct us away from a politics centered on the state. Reflective solidarity calls on us to challenge exclusionary notions of citizenship that fail to account for the variety of types of political action. Identity politics further commits us to the expansion of opportunities for democratic participation. Attuned to the presence and location of power in societies stratified along lines of sexuality, race, and gender, reflective solidarity instructs us to look for possibilities of freedom and inclusion that do not ignore or subvert the interdependencies constitutive of our identities. These spaces and possibilities for a democratic politics of difference and solidarity can be found in a revitalized civil society, a civil society conceived not in terms of an opposition between public and private spheres but as a variety of interconnecting discursive spheres.

Until quite recently, most feminists have ignored the concept of civil society. A critical awareness of the dichotomy between the public and private spheres, however, underpins most Anglo-American feminist political theory. In fact, one is hard pressed to find a text in this area that does not appeal to or challenge women's position in the intimate or domestic sphere. The silence regarding civil society and the "noise" over the public/ private split are linked in an important way. Far from betraying some conceptional oversight on the part of feminists, the stress on the public/private distinction exposes a fundamental problem at the heart of democratic theory — the difficulty of integrating women in notions of civil society.[1]

The most helpful contemporary theory of civil society is offered by Jean Cohen and Andrew Arato.[2] This model conceives civil society as a space of social interaction between the state and the economy. Following Habermas, Cohen and Arato suggest the idea of a decentered society in which societal integration arises through the systematizing forces of the economy and institutionalized political power as well as through various social solidarities. These social solidarities, often formed around the new social and political movements thematized as identity politics, open up a broad terrain of political contestation. The space demarcated as civil society includes these movements as well as associations such as schools, churches, families, clubs, museums, and, in part, the media.

This is not a theory of civil society commonly used in feminist discussions. As Carole Pateman points out, feminist conceptions of what exactly belongs in the public sphere and the relation of this sphere to civil society are complex and historically variable.[3] Usually, feminists juxtapose the private, domestic sphere to the public sphere of the state and/or economy. In these instances, civil society is conflated with the state, the economy, or both, a move that often leads to the neglect of other, more intermediate forms of association. At other times, feminists view civil society in terms of the public sphere of political debate. What remains constant throughout feminist discussions is the critique of the separation of the particular and private world of the family from the universal world of the public, a critique that challenges the worth of democracy for women.

Gendered Spaces

Claude Lefort provides a helpful way of understanding the relationship between democracy and civil society. Looking at the birth of democracy, Lefort contrasts this new form of political power with the older monarchical form. He describes the prince as "a mediator between mortals and gods or, as political activity became secularized and laicized, between mortals and the transcendental agencies represented by a sovereign Justice and a sovereign Reason."[4] For Lefort, this mediation has two key repercussions. First, the power of the prince refers to something outside of society itself. It points toward an otherworldly force that justifies the power of the king, be it the realm of the gods or of some sort of absolute law or knowledge. Second, insofar as the prince acts as mediator, the body of the prince itself becomes the locus of power, symbolizing and guaranteeing the unity of the kingdom. In stark contrast to this idea of an embodied power, which always refers to an outside or to an *Other,* power in a democracy is decentered, represented as an *empty place.* Since power is no longer justified by a reference to an *outside* or centered in the monarch, it can no longer be represented in terms of a substantial determination of an *inside,* be it in the form of an individual, group, or conception of the community. Disentangled from the certainties of law and knowledge, power in a democracy is limited. It opens itself up for questioning and periodic contestation and redistribution within institutionalized forms of conflict. Elaborating on this idea of an empty place, Lefort explains:

It is because there is no materialization of the *Other*—which would allow power to function as a mediator, no matter how it were defined—that there is no materialization of the *One*—which would allow power to function as an incarnation. Nor can power be divorced from the work of division by which society itself is instituted; a society can therefore relate to itself only through the experience of an internal division which proves to be not a *de facto* division, but a division which generates its constitution.[5]

We see here in Lefort's reference to the division that generates the democratic constitution the idea that power "belongs to no one." Since the exercise of political power in a democracy is always the result of a contest, diversity and opposition become visible. This division erects "a *stage* on which conflict is acted out for all to see," a stage on which division is demonstrated to be "constitutive of the very unity of society."[6] Structured by the norms of publicity and the rights of free expression and association, in a decentered society the competition among differing opinions becomes a legitimate form of political conflict and struggle. Our enemy is no longer some outside "other" or stranger whom we must exterminate or banish. Rather, she is one of us, someone with whom I compete, someone with whom I live. The diversity within civil society itself is thus institutionalized in a political constitution based on the recognition and legitimation of difference.

I want to use Lefort's discussion of democracy as a framework for approaching the feminist critiques of civil society. To this end, I present three rather broadly drawn lines of feminist argument. In its most traditional form, feminist critique has shown how women have lacked the opportunity to become opponents in political debate. The diversity institutionalized within democratic political forms, be it within the sphere of public opinion or actual representation, has been the diversity of male views and opinions. Although women may have been active in various nonofficial capacities, they have lacked the opportunity to take their place in the exercise of power. Instead—and here I shift to the second type of feminist critique—women have been construed as a silent audience witnessing the events enacted upon the political stage. On this stage, democracy is depicted as a struggle and a competition. To be an actor, one must be cast as independent and aggressive. One must possess the strength of will necessary to fight to protect and secure one's freedom and to recognize the reasonable claims of others to do the same. Since the role of active political agent is a masculine one, women occupy a space of supportive passivity. The political stage thus divides not only the actors who perform upon it but also the actors and the silent audience.

This leads to the third and more radical form of feminist critique. Rather than occupying an empty place, power in a democracy is embodied in a particularly masculine body. This masculine body mediates between an outside that has been moved into civil society itself—the private, familial, and domestic sphere to which women are confined—and the inside world of political action. As citizens, men are inside, within the public sphere of debate and competition. As heads of families, their power appears to stem from a realm outside of this discursive public. Since women remain excluded and "other," the masculine form can be constituted as the "one," a form in which women cannot recognize themselves. The division to which Lefort refers takes place not only within the opinions of men but also within the public and private spheres of civil society. Indeed, this division can be seen as a division that generates the constitution of democracy not only in that it separates out a realm free of public or state intervention, but also because solidarity in a society of conflict requires the establishment and protection of relationships of love, care, and affection. Yet—and herein lies the contradiction within this democratic conception of civil society—how can these relationships be said to be protected when they themselves are products of a political division that must remain suppressed if the myth of the intimate is to retain its integrating function?

Three Forms of Feminist Critique

When one separates the three forms of feminist critique that I have melded together in the discussion of Lefort, one finds that they rely on differing conceptions of exclusion and differing notions of recognition. Turning first to the idea of exclusion, we can distinguish between *practical exclusion* and *constitutive exclusion*. I use practical exclusion to refer to a restriction from the public and official economic institutions of civil society imposed by particular sorts of situational obstacles. This allows for practical exclusion to be understood in both a weak and strong sense. One is practically excluded in a weak sense when traditional legal and economic barriers prevent one from being included. Practical exclusion operates in a stronger sense when symbolic forms of cultural interpretation function so as to limit notions of inclusion. In contrast, I use constitutive exclusion to mean that there is something inherent within the categories of civil society themselves that prevents full inclusion. The conceptual coherence of the categories themselves requires the creation of an other to be excluded. Thus, practical exclusion refers to the levels of institutionalization and cultural interpretation, whereas constitutive exclusion operates on the conceptual-theoretical level.

In contrast to exclusion, recognition functions as the correlative concept of inclusion. It highlights those characteristics through which social membership is attributed to individuals. Within the feminist critiques, one can find three distinct notions of recognition operating in conjunction with the concepts of exclusion. The first type is *universal* or *juridical recognition*. It refers to the recognition of the supposedly universal characteristics of citizens, such as equality and autonomy, that are secured by rights. Individuals are considered social members because they possess a capacity for judgment and agency that makes them the equals of all others with these capacities. The second type of recognition is *attributive* or *role recognition*. This is the recognition granted persons on the basis of particular attributes that are culturally interpreted through social roles. The idea is that persons are included as members of society with reference to their memberships in other groups, to their already given social roles as, say, heads of families or providers of care and nurturance. Finally, the third type of recognition is *particular recognition*. Rather than appealing to universal characteristics or generalized group attributes, particular recognition relies on the appreciation of the differences among individuals. As we see in the second phase of identity politics, particular recognition emphasizes that individuals can only be understood as social members when their particular needs and experiences are taken into account. This third sort of recognition serves as a critical ideal with which to confront generalized forms of recognition with their exclusionary tendencies.

These two axes of exclusion and recognition enable me to reconstruct the feminist critiques of civil society in terms of three different types of arguments. I use the term "reconstruct" for three reasons. First, feminist literature is rich, complex, and varied. I am only thematizing particular aspects of the feminist argument, rather than exploring all the nuances and variations within feminist debates. Second, different types of criticisms are often interwoven within one particular critique. Feminists who disagree on some levels often employ similar reasoning on others. Third, my intent is to draw out the commonalities in feminist writing to uncover the consequences and side effects they have for a democratic theory of civil society. Thus, although there are important historical and cultural differences in the way women have been included or excluded from civil society, I am interested in feminist discussions of the underlying theory of inclusion and exclusion.[7] For the sake of clarity, then, I designate these three types of feminist critique simply as FC1, FC2, and FC3.[8]

FC1 focuses on women's practical exclusion in the weak sense of legal and economic barriers to inclusion. Viewing civil society as either the public political sphere or the economy, it argues that women should be granted universal or juridical recognition. The norms of rationality, autonomy, fairness, and equality underlying idealized versions of both the political and economic public spheres are said to apply not just to men, but to all reasoning persons as such. Extending universal recognition to women in the form of rights, then, will permit their inclusion into civil society.

The critical efforts of FC1 are empirically oriented toward revealing existing inequalities and providing arguments for legal solutions to sex discrimination. In its early versions, FC1 centered on women's rights to education, to vote, and to own property.[9] Later versions have sought to extend these rights to include reproduction, broaden the notion of equal protection, and end forms of sex segregation.[10] These later versions stress the importance of labor legislation for the establishment of fair employment opportunities, equal pay for equal work, and compensatory welfare benefits.[11] In short, FC1 claims that the term "men" or "mankind" includes women.

FC2 stresses women's practical exclusion in the strong sense. Rather than simply emphasizing the institutional barriers to women's inclusion in the public sphere, this critique draws attention to the cultural interpretations that have subordinated women. In the American debate this often takes the form of a critique of the classic works of liberal and republican political theory.[12] These arguments stress the division between the private and public spheres underlying various versions of contract theory. They show how this division is not simply a distinction between the familial and the political worlds, but more deeply a separation of what is seen as natural and dependent from what is viewed as cultural and free. Because familial relationships have been viewed as natural rather than civil forms of association, this division has prevented issues of sexuality, child care, and domestic violence from entering the public political debate. With private interpreted as "free from state intervention or public concern," most of the activities and needs of women could not be understood as political issues. The interpretation of the private sphere as a realm of dependency has led to a definition of women at odds with the conception of agency operating in both the liberal possessive individualist notion of civil society and the republican conception of the public sphere as an arena for the exercise and development of masculine virtues. Associated with particularity, sentiment, and dependence, women are viewed as lacking the capacities for dispassionate judgment, pragmatic self-assertion, and autonomous action required in civil society.[13] As it challenges liberal and republican interpretations of the institutions and norms within the public and private spheres of civil society, FC2 aims to eliminate gendered representations that exclude women from democratic discourse.

FC2 extends its questioning of cultural interpretations by combining it with the notion of attributive or role recognition to explain why the guarantees of equal rights have not by themselves succeeded in ending women's subordination. Much of the work in this area looks at the way gender structures our understandings of persons and the social spaces within which they interact. Defined in terms of their domestic and child-rearing functions or as primarily emotional or sexual beings, women have not been able to overcome the force of a gendered set of social roles and become fully included in civil society. Instead, they are included *as women*. In the workplace they repeat their roles as care givers, supporters of masculine activities, and objects of male sexual desire. Their child-rearing and household activities are not seen as economic contributions or personal options, but as part of who and what women are — wives and mothers. Women's functional position in the domestic sphere and their biological reproductive capacity have been used as grounds for blocking their employment in potentially toxic but high-paying workplaces, sanctioning their being laid off on grounds of pregnancy, and justifying their exclusion from juries.[14] Additionally, as Deborah Rhode illustrates in her discussion of litigation involving the airline industry, and as Naomi Wolf explores in her treatment of suits involving workplace dress codes, cultural understandings of women as sexual objects have been determining factors in interpretations of women's occupational roles.[15]

FC2 also points out the effects of gender on public debate. Women face the devaluation of their speech as they are ignored, derided, or interrupted. They suffer from a cultural preoccupation with their bodies and appearance. In the military, women until the late 1980s have been considered liabilities, turning fighting units into hotbeds of sexual activity and propelling the breakdown of the family at home. Not only does the issue of military service reveal the difficulty of seeing women as citizens, but also it indicates the problematic way in which masculinity has been constructed and interpreted. Thus, FC2 does not limit itself to exploring the problems of gendered role definitions for women. It also questions the fear of connection and rigid insistence on separation and self-sufficiency that typify notions of masculinity, and it explores the effects of these notions on conceptions of the public and public debate.[16]

To sum up, FC2 argues that because of the effects of gender and gendered role interpretations, women have not been seen as equal participants in political discourse. Ultimately, FC2 claims that women's place in the private sphere (their position in the sex/gender structure) determines their position in the public. With provisions for better day-care and shared child rearing (both of which could affect the psychological construction of gender) and for the continued questioning and critique of cultural interpretations of social institutions, roles, and norms, however, women will be able to escape from attributive recognition and enjoy recognition as universal subjects. FC2 shows why the notion of "men" does not include women and what to do to change it.

FC3 builds from the stress on the private sphere that characterizes FC2, but radicalizes the argument to claim that the division between the public and private constitutively excludes women from the public sphere of civil society. Because the ideas of publicity, justice, and rationality are formed in opposition to notions of privacy, the good life, and emotionality, these conceptions cannot serve as regulatory ideals for women.[17] Already part of a masculine way of defining and interpreting the world, they establish a system of law, right, and order that institutionalizes inequality by masking it under claims of fairness and impartiality. The very fact of sexual difference renders the ideal of equality suspect — there is no sexless or genderless body that could provide a standard for comparison. Indeed, the estrangement of such an idea from our experience as embodied beings in the world presents itself as, at best, hopelessly naive, and, at worst, a potentially dangerous denial of the physicality of our existence. Insofar as it relies on an abstraction from the relationships of need, care, and interdependency in which human beings are situated, the masculine fiction of autonomy leads to a concept of civil society based on atomized selves.[18] It is a fiction that itself constructs the problem of democracy as a tension between freedom and social order, as a balance between political disintegration and coercion.

For FC3, objectivity and neutrality themselves are oppressive in that they attempt to establish standards for what can be said and what must remain unsaid.[19] To speak under these conditions, women have had to conform to a set of standards and expectations that men alone established. Even with efforts to open up the debate as to what is legitimate and what is not, women remain excluded because of the very rules that give form to this debate. These rules have determined which topics can be seen as worthy of political debate, which themes are universal or general enough to warrant public interest. Further, they have structured public debate on the model of warfare by other means. In so doing, they limit public discussion to a particular range of issues, remaining blind to the multiplicity of debates and discussions occurring outside the "official" domain of the public.

Extending the FC2 idea that women have been associated with the emotional and particular, FC3 argues that women's experiences *are* emotional and particular. This is not simply a revaluation of those characteristics traditionally attributed to women. On the contrary, it is part of a more far-reaching critique of the already gendered, particular, and hence coercive nature of ideals with a claim to universality. There is no sexless point of view; sexual domination extends "all the way down." We are *all* emotional and particular.

FC3 denies the very possibility of universal or juridical recognition. The rights that structure juridical recognition are based on particular cognitive properties. These properties, which include rationality and autonomy, are masculine characteristics. When women have rights, women are recognized only to the extent that they, too, are masculine or conform to a masculine standard. But, because rationality and autonomy are already masculine, women are constructed as feminine; they are defined as having their own distinct characteristics and are seen as embodying those capacities viewed as masculine in a different way. They thus can neither see themselves nor be seen as bearers of rights that fundamentally deny their difference. FC3 concludes that, given the differences between men and women, and among people in general, one must accept that universal recognition is a fiction that presents particular interests as general. FC3 thus stresses the importance of particular recognition based on the idea that people are not the same. Any attempt to find similarities always privileges a particular point of view or winds up ignoring those traits, attributes, or experiences that some groups hold dear. One can sum up FC3 as claiming that the term "men" cannot possibly include women (and usually only refers to a few straight, white, rich, and powerful men at that). Or, better yet, FC3 moves from "the personal is political" to "the theoretical is political."

The Consequences and Side Effects of the Feminist Critiques

The first two forms of feminist critique expose the important side effects that the inclusion of women has for democratic conceptions of civil society. Focusing on problems of institutionalization, FC1 calls our attention to arrangements that have excluded women from public discussion, encouraging efforts in the development and expansion of spaces for democratic participation. Additionally, it recognizes the continuing importance of rights claims as vehicles for emancipation. Focusing on problems of interpretation, FC2 appeals to processes of democratic debate as we question the cultural representations of the institutions, roles, rights, and needs that can effectively block women's inclusion. It shows how the claim of universal reason has been juxtaposed against feminine emotionality, how norms with claims to universality not only have coincided with particularly masculine traits, but also have had completely different meanings for women, and how the description of the public sphere as a realm in which only "universal" interests could be discussed has prevented women's concerns from entering public debate. In short, FC2 shows how masculine discursive frameworks have led to a particular, limited, and gendered conception of civil society. On both the level of institutions and that of interpretation, the wide-ranging side effects resulting from the inclusion of women as full and respected agents in civil society deepen and enhance notions of democracy as they help to realize its "supposition of reasonableness." Habermas writes:

The supposition of reasonableness rests on the normative sense of democratic procedures which should guarantee that all socially relevant issues can be thematized, treated with reasons and imagination and worked through to resolutions which — with equal respect for the integrity of each individual and each life form — suit the equal interests of all.[20]

With its focus on problems of justification, FC3 forces us to deal directly with the consequences of women's constitutive exclusion. I use the negative concept of exclusion at this point because it is not yet clear whether from the perspective of FC3 it is even possible to include women within a theory of civil society. As I have shown, FC3's claim that women are constitutively excluded hinges on the seemingly irreconcilable opposition between the universality of the public and the particularity of the private. This claim admits of at least two different interpretations. The first interpretation locates the problem in the notion of universality. The second sees the problem as arising from the association of universality with the public and its opposition to a private sphere of particularity. If the second interpretation is convincing, then it should be possible to retain a democratic notion of civil society, that is, a conception that includes the categories of rights and the ideals of universality and impartiality.

Iris Marion Young's critique of the universality of the public sphere, for example, contrasts the public realm with private particularity:

The public realm of citizens achieves unity and universality only by defining the civil individual in opposition to the disorder of womanly nature, which embraces feeling, sexuality, birth and death, the attributes that concretely distinguish persons from one another. The universal citizen is disembodied, dispassionate (male) reason. . . . Precisely because the virtues of impartiality and universality define the civic public, that public must exclude human particularity.[21]

Young could be arguing that there is something inherently suspect or wrong with notions of universality and impartiality. Or she could be saying that universality and impartiality are exclusionary under specific conditions. They are exclusionary when they obscure our differences and particularities; are opposed to our common experience as embodied, emotional beings; and remain confined to a particular aspect of social life, a civic public sphere.

Although some might want to stress the first interpretation and challenge the viability of concepts like justice and impartiality for feminist theorizing, I claim that the strengths of this critique can be found in the second interpretation. The problem with ideas like justice and impartiality arises from *limiting* them to the public sphere and *opposing* them to the private sphere. Were FC3 to reject the ideals of justice and impartiality, it would get caught up in its own strategy. What is raised as a critical point against false or premature universalization would itself be universalized into a totalizing embrace of the particular. Furthermore, were FC3 to limit its critique to a challenge to justice, it would accept precisely that dubious part of the liberal tradition that claims that what is public is universal and what is private is particular. A more promising strategy is thus to extend the critique to these associations themselves — we do not need to swallow the view that the public sphere is a sacred, universal sphere immune to particularity nor the presumption that the bodily, sexual, affective aspects of our private lives are particular with no universal status. Indeed, part of the oddness of Young's position is the assertion that the attributes of birth and death concretely distinguish persons from one another. I would have thought that these are general characteristics that we all share.

Thus, the second interpretation tells us that women are constitutively excluded by concepts of civil society that are constructed in terms of oppositional categories. The challenge to the theorist of civil society is to break down these oppositions — showing how particularity is not confined to the private sphere but is already a component of the public — and extend the claims of universality that were previously confined to the latter sphere into the former. To be sure, with this move FC3 might start to look a lot like an instance of FC2, an instance that either rhetorically overstates its case or somehow misunderstands its own project. Nonetheless, by presenting the issues in an extreme form, FC3 pushes FC2 to a more coherent position. This new, more coherent position ends up eliminating the distinction between the public and private spheres by removing their defining characteristics. Reformulating the insight gained from the second interpretation of Young, we see the consequences of FC3 for a democratic conception of civil society: Universality and impartiality are inclusive when they recognize our differences and particularities; are conceived in light of our common experience as embodied, emotional beings; and are extended to and components of our intersubjective relationships.

Ending the association of particularity with the private and universality with the public has important consequences for the universal recognition captured by rights claims. The universality within the notion of rights does not have to mean that people are primarily or merely beings with particular sets of cognitive characteristics that override their feelings and physicality, their particularities and differences. Rather, rights provide a useful way for thinking about persons in particular sets of situations, situations where they may be harmed, oppressed, or exploited, situations that arise in a wide array of contexts, including intimate and familial ones. As the organized expectations of generalized others, rights are always in need of interpretation. The very abstractness necessary for the intersubjective dimension of rights both enables and requires an attention to concrete differences in the application of rights. To argue for the universality of rights does not mean that one thinks every social member is identical. If we were all the same, we wouldn't need individual rights because there would be no differences to contest. The normative claim of universality within the notion of rights respects individual differences. It guarantees that each, because of her very particularity, is valued and her differences secured.

Universality and impartiality can also be conceived in light of our common experience as embodied, emotional beings. Habermas offers such a conception of universality in his discourse ethics. Discourse ethics relies on the idea that valid norms are those that can be universalized, that is, freely accepted by each and every person affected by them.[22] The idea of universality in discourse ethics functions as a "bridging principle" in the discursive justification of a norm. It establishes the link between the reasons given by participants in a discourse and their conviction that a particular conclusion regarding the validity of a norm is warranted.[23] In discourse ethics, then, "warrant" refers to the normative relationship among the participants in argumentation. A norm that warrants the acceptance of each and every person affected cannot be one that would, as Seyla Benhabib puts it, "deny our embodied and embedded identity."[24] A norm that depends for recognition on the suppression or denial of our basic feelings and experiences, our ties and commitments, or our fundamental physicality, does not warrant acceptance. Such a norm would destroy the very relations of intersubjectivity upon which its validity depends. This understanding of universality as requiring consideration of the emotional and physical attributes of persons thus makes possible the critique of institutions or interpretations that exclude others by suppressing their feelings or denying them the integrity of their bodies.

Such a view of universality has important consequences for an inclusive theory of civil society. It enables us to distinguish between those differences we want recognized and those that have been constructed as vehicles for subordination or devaluation. As it evokes the recognition of differences, it reminds us of the role of the situated, hypothetical third. Breaking through traditional interpretations of generalized others presupposes that we are not institutionally constrained to a given domain. We have to be able to participate in a variety of groups to develop the very capacity to distinguish among and question the valuations of difference already given.

Traditionally, justice has been characterized as a virtue and confined to the public sphere. What this has tended to mean, however, is that the private sphere has been open to injustice. Once justice is viewed as a dimension of validity, however, it need not and cannot be confined to one particular sphere of human interaction.[25] It stretches throughout all of our normatively structured relationships and interactions. Of course, this does not mean that every interaction is to be judged in the same way or that the establishment of the validity of a norm determines the proper action in a given case. Rather, the ideal of impartiality within the dimension of justice extends to the application of a norm in a particular situation.[26] Through discourses of application, those affected in a particular situation can bring to light all those considerations they view as decisive for the outcome of the situation. Further, as they seek for common understandings, they can call upon one another to justify their descriptions and accounts of the situation and to give reasons for their preference for one of several competing valid norms.[27]

Conceiving justice as a dimension of validity that extends throughout our intersubjective relationships does not mean that our intimate ties are simply subsumed under legal rules and principles. On the contrary, the consequences of this understanding of justice involve the expansion of the rationality of communication. Previously, to say that a dilemma was private was to limit the sorts of norms that could play a role in determining its resolution. FC3 shows that a theory of civil society that includes women cannot be based on a distinction between the public and the private. Thus, our conception of civil society itself must be reformed to allow for this expansion of communicative rationality. And this requires that we jettison the very distinction between these spheres in favor of a civil society based on multiple, interconnecting, discursive spheres.

Moving beyond Public and Private Spheres

On the descriptive or empirical level, the distinction between the public and private spheres has already broken down.[28] The political recognition and legal guarantees that created the domestic sphere demonstrate that the family is not a domain free from state intervention. The state has always played a major role in defining the family.[29] For example, the difficulties encountered by lesbians and gay men as they seek to acquire custody of their children, marry, and adopt indicates the way in which the state defines the family in exclusively heterosexual terms. Moreover, as child abuse, domestic violence, and marital rape have become issues for political debate and legal regulation, even the illusion of a division has begun to fade away. With the increase in divorce, the number of single-parent households, and the variety in living arrangements, one can no longer think of the private sphere as referring exclusively or even predominantly to male-headed families. Such a conception hinders public attention to the need for new ways of dealing with reproduction, the care and socialization of children, the medical needs of those not part of traditional families and thus outside of conventional health insurance policies, and the challenges presented by the growing number of senior citizens. Furthermore, as the work of women of color has taught us, the very notion of a male-headed family blinds us to race, to the extended kinship arrangements in nonwhite families and the leadership role taken by many African American women in the home.[30]

Additionally, the idea of *the* public sphere fails to capture the diversity of public spheres within modern civil society.[31] Criticizing Habermas's conception of the "liberal model of the bourgeois public sphere," Nancy Fraser cites recent historiography that illustrates that this sphere was one among a plurality of competing discursive spheres. To be sure, Fraser misinterprets the Habermasian conception of the public sphere. Rather than referring strictly to the public debates among eighteenth- and nineteenth-century bourgeoisie, Habermas emphasizes the formal norms of publicity, equality, and reciprocity, which served as critical ideals of democratic debate. What is significant about Fraser's discussion, however, is that she highlights how women, workers, ethnic groups, and lesbians and gay men have continuously created spaces in which they have published, voiced, interpreted, and debated their concerns. The conception of one particular space in which citizens disregard their particular concerns and discuss matters of general interest thus fails to reveal, and hence denigrates, the participatory activity of large numbers of agents in civil society. It elevates one aspect of civil society above the others, furthering their exclusion by focusing on the words and actions within this restricted "public" sphere.

How the dissolution of the boundaries between the public and private spheres is to be worked out on the conceptual level is a more difficult problem. Some feminists have voiced the fear that the demise of the intimate sphere implies the loss or devaluation of the nurturing and maternal values associated with women. Others have claimed that women's values can solve the problems of a masculinely constructed civil society (such views often come very close to communitarianism).[32] Both positions arise out of the binary terms in which traditional conceptions of civil society have been drawn. They posit the difference between male and female attributes and virtues so strongly that they neglect the elements of power and struggle within the private sphere and the potential for connection and recognition within the public. Types of action are reduced to spheres of action, making it impossible to acknowledge either the role of communicative action in both intimate and public spheres or the presence and problem of strategic action in each of these spheres. In short, such a reduction fails to allow for the possibility of associations of reflective solidarity.

A better approach to civil society involves beginning not with a division between the public and the private but with the goal of including women. With this as our goal, we attempt from the start to conceive of solidary relations in which difference is both respected and part of our mutual accountability.

Cohen and Arato's theory of civil society is helpful in this regard. Relying on Habermas's system-lifeworld distinction, they conceive of civil society as a communicatively integrated sphere differentiated from the state and the economy. Through institutions that preserve and renew cultural traditions, group solidarities, and individual and social identities, civil society mediates between the lives of social members and the state and economic systems. This complex model of state, economy, and civil society thus depicts contemporary societies as drawing from three resources to secure integration — money, administrative power, and solidarity.[33] Accordingly, despite the fact that civil society is understood as influencing the state and the economy, it does not control them. Both the state and the economy are crucial for the systemic integration of complex modern societies. Unlike approaches that challenge the continued existence of the state and the economy, by focusing on the political dimensions of civil society, Cohen and Arato can argue for an extension of radical democracy that does not threaten overall social stability.

This model of civil society, then, relies on a reconstruction of the normative dimension of traditional theories of civil society. It is based on an ideal of democratic legitimacy rooted in discourse ethics and a framework of basic rights.[34] Accordingly, Cohen and Arato stress that the fundamental coordinating mechanism within civil society is communicative action. Of course, communicative action is not the only source of social solidarity—if it were, the advocation of "town meetings" for millions might be a sound strategy instead of a naive idea. Rather, associations in civil society are part of a complex network of relationships. The expansion and differentiation of discursive spheres and the institutionalization of democratic decision-making procedures throughout and within these associations, then, are what enable this network to secure the conditions necessary for the development of reflective solidarities. So, despite their insistence on a separation between public and private spheres and their use of concepts like the juridical subject and the autonomous individual that have come under feminist attack, Cohen and Arato's model nonetheless asserts the primacy and centrality of democratic participation and discursive questioning within an inclusive notion of civil society.

Relying on this model, I reinterpret those categories Cohen and Arato see as constitutive to a democratic, participatory conception of civil society from a feminist perspective aimed at including women.[35] My reinterpretation is structured in terms of the ideas of recognition and exclusion that lie at the heart of the feminist critiques. To overcome the opposition between universal and particular recognition and to emphasize the importance of the social questioning of traditional conceptions of roles, I revise Cohen and Arato's categories of the autonomous, self-reflective, moral individual and the juridical subject by stressing the notion of the embodied person and the importance of discursive rights. This revision appeals to the importance of the intersubjective questioning of interpretations of social norms, roles, rights, and needs for reflective solidarity while emphasizing the necessity of securing the conditions required for such questioning. To capture the feminist insight into continuing instances of practical exclusion at the levels of institutionalization and cultural interpretation, I stress publicity, democratic participation, and plurality. Publicity serves to expose those interpretations that have excluded women and others from civil society. Democratic participation and plurality help to create the spaces and anchor the potential for the active inclusion of each social member. These reinterpretations, then, move beyond the distinction between the public and private spheres and enable us to conceive of a civil society that includes women as one made up of a series of interconnected discursive spheres.[36]

Recognizing Embodied Persons

Feminists have rightly pointed out that the category of *autonomous, self-reflective, moral individual* has functioned as a mechanism for women's exclusion. Construed in terms of masculine detachment and rationality, it has enabled the bodily and emotive aspects of all of our lives to remain immune to questioning and to escape politicization. It is falsely universal, rooted in a notion of subjectivity that denies human particularity, relationality, situatedness, and multiplicity. I replace this category with the *mutual responsibility of embodied persons*.

I stress embodiment because of the importance of bodily integrity. Our bodies are not merely possessions that we use and enjoy; nor are they simply extensions of ourselves. Our bodies are integral components of who we are, how we see ourselves in the world, and the way we interact with others. Consequently, free control over our bodies is vital to our capacity to acquire the sense of self-trust and self-esteem necessary for responsible relationships and to develop the self-confidence to engage in critical questioning and discourse. We can trust neither others nor ourselves if we are plagued with fears of vulnerability and physical exploitation, if we find that others can and will exploit and manipulate our bodies and needs. But once social membership is premised on persons secure in their own bodies, we can anchor in our conception of civil society the idea that being a member in solidary connection with others can only arise among individuals who respect themselves and others as physically inviolate.

Emphasizing embodiment draws attention to the sex and gender of persons in civil society. Issues of sexuality, pregnancy, and childbirth are thus no longer confined to a private sphere. Instead, they are fundamental themes for society as a whole. Since the disembodied, disconnected, and egoistic autonomous agent is eliminated as a normative ideal, the institutions of civil society as well as of the state and economy are forced to assume that persons are already connected with other people and to find alternative forms of organization. These institutions thus have to include within their basic structures arrangements that allow for the care of others — for example, domestic partnership arrangements, time-sharing plans that do not penalize those with children, day-care facilities at the workplace, provisions for children at club and group meetings, and the coordination of the school day with the working day.

The moral responsibility of the individual in civil society reminds us that autonomy always arises out of intersubjective relationships. Not concerned merely with carrying out their own projects, morally responsible agents recognize the need to attend to the connections sustaining individuals and groups within society. This sense of responsibility supports the idea that reflection is never an isolated activity, but one carried out dialogically. The risky process of questioning social roles and cultural interpretations can avoid disruptive fragmentation and generate solidarity only when it is supported by a network of communicatively mediated relationships.

As I have shown, the category of *juridical subject* presents a particular problem for feminists. The extension of basic rights to women was significant, to say the least, as it allowed women to claim that same freedom previously enjoyed by men. Yet the ideal of equality of all before the law has prevented experiences particular to women from receiving full consideration. These experiences have appeared only as exceptions to a masculinely defined norm. The idea of two juridical subjects, one masculine and one feminine, suggests a sexual apartheid in which citizens are divided into two groups with two sets of laws. Additionally, this formulation remains rigid in its insistence on essential and knowable sexual identities. Ignoring the insights of the critics of identity politics, it fails to question precisely those structures of power and meaning in which identities are constructed and intelligible. With these difficulties in mind, I argue for a limitation of the concept of the juridical subject to refer to the *embodied person as a bearer of discursive rights*.

In a democratic civil society, persons have to be recognized as possessing those rights that are necessary for communicative freedom and that guarantee sufficient human dignity to permit full participation in society.[37] Once individuated selves are viewed as developing in the context of their relations with others, we no longer have recourse to a notion of rights premised on autonomous subjectivity. Instead, we have to secure the potential for participation within those discursive relationships capable of protecting concrete and fragile identities. Attributing discursive rights to embodied persons, then, allows us to view selves as in process in that it does not require us to limit or fix the content of these selves. The definitions generated in law are themselves up for democratic interpretation and negotiation. Designed to capture the insight that in certain contexts rights secure the protection of basic liberties, the notion of the embodied person as a bearer of discursive rights is premised on the idea that self-determination presupposes the psychological integrity of embodied persons.

The concept of discursive rights emphasizes the continued questioning and confrontation of cultural interpretations that cheapen the value of these rights for particular groups in civil society. To this end, it focuses on the forum and context in which rights claims are made. This contributes to the ability of discursive rights to secure reflective solidarity. Discursive rights establish an idea of membership as being part of a community that argues. By recognizing the right of each to challenge and contest exclusionary meanings, they provide spaces for the inclusion of different voices. The stress on the context in which right claims are made draws attention to the situatedness of those others, those hypothetical thirds, who continue to remain outside the boundaries of given articulations of rights. As we seek to hear them, and as they endeavor to disrupt our traditional understandings, these others transform our notions of discourse and rights even as they claim them.

The concept of the embodied person as a bearer of discursive rights thus takes seriously the limits of and problems with rights in contemporary democracies. Clearly, not every dispute between individuals or groups involves or must involve a rights claim. Indeed, a restricted focus on rights often conceals other morally or ethically significant features of the context in which a dispute is situated. The mere existence of a right, then, cannot be the singularly decisive element within a dispute. In fact, it is more often the case that *everyone* involved has a compelling rights claim. Further, the feminist critique of the opposition between universality and particularity tells us that we have to acknowledge that specific needs and interests can exist *alongside of* more generalizable concerns without always being subsumed. Attending to and exploring the relationships and contexts involved in a dispute, then, is a process parallel to that of establishing the rights of the parties involved. One could describe this process as thematizing particular aspects of situations in order to find "the best fit." It requires a multiplicity of interpretations and the potential for discursive participation and questioning. Such a process creates a space for a decision as to whether a dispute is best resolved in terms of rights, needs, or the advantages or disadvantages (the benefits or harms) that could foreseeably result from any given decision.

Admittedly, this process might require that some rights be overruled. But this is often already done (as in cases of libel or slander). And we no longer have recourse to traditional conceptions of civil society where supererogatory acts and acts of compassion or care were confined to the private sphere. Without such conceptions to fall back on, we have to allow that in certain cases the mere existence of rights cannot function so as to "trump" the needs of others involved in a dilemma. As Rhode argues "Debates over rights often simply restate rather than resolve fundamental tensions in cultural ideals; reliance on formal entitlement may obscure the broader institutional structure that contains them."[38] Thus, at the procedural level, the rights appealed to themselves would have to be explained and justified with reference to the normative context of the situation — that is, the intersubjective needs and relationships constituting the background of the problem and the foreseeable consequences that would arise from a given application.

The interpretation of the juridical subject as an embodied bearer of discursive rights strengthens solidarity in ways lacking in its earlier form. Rather than mediated through relationships structured in terms of rights, social ties in civil society are created through an appreciation and recognition of the needs of particular others. In other words, one can know that one will be treated not simply in general terms but with regard to those circumstances that make one's position unique. Social membership within a reflectively solidary society thus comes to imply that one is accorded not simply the universal recognition of one's rights but also, and *even consequently*, the particular recognition of one's needs.

Toward Constitutive Inclusion

When understood in conjunction with the notions of embodied persons and discursive rights, the category of *publicity* becomes much more than "the means by which society controls the state."[39] Publicity is the way members of civil society expose, question, and confront those cultural interpretations that have devalued the speech of particular groups. Agents in civil society are always situated within a context of traditions that constitute the background of preconceptions, values, and norms that they bring into their daily interactions. These cultural symbols construct their views of themselves, others, their community, and society as a whole. As the various phases of identity politics attest, by bringing to light and thematizing certain aspects of their traditions and the traditions of others, groups in civil society acquire a better understanding of the differences among members and the capacity to recognize those cultural interpretations that practically exclude groups and individuals from full democratic participation. This heightens awareness of the ways in which difference is created, destroyed, attributed, claimed, valued, and devalued, enabling groups in civil society to take the perspective of hypothetical, situated thirds. Insofar as it guarantees the existence and the openness of contents for democratic questioning, publicity becomes a constitutive element in securing the value of discursive rights.

Clearly, this notion of publicity has a complicated relationship with a number of traditional interpretations that have helped to secure the normative and symbolic integration of civil society and give meaning and coherence to various groups within it. However, when we keep in view the goal of including women, we have to confront the fact that a key aspect of the conventional solidarity of civil society involved the cultivation of the notion of the domestic sphere and women's nurturing qualities. Challenging these ideas required and continues to require making the internal dynamic of families public. Michael Dyson makes a similar argument against those who claim that "critical news about black folk, especially if its source is other blacks, must be handled in secrecy away from the omniscient gaze of white society." "When it is secret and closed," Dyson notes, "cultural criticism threatens to become elitist and anti-democratic. Making criticism public encourages the widest possible participation of a diverse audience of potential interlocutors."[40] Insofar as not every aspect of traditional or group values comes under investigation at the same time, neither the groups within civil society nor the society as a whole face complete fragmentation and disintegration. On the contrary, through their encounter with different cultural forms and practices and their increasingly open communicative engagement with others, groups discover that new patterns of symbolic integration emerge, patterns created and furthered through democratic participation. Thus, publicity does not have to lead to disintegration. As it shows us the openness within the organized expectations of generalized others, it can help secure the conditions necessary for reflective solidarity.

In conjunction with publicity, *democratic participation* guarantees and anchors the inclusion of social members. Rather than simply implying parliamentary democracy (with its problems of low voter turnout and general passivity on the behalf of the electorate) or a reliance on discourse in "the official public sphere," participation in a democratically conceived civil society operates on a variety of levels and calls for the further formation of spaces for democratic will-formation and participation.[41] The existence of discursive rights, then, has to be strengthened and supported through an increase in opportunities to exercise these rights. Indeed, recognition of the particular needs and interests of others is not a precondition for discourse, but arises through those active discussions open to the participation of those representing a variety of perspectives. Accordingly, a variety of existing institutions present themselves as potential spaces for increased democratization. According to Cohen and Arato, "The functioning of societal associations, public communication, cultural institutions and *families* [emphasis added] allows for potentially high degrees of egalitarian, direct participation and collegial decision-making."[42] How they can reconcile this claim with an emphasis on the private sphere is unclear and, I think, unnecessary. In fact, their inclusion of families as spaces for democratization tells us that all associations within civil society are, to a certain degree, public. All associations, be they those into which we are born or those which we choose to enter or those somewhere in-between, can be challenged in light of principles of democratic legitimacy.

This leads to a notion of civil society constituted not by a division between the public and the private but by a multiplicity of differing spheres. We are already members of a plethora of ever-changing and evolving spheres of discourse, spheres that are open and closed to others in a variety of different ways. For women, this takes on a special import as they can champion their right and worthiness to speak in a variety of fora. Of course, not every discursive sphere concerns itself directly with political concerns in the sense of matters requiring legislation. However, as women have questioned a variety of issues — including the tendency of men to interrupt them or dominate their speech in intimate and social contexts, the division of labor in the household, the reluctance of museums to include women's art, the masculine bias within the natural sciences, and even the sexism in types of rap music — they have drawn attention to the fact that, regardless of content, the discursive spheres within civil society can and must be subject to democratic norms.

Through publicity the various spheres and institutions of civil society acquire a degree of porousness. Previously, families, churches, schools, and clubs were seen as relatively closed institutions, immune from outsiders and questioning. Once publicity is understood as a constitutive category of civil society, such closed groups can be viewed as already situated within an ongoing discussion about democracy, a discussion that is itself part of democratization. Of course, particular organizations will reasonably want to maintain a degree of closure to secure the substantive coherence of their group. Issue- and theme-oriented groups like women's health organizations, biking clubs, or animal rights foundations might justifiably balk if pressed to broaden their concerns beyond their specific area of interest. Nonetheless, all groups and organizations come under the pressure for greater democratization and inclusiveness because of their location in civil society. Since the members of organizations are always involved in a plethora of relationships and discussions, and through publicity are exposed to debates outside of their own circle, their own preconceptions and interpretations, the issues and patterns they see as relevant, come into question.

Institutions also become more porous as outsiders begin looking in and exposing and challenging particular practices or representations. This has been one of the major contributions of identity politics. For example, Native Americans have criticized the mascots of several U.S. sport teams for fostering racist and biased conceptions of Indians. Radical feminists in the seventies fought against the "bunny image" propagated by the Playboy Clubs. Indeed, the porousness of exposure is what enables a democratic civil society to coexist with right-wing and extremist organizations. Publicity entails that such groups cannot rely on secrecy. Instead, they are constantly challenged, confronted, and, in a way, forced into democratic discussion. To this extent, publicity ends up playing a key role in the prevention of violence.

The interconnection between publicity and democratic participation naturally leads to questions regarding legislation, or the possibility of achieving a consensus on a variety of controversial concerns and particular cultural values. Of course, when civil society is conceived as a multiplicity of discursive spheres connected through the communicative practice of rights-bearing members and made porous through the guarantees of publicity, at least some issues can be decided without legislation. The forces of investigation and critique can effect a great deal of change. Without relying on legal means, women have made inroads into leadership positions in numerous churches. By contesting the biases within the classical texts of political theory and philosophy, they have helped to transform university curricula so as to challenge traditional representations of women. By confronting the racism and homophobia dominant in American popular culture and the media, people of color and lesbians and gay men have opened up new spheres of debate and uncovered previously submerged histories.

Still, as various groups in civil society struggle to convince others that their values or interpretations deserve or require legally secured protection, a wide range of issues will become matters for democratic legislation. For a number of concerns, the basic forms of parliamentary democracy and majority rule will suffice. Yet I would also suggest that with regard to those cultural interpretations that limit the worth of the discursive rights of some members of civil society, the requirement of inclusion may override democratic decision making and, further, entail that the issue be handled with regard to the needs of those excluded rather than the rights of those already included. I was thus appalled by the media treatment in 1994 of Antioch College's consensual sex provisions. Rather than addressing the needs of women students (as well as their male counterparts) to feel safe in sexual situations, most newscasts and reports focused on the rights of men to sex without asking, assuming that women's bodies are there for the taking. (Indeed, what was often overlooked was the fact the Antioch decision did not even override democracy—the measures were voted in by the students themselves.)

We may not be able to come to a general consensus on those symbolic forms transmitting cultural values. But the notion of discursive rights requires that we seek to ensure that the value of these rights be the same for all. We have to acknowledge the consequences and side effects of cultural interpretations: Those forms of symbolic representation based on the explicit degradation of specific groups or the deliberate and sustained denigration of particular ways of life serve to exclude these groups from full participation in democratic society. Simply put, images can hurt. They participate in the construction of concrete identities and, in so doing, give persons a sense of their own worth and efficacy. Tied within larger structures of interpretation and meaning, biased and derogatory images prevent the beneficiaries of positive cultural reinforcement from recognizing their privilege. Thus, heterosexuals benefit daily from the degradation of homosexuality, which blocks inquiry into the conditions for and construction of heterosexuality. Whites benefit daily from associations between blackness and criminality. On a more personal level, only recently, upon reading Dorothy Allison's novel *Bastard Out of Carolina,* did I realize how I, growing up white in the South, benefited daily from the designation of other white people as "poor white trash." My family's changing class status took on value to the extent that it distanced itself from our less-well-off, less-educated, less-cultured (yes, always *less*) cousins.

Negative cultural representations prevent us from recognizing the needs and interests of the denigrated and excluded. They prevent us from acknowledging our own privilege and complicity. They undermine solidarity and democratic discourse, forcing both to remain partial and exclusionary. The inclusion of women and others who have been disadvantaged and maligned—indeed, the preconditions for democracy itself—will thus sometimes entail that the self-expression or self-realization of some become secondary to the self-determination of others. And this move, far from requiring the suppression of speech, calls for more speech. In a democratic civil society, limitations on arts funding for radical or alternative projects cannot appeal to the self-realization of a closed community. Theaters and television networks cannot worry about confronting the sensibilities of some unseen majority. Instead, spaces and opportunities have to be developed and expanded that will facilitate the criticism of prejudices and allow for the emergence of alternative, more positive, images.

This conception of an inclusive civil society, then, does not depict the role of the media as one of increasing the complacency and fragmentation of society. On the contrary, new participatory and interactive media forms can facilitate reflection, although they often fail to do so. "Channel surfing," while often a form of passive consumption, also reflects active choices and valuations. Even tabloid journalism has its place—talk shows like *Geraldo, Oprah,* and *Donahue* provide opportunities for confronting and investigating ways of living that have long remained hidden below the surface of society. Conservative call-in radio shows allow listeners actively to participate in politics. Media scandals bring to light problems in the traditional, patriarchal family that many would prefer to ignore. Underlying the first *Menendez* trial was the issue of child abuse. The O. J. Simpson story, despite its weirdness, centers on domestic violence. So, while some stress the ability of popular media to manipulate viewers, I think that this overstates the issue: Many Americans are capable of actively reflecting on what they hear, read, and see.

Finally, to address the idea of *plurality,* once we have interpreted the categories of civil society with the goal of including women, the presumption and recognition of a multiplicity of views and practices appear in their constitutive force. As long as the private remains a sphere conceptualized in opposition to the public, plurality signifies little more than a plethora of masculine associations and representations; there is no guarantee that the concerns and interests of all will be included in discourse. Yet when seen in terms of an always expanding and interconnecting number of discursive spheres, plurality emerges as the guiding recognition of difference within civil society. No longer attached to already given interests, previously delineated spheres, or naturalistically determined groups, plurality in this model of civil society refers to the irreducible differences flowing within and among changing differences, spheres, and identities. It captures our understanding that disagreement, and even struggle, occurs within and between groups in civil society, whether they consist of two or three individuals or the entire population. It reminds us that disagreement and struggle themselves must be part of our notion of solidarity. Thus, plurality also entails the demand that we hear the voice of others and recognize their needs. Insofar as difference is claimed by persons secure in their own mental and physical integrity—persons guaranteed a voice through the establishment of discursive rights and brought into the open through publicity—difference can itself take on an integrating role in civil society. Indeed, it is the attempt to suppress or deny difference that has disintegrating effects, that disrupts our already fragile solidarity.

I began by situating my discussion within the context of Lefort's account of power in a democracy as represented by an empty space. For this space to be truly empty, it can no longer be understood in terms of a division between outside and inside; the markers of certainty designated by the public and private spheres themselves must be dissolved. Further, the dominance of the masculine body as the mediator between two separate and distinct spheres must be replaced by the interaction of differently sexed and gendered bodies reciprocally connected through their communicative engagement in a multiplicity of overlapping discursive spheres. In this way, the division that generates the democratic constitution is not predetermined as an essential division between men and women, but is opened up to allow for the thematization of a variety of ever-changing opponents and alliances. The division itself thus becomes a source of reflective solidarity. With this increase in differentiation, the masculine conception of the role of an actor on the political stage falls away. We now have a more complex understanding of action capable of highlighting cooperative relations of mutual recognition and more subtle displays of power within and among the various spheres in civil society.

With an end to the separation between the public and private spheres, women can be included on the stage of civil society. More fundamentally, we can begin to create the conditions necessary for the emergence of reflective solidarity.

CHAPTER 4

Solidarity and Legal Indeterminacy

The Shift in Privacy from Sphere to Boundary

Democracy is instituted and sustained by the dissolution of the markers of certainty. It inaugurates a history in which people experience a fundamental indeterminacy as to the basis of power, law, and knowledge, and as to the basis of relations between self and other, at every level of social life (at every level where division, and especially the division between those who held power and those who were subject to them, could once be articulated as a result of a belief in the nature of things or in a supernatural principle). It is this which leads me to take the view that, without the actors being aware of it, a process of questioning is implicit in social practice, that no one has the answer to the questions that arise, and that the work of ideology, which is always dedicated to the task of restoring certainty, cannot put an end to this practice.

Claude Lefort[1]

Reflective solidarity is an ideal for associating within pluralist, democratic societies. With reflective solidarity, disagreement and
dissent shed their disintegrative connotations and become characteristics of the bonds *connecting* people. Rather than tearing people apart,
questioning — adopting a hypothetical perspective toward shared norms
and expectations — calls on us to respect the other in her difference.
Questioning relies on and furthers relationships of mutual recognition
as it challenges us to take accountability for the exclusions within already
given practices and interpretations.

But, reflective solidarity is an *ideal*. Though we may strive to achieve it, we will often fail. Yet *here and now* we encounter pressing problems of social and systemic integration that cannot be set aside. Under these "real-life" conditions, law, as Habermas reminds us, functions as a "transformer" that guarantees that the net of communication woven throughout society remains intact.[2] In other words, law helps secure solidarity. When understood in the context of contemporary democracy, a context that highlights law's indeterminacy, law can also be seen as transmitting and generating *reflective* solidarity — that is, by emphasizing the context and conditions of law, we can understand how it contributes to the realization of an ideal.

Contemporary constitutional democracies are based on the idea that the legitimacy of law depends on the will of the governed. Habermas explains this idea in terms of "the principle of democracy." This principle states that only those laws are valid "which can meet with the agreement of legal consociates in a discursive law-making process that in turn has been legally constituted."[3] The principle of democracy thus refers to the way political opinion- and will-formation is institutionalized: Democracy requires a system of rights guaranteeing the equal participation of each individual in a communicative lawmaking process.

The connection between democracy and the legitimacy of law draws our attention to the contexts and conditions of legislation in contemporary pluralist societies. Lawmaking is a project undertaken by citizens situated within a historically given society. It relies on a store of traditions and narratives, on the language that citizens use to understand the meaning of their association and to communicate the expectations associated with this meaning. More specialized than the language of everyday communication and interaction, *legal language* provides a vehicle for transmitting citizens' understandings and expectations throughout civil society, the state, and the economy. Because they are constructed in legal language, laws and legal norms are abstract and indeterminate — they always require interpretation. Laws do not regulate interactions among persons as concrete and irreplaceable members of specific communities; rather, they govern interactions among actors who recognize themselves as members of an abstract community produced by law.[4] Just as legal norms are abstract, so are legal persons. Because they embody the organized expectations of a legal community, legal persons are generalized others. Similarly, their mutual recognition is also abstract. Legal persons respect each other as equal participants in a collective debate regarding the character of the legally constituted community. This equality of respect embodies the intersubjective sense of rights, the way they express a relationship of recognition as well as a social practice rooted in social and political commitment.[5]

The democratic ideal at the heart of legal legitimacy explains how law can transmit reflective solidarity: Law is both a repository of collective social understandings and a set of enforceable behavioral expectations. It maintains a store of histories, values, and principles that give meaning to citizens' mutual recognition of each other as consociates in a shared life practice, and it establishes the rights and procedures necessary for playing out, guiding, contesting, and changing these histories, values, and principles. In its latter role, law secures solidarity in an empirical sense; it helps to integrate disparate and differentiated persons by allowing for a variety of forms of association and participation. It is a system of action, establishing generalized sets of behavioral expectations whereby conflicts can be settled according to the binary code lawful/ unlawful.[6] Yet because this code is not fixed, because democracy itself is "founded upon *the legitimacy of a debate as to what is legitimate and what is illegitimate,*"[7] law makes possible the achievement and re-achievement of solidarity in its reflective and normative sense: We are constantly called to question and interpret the meaning and content of "our" expectations. Here, law serves as a system of knowledge, providing an institutionalized history of decisions interpreted with an orientation toward the future. The "certainty" of behavior that law is supposed to guarantee always depends on the "rightness" or acceptability of the expectation in question. More precisely, "certainty" shifts from something guarantable as the outcome of any one specific legal principle or judicial decision to become the characteristic of legal procedures.

Although the democratic context of contemporary law requires that legal norms remain open for interpretation, recent critics have been wary of this abstractness. The objectivist rhetoric of legal decisions and the influence of legal positivism (which stresses the separation of law from value and the ability to establish a system of legal rules capable of facilitating consistent and predictable outcomes)[8] have led some writers to argue that there is a contradiction between the abstract character of rights and their consistent application in concrete cases. Scholars associated with the Critical Legal Studies movement ("Crits," as they are sometimes called) stress that legal principles and doctrines "depend on historically contingent assumptions and values rather than eternal or objective truths."[9] They argue that whatever consistency legal applications appear to have stems from partisan constructions of social reality, constructions that both belie the universalist claims associated with rights and reflect the interests of the powers-that-be.[10] For Crits, the "indeterminacy thesis" is that rights, far from determining any outcome, are indeterminate, dependent on a particular restriction of context and contents for their meaning. "Therefore," as Drucilla Cornell explains, "no line of precedent can fully determine a particular outcome in a particular case, because the rule itself is always in the process of reinterpretation as it is applied. It is interpretation that gives us the rule and not the other way around."[11]

As developed by the Crits, the indeterminacy thesis could lead us to think that law is incapable of providing a system of action. We might presume that the contradictions appearing in legal applications demonstrate its arbitrariness, an arbitrariness nonetheless suppressed temporarily by a particular dominant and dominating legal discourse. In contrast, Cornell offers a different interpretation of indeterminacy, one that supports an ideal of reflective solidarity: "The concept of indeterminacy is meant to indicate that we do not question by gazing down on institutionalized standards of communicability from a transcendental viewpoint; rather, we question from within our shared context. Yet, as we question, we also inevitably affirm meaning as the "basis" for our understanding of the process of questioning itself."[12] We question legal norms and principles with regard to their concrete application in a given case. In so doing, we provide an interpretation of both the situation at hand and the norm itself.[13] Questioning, then, is already contained within the very notion of an abstract norm, which must be interpreted for its meaning to be realized in practice. Furthermore, because this "meaning" is at the heart of an interpretive process, it is not fixed, but is itself temporarily achieved through our discursive efforts of understanding. The affirmation of meaning is an affirmation of a collective enterprise of "re-imagination." "We" affirm meaning through our participation in interpretation and contestation. And since this meaning only arises through our shared questioning, what we are actually affirming is the process of questioning itself. With this understanding of meaning, indeterminacy contributes to law's capacity to transmit and generate reflective solidarity.

Discussing the creation of the meaning of law — "jurisgenerative politics" — always part of dialogic constitutionalism, Frank Michelman makes a similar point:

Jurisgenerative political debate among a plurality of self-governing subjects involves the contested "re-collection" . . . of a fund of public normative references conceived as narratives, analogies, and other professions of commitment. Upon that fund those subjects draw both for identity, and by the same token, for moral and political freedom. That fund is the matrix of their identity "as" a people or political community, that is, as individuals in effectively persuasive, dialogic relation with each other, and it is also the medium of their political freedom, that is, of their translation of past into future through the dialogic exercise of recollective "imagination."[14]

In contemporary pluralist societies this fund of histories and values is always open to interpretation. Indeed, to serve as a source of and vehicle for reflective solidarity it must remain indeterminate, allowing for the possibility of varying normative outcomes and futures: "Legal indeterminacy in that sense is the precondition of the dialogic, critical-transformative dimension of our legal practice variously known as immanent critique, internal development, deviationist doctrine, social criticism, and recollective imagination."[15]

The democratic context of law thus tells us that all legal rights, standards, and principles are indeterminate. This indeterminacy, moreover, points toward collective efforts at constructing and ascertaining meaning. Under democratic presuppositions in which meaning is never fixed and is itself the product of dialogue, indeterminacy is necessary for reflective solidarity. Because reflective solidarity holds that responsibility means that our mutual expectations must remain open, as the lawmaking process generates abstract norms it protects and extends our communicative ties. Law transmits opportunities for the contestation of meaning because legal norms require interpretation.

To be sure, these opportunities are constrained by the very legal language that allows them to penetrate the diverse spheres of civil society and systems of state and economy. On the one hand, this constraint is reflexive, applicable to the law and legal language itself. The semantic content of a legal norm establishes boundaries as to what sorts of concerns and contexts it is meant to govern. In turn, these boundaries regulate the discourse regarding the meaning of the norm in question. Nonetheless, the legitimacy of any effort to establish a boundary is itself constrained by the preconditions of democratic debate. Legitimacy always takes us back to the discourse of legal persons. For example, sexual harassment law applies to harassing behavior in the workplace. Here, semantic content refers to the meanings of the terms "sexual" and "harassment" in the context of a "workplace." These terms establish the boundaries, or the field of application, of the law — to interpret the law, we have to know what these terms mean and work within them. Finally, as they interrogate the legitimacy of these boundaries, courts look to the legislative history of sexual harassment regulation.

On the other hand, more substantial constraints often become deeply connected with legal norms. In contrast to the reflexive constraints that take us back to the legitimacy of a given law, these "interpretive constraints" affix themselves to norms as a way of narrowing their field of application. By interpretive constraints I mean the domination of a particular vocabulary or mode of discussion, a crystallization of meaning and interpretation that establishes the parameters of questioning. An interpretive constraint determines which terms can be used to interpret a legal principle or rule and what these terms mean. It installs the standards for the admissibility of arguments, the criteria of truth and falsity. Although interpretive constraints enable us to collect and order the "facts of the matter" or describe the situation at hand in accordance with already given norm interpretations, they often end up erecting barriers to the inclusion of new descriptions and interpretations.[16] Interpretive constraints often cut off interpretation and substitute tradition for reflection. They endeavor to make us see what is indeterminate as determined.

My examination of the role of law in transmitting reflective solidarity addresses the continued impact of interpretive constraints that determine legal concepts. I focus on the reasonableness standard in sexual harassment law and the right to privacy as articulated in the struggle for abortion rights and the rights of gay men and lesbians (for numerous commentators continue to emphasize privacy despite the Supreme Court's holding in *Bowers v. Hardwick* in 1986).[17] I address reasonableness and privacy to clarify my argument that we should jettison the dualistic, public/private model of civil society. My rejection of a sociological separation of spheres on empirical and normative grounds does not necessarily entail the rejection of a legal concept of privacy. It does not mean that the right to privacy itself must be discarded. Nor does it deny the continued critical force of either a notion of privacy or an evocation of the private/public dichotomy. Instead, the idea of multiple spheres entails reformulating legal conceptions of privacy to eliminate their association with the patriarchal private sphere, protect our intimate and ethnic solidarities, and secure the potential for each individual to participate in the various spheres already part of civil society. Thus, I use the idea of a divide between the public and private spheres critically in order to articulate the shift in privacy from sphere to boundary.[18]

Sexual Harassment and Reasonableness

By the late 1970s, the Circuit Courts of Appeals had acknowledged sexual harassment as a form of sex-based discrimination proscribed by Title VII of the Civil Rights Act of 1964.[19] With the Supreme Court's holding in *Meritor Savings Bank, FSB v. Vinson*[20] in 1986 and the Equal Employment Opportunity Commission's establishment of guidelines for impermissible conduct in 1990, the harm of sexual harassment came to be recognized as undermining women's equality in the workplace.

Nonetheless, courts have had problems deciding what kind of behavior is harassing. Since quid-pro-quo (sex-for-favors) and retaliatory harassment are relatively straightforward, most of the problems occur in hostile environment cases. In *Meritor* the Court proposed the following test: To succeed under the hostile environment theory, a claimant must establish that the alleged behavior was "unwelcome" and that it was "sufficiently severe or pervasive 'to alter the conditions of [the victim's] employment and create an abusive working environment.'"[21] Deciding that the behavior in question in *Meritor* was clearly sufficiently severe and pervasive, the Court focused on welcomeness. Lower courts were left to establish the tests and standards by which to judge the actual abusiveness of the workplace — to what extent the workplace was altered by harassing behavior. The standard they chose was one familiar to tort law, that of the reasonable person.[22]

As the dissent in *Rabidue v. Osceola Refining Co.* in 1986 pointed out, however, the reasonable person standard "fails to account for the wide divergence between most women's views of appropriate sexual conduct and those of men" and thus implicitly reinforces the masculinity of the reasonable person.[23] Indeed, the *Rabidue* court ruled that a reasonable person would not find a work environment hostile and abusive in which a woman was repeatedly referred to as "whore," "cunt," "pussy," or "tits," and in which her supervisor remarked, "All that bitch needs is a good lay."[24]

Explicitly rejecting this reasonable person approach, in *Ellison v. Brady* in 1991 the Ninth Circuit Court of Appeals adopted the reasonable woman standard.[25] It argued that the reasonable woman standard would not only put women on more "equal footing" with men by taking into account their different experience of rape and assault, but also "shield employers from having to accommodate the idiosyncratic concerns of the rare hyper-sensitive employee."[26]

THE CRITIQUE OF REASONABLENESS

Feminist legal theorists have raised substantial criticisms of both standards. Generally agreeing that the reasonable person as currently conceived reinforces the male perspective of the status quo, they have stressed a number of problems with the reasonable woman standard. Their critiques tend to fall into two broad categories: those which focus on application, on the standard's inability to accommodate difference; and those which target the conceptual problems within the notion of "reasonableness." Those critics who emphasize application usually support a revised notion of the reasonable woman, while critics who concentrate on conceptual problems often reject the reasonableness standard entirely. My claim is that whereas the application critique mistakenly worries about the determinations installed by a standard that challenges the masculinity of the reasonable person, the conceptual critique fails to attend to the problem of gender at all. The conceptual critique dismisses reasonableness for the wrong reasons, and, in so doing, overlooks the place of the public/private distinction in sexual harassment law. Once this understanding is uncovered, we can grasp the way that recent decisions, rather than relying on reasonableness, employ and problematize a notion of the private sphere.

Three basic arguments characterize the application critique. In the first place, application critics point out that the same lawyers, judges, and juries who have perpetuated the reasonable person standard apply the reasonable woman standard. As Eileen Blackwood remarks:

Given that men and women experience sexuality differently, how then can decision makers determine how a reasonable woman would have reacted without resorting to male defined culturally biased perspectives? They will have to draw on their own experiences and views of what conduct is reasonable for a woman. The current need for sexual harassment law demonstrates that men and women do not agree on what is reasonable. It seems naive to assume that the legal decision makers will be different.[27]

Consequently, this strand of critique holds that the notion of the reasonable woman is ultimately indistinguishable from that of the reasonable man.[28]

In the second place, application critics argue that the reasonable woman standard "does not accommodate the experiences of all women."[29] Women differ among themselves as to what sorts of behavior they find harassing. This line of argument often finds itself caught in a train of identifications, wondering if the next step will be the standard of the reasonable Chicana lesbian or that of the single, Anglo mother.[30]

In the third place, application critics maintain that the reasonable woman standard risks reinstating the stereotype of the delicate, passive victim in need of protection from the coarse world of the workplace.[31] Courts tend to presume that the expectations of the reasonable woman are that she will not be exposed to explicit images or coarse behavior. The embodiment of virtue, she establishes the limits and boundaries of respectable behavior. She is a Lady or Madonna caught in a world of whores. For these critics, the reasonable woman is a static symbol, the complexity of her experiences and desires negated by a standard that demands perfection.

Ultimately, all three of these arguments address the inability of the reasonable woman standard to acknowledge difference. They claim that when applying the standard, courts risk underestimating the importance of difference in three dimensions: the differences between men and women, the differences among women, and the differences within each woman. For the application critics, then, the goal is finding an appropriate way to include difference and specificity.

In focusing on the proper formulation of the reasonable woman standard, the application critics become enmeshed in the dilemmas of difference plaguing identity politics. Underlying their arguments is the idea that law has the potential to recognize concrete differences. They suggest that the legal meaning of the recognition of difference is not an abstract guarantee of respect, but the concrete acknowledgement of specificity. They are forced into this position, however, because of the intransigence of the masculine determination of reasonableness. When the reasonable person appears to be the reasonable man, opening up the standard to include women seems to direct us to a reasonable woman standard. But this standard, the critics argue, installs its own set of exclusions. On the one hand, the critics are right: seeking to overcome the determinations of one standard through yet another set of determinations can only lead to further exclusion. Yet, on the other hand, if we focus on the remedy the standard seeks to provide, on the reasonable woman as a critical perspective toward a masculinely determined notion of reasonableness, we can read the call for the recognition of difference as a call to greater indeterminacy.

I am suggesting that in law identity politics is a response to interpretive constraints. So, rather than reading the call for inclusion at the heart of identity politics as a call for greater legal specificity, we should understand it as indicating the need for a perspective both hypothetical and concrete—in other words, the perspective of the situated, hypothetical third.

The reasonable man is a generalized other, an organized set of social interpretations. Taking a hypothetical attitude toward him means that we open him up, dissecting him in light of the plurality of meanings already present in reasonableness. If we concretize this perspective, attributing to it "femininity," we reveal the biases already present within our notions of both "reasonableness" and "person." We can continue our concretization, adding race, class, ethnicity, the whole "string of hyphens" to challenge exclusions as they arise. This will become clearer after I outline the conceptual critique of reasonableness.

The conceptual critique of reasonableness addresses the operation of interpretive constraints on the very idea of reasonableness. It holds that neither the reasonable woman standard nor the reasonable person standard can successfully address the problem of sexual harassment because the very idea of reasonableness presupposes a notion of consensus ultimately incapable of accommodating difference.[32] Since Nancy Ehrenreich has offered a rich and nuanced version of this argument, I will focus in some detail on her discussion of the inability of reasonableness to mediate between diversity and conformity.

Constructing her argument by means of an analogy between the function of reasonableness in the private law concept of negligence and in public antidiscrimination law, Ehrenreich asserts that

(unfounded) pluralist assumptions support the courts' use of the reasonable person concept to define discrimination in the sexual harassment setting. Such assumptions allow reasonableness to be seen as mediating a fundamental contradiction between liberty and security in liberal legal thought— a contradiction expressed in this context as the conflict between our desire to promote social diversity by providing autonomy to individual groups and our need to protect vulnerable groups from discrimination by coercing a certain amount of conformity to general standards of conduct.[33]

For Ehrenreich, a "pluralist ideology" underlies both negligence and antidiscrimination law. This ideology is characterized by the following beliefs: that diversity is a positive good, a guarantee of democracy insofar as it prevents any one perspective from gaining dominance; that diversity is an accurate description of existing American society, which means that the commonly held belief in pluralism serves as a unifying, overarching value in America; and that the role of government is to preserve heterogeneity and maintain a relativistic stance vis-à-vis diverse groups.[34] Accordingly, antidiscrimination law is supposed to serve as a protection of diversity, intervening in those instances when coercive practices and stereotypes disadvantage members of protected groups in the broader society's discussions and exchanges. Because the courts must remain neutral, they use the reasonableness standard as a guide for intervention, a way of "identifying a point along a continuum of conduct that separates (prohibited) discrimination from (protected) freedom."[35] Reasonableness is thought to provide such a standard because of its indeterminacy. Since what is reasonable cannot be defined once and for all, reasonableness must itself be the product of pluralism, the result of an already given societal consensus. The courts are neutral, then, because they are applying a test that owes its legitimacy to its origins in the free discussions of a pluralist society.

Ehrenreich uses *Rabidue v. Osceola Refining Co.* to show the inability of reasonableness to perform this mediating function. She addresses three aspects of the majority decision: "its 'privatization' of the plaintiff, its recasting of the group conflict in this case, and its equation of reasonableness with consensus."[36] First, the majority opinion privatized Vivian Rabidue's complaint by describing her as "an overly sensitive obnoxious woman" and by stressing her voluntary entry into the workplace. This erased her group membership, constructing her as an atypical, unreasonable woman who had chosen to work in an obscene environment and must consequently bear the responsibility for this choice. With this act of privatization, the court avoided "visualizing the case as a conflict between men and women" and "undermined the legitimacy of the plaintiff's claim by making it seem not to implicate pluralist concerns (since she did not represent the interests of women as a group)."[37]

Second, having effectively eliminated the possibility of a conflict between men and women, the court recast the issues at stake in *Rabidue* as involving class conflict — the values of "American workers" versus those of some vague but powerful elite. Douglas Henry's verbal abuse of Vivian Rabidue (which led her to file a sexual harassment complaint) was not the particular and idiosyncratic behavior of a lewd employee, but a characteristic of working-class culture as a whole. As such, tolerance of diversity would demand that this culture be protected against the incursions of the powerful.

Third, in determining the content of the social consensus regarding reasonable behavior, the majority equated consensus with prevailing social practices.[38] They reasoned that since "pictorial erotica" is widespread in America — to be found on newsstands, in the movies, and on television — sexually graphic images in the workplace cannot reasonably be viewed as having significantly harmful effects. To be sure, the poster in question in *Rabidue* "showed a prone woman who had a golf ball on her breasts with a man standing over her, golf club in hand, yelling 'Fore.'"[39] Nonetheless, because of the pervasiveness of derogatory images in American society, the majority held that such a poster would not impair a woman's equal participation in her place of employment. With this reading of *Rabidue*, Ehrenreich concludes that far from mediating the divide between diversity and conformity, reasonableness conceals and displaces it.

Given Ehrenreich's critique of reasonableness, it is not surprising that she views the reasonable woman standard as no less problematic than that of the reasonable person. Like the latter, the reasonable woman standard relies on a distinction between prohibited discrimination and protected freedom via the opposition between the regulable behavior of the "neurotic" woman — "the rare hypersensitive employee" — and the legitimate concerns of the reasonable woman. And, like that of the reasonable person, the notion of the reasonable woman relies on the assumption that there is a preexisting consensus regarding reasonableness that can supply a neutral standard.

While Ehrenreich's critique is frequently illuminating and provocative, it misreads the problem of the public/private distinction in *Rabidue*. Because she draws her conception of the private sphere from negligence law, Ehrenreich fails to recognize the different notion of the private at work in sexual harassment cases. In fact, Ehrenreich's conception of the divide between the public and private spheres conceals the domestic and sexual view of the private at work in *Rabidue* (and in sexual harassment cases generally). Consequently, she cannot distinguish between a valid consensus and a merely existing consensus, between one that is culturally or societally presumed to be held and one that *deserves* to be held because it reflects the interests of all concerned. By adopting a voluntarist notion of the private sphere, by concealing the importance of sex and domesticity in sexual harassment cases, Ehrenreich fails to see the potential of privacy as a shifting, negotiable boundary. She is prevented from accounting for the unstated ideal that emerges in recent cases, an ideal that moves beyond an empirically given consensus and points toward a valid one.

As she builds from her analogy with negligence law, Ehrenreich conceives the private sphere as characterized by freedom of contract and unfettered interaction. In contrast to the public sphere, which regulates and protects such "natural" exchanges, the private sphere is a consent-based realm of individual freedom. Beginning with this view of the private, Ehrenreich can move quite easily to her critique, which resembles familiar marxist critiques: Such a realm is neither free nor voluntary, but fundamentally hierarchical. Any gain on behalf of one group is necessarily a loss for another.[40] In short, since interactions remain strategic, we (and the courts) are left with strategic choices regarding whose interests will be served or protected. So, of course, the reasonableness standard could not serve as a mechanism with which courts could distinguish protected exercises of freedom from regulable interferences with collective security. With such a reading of the private, no norm or standard could ever provide a mediation capable of bridging the divide between the public and the private, for, as Ehrenreich asserts, the relational and hierarchical construction of groups in American society entails that "part of each group's identity is its awareness of its position in a hierarchy of groups. Because groups are mutually defined in this way, it is simply impossible to accommodate one group without in some way affecting others."[41] Ehrenreich's conception of the public/private distinction thus prevents her from moving beyond an agonistic vision of competing identities.

But this analogy between negligence and antidiscrimination law, although an important reminder to feminists who often forget about the continued impact and use of a market notion of privacy,[42] cloaks the understanding of the private at work in sexual harassment law. Sexual harassment law is designed to locate and eliminate conduct that alters the plaintiff's work environment, unreasonably interfering with her ability to work. Furthermore, this conduct is viewed as based on sex—on the sex of the plaintiff and on the sexualized character of the interaction.[43] As it identifies and punishes sexualized conduct, the court relies on a particular conception of appropriate performance. Decisions in sexual harassment cases hinge on how plaintiffs' and defendants' performances are interpreted. How a court constructs this interpretation thus depends on how it uses the notion of privacy. In other words, since the issue is sexualized performances, or the way in which particular performances sexualize and are sexualized, how the court reads the boundary established by privacy determines its decision. The private is the boundary marking the admissibility of performances.

PRIVACY AS BOUNDARY

With this understanding of privacy as a boundary, we are able to grasp what is at stake in sexual harassment cases—namely, the problem of women and sex. If women are viewed from the outset as sexual, privacy cannot provide a boundary marking sexualized performances as inadmissable. Instead, they are already within the old traditional private sphere of domesticity, sexuality, and intimacy. The boundary that privacy establishes is pre-interpreted in terms of an already given understanding of the opposition between the sexuality and domesticity of the private sphere and the "neutrality/neuter-ality" of the more public sphere of labor and interaction. Yet when women are not preinstalled in a private sphere, privacy provides a more free-floating boundary between their performance as employees and workers and their performance as particular persons. Once freed from the private sphere, women are able to use privacy as a protection, as a boundary establishing the appropriateness of particular performances.

The tension between this boundary notion of privacy and traditional interpretations of the private sphere becomes clear when we look at some of the conceptual difficulties present in the idea of the reasonable person (or the man from whom this person derives). The reasonable person or man cannot mediate between the public and private spheres because he brings with him the typical trappings of masculinity. As Ehrenreich explains, the image of the reasonable man used in negligence literature is often concretized as "the man who takes the magazines at home and in the evening pushes the lawn mower in his shirtsleeves."[44] Situated between the traditional domestic and public spheres, this man becomes himself the boundary marking admissible performances as he moves from his position as head of household into the workforce and back. In fact, his placement at home yet outside establishes not only his ability to shift freely from one domain to the other, but also his capacity to demarcate with his movement the perimeter and assumptions of each of those domains. He takes his magazines at home, bringing the outside world of paid labor into the domestic sphere and inserting an element of publicity into the realm of intimacy. Similarly, he takes with him into the workplace his attributes of paternal and masculine dominance. By bringing with it these connotations of male superiority, the boundary established by the reasonable man fails to provide women with relief in sexual harassment cases. Harassing behavior simply repeats traditional male expectations of sexual access to women. It reinserts women in the home, setting up modes of behavior perhaps private for the "reasonable" man as appropriate male/female interactions.

The image of the "man in his shirtsleeves" also shows us why the standard of the reasonable woman fails to mediate between the domestic and public realms. The reasonable woman herself eludes representation, for how would we depict her? Is she a homeowner, even though vast numbers of American women live below the poverty line? Is she also white, like the gloss over the race of the reasonable man leads us to believe he is? Is someone attending to her intimate and sexual needs, perhaps a maid or househusband, when most women bear the weight of child rearing as well as wage earning? If she is the concealed wife of the reasonable man, the reasonable woman is configured as heterosexual, excluding the reasonable lesbian. As a wife she remains confined indoors, perhaps nagging her husband to mow the lawn. Her privacy is not a boundary, but a sphere—her only bridge to the outside world is him, the bringer of the magazines. She, if reasonable, does not enter the public sphere of the workplace. Precisely because she remains caught in the domestic private sphere, already enmeshed in various coded meanings, the privacy of the reasonable woman cannot but fail to reinstate women within the private sphere.

Returning to *Rabidue,* we find this tense and ambiguous reading of the private informing the court's reasoning. Its narrative begins with a recollection: Vivian Rabidue was first employed at Osceola Refining Company as an executive secretary. Later, she advanced to the position of administrative assistant.[45] By recalling her past with Osceola, the court casts Rabidue in a supportive role. Her occupational performance suggests that of a housewife. Her duties were to attend the telephone, purchase office supplies, make contacts with customers—the caretaking and social responsibilities of the good wife and mother. Yet in the story the court tells, Rabidue was not a good wife; she could not work "harmoniously with others." Instead she was an "independent, aggressive, intractable, and opinionated individual." Furthermore, she "disregarded supervisory instruction and company policy whenever such direction conflicted with her personal reasoning and conclusions."[46] By bringing in Rabidue's occupational history, constructing it in domestic terms, and showing how Rabidue failed to perform her role as cast, the majority on the court relies on a particular reading of the boundary established by privacy: it is the boundary provided by the reasonable man as he moves from the domestic to the public sphere.

Not surprisingly, this reading enables the majority to view Douglas Henry as performing appropriately. The domestication and sexualization of Rabidue that accompany the court's assessment of the boundary of privacy prevent Henry's behavior from being seen as itself an act of sexualization, as an effort to place Rabidue in the private sphere. Only the dissent acknowledges that Rabidue was prevented from taking customers to lunch because of her sex, because it was "inappropriate" for a woman to take out male clients.[47] Moreover, in faulting Rabidue for an aggressive and independent performance, the court implicitly endorses Henry's (and the company's) efforts to keep a wayward wife in line. Pornography and obscenity remind women of their status as sexualized objects and serve to punish them for daring to perform a role not assigned to them. In fact, what becomes clear in the dissent is Osceola's inability to escape from a domesticized/sexualized conception of Rabidue's role despite the requirements of her job, a conception on which the majority relies: Although she was said to be abrasive and aggressive, she was "not forceful enough to collect on slow-paying jobs"; although she was required to improve efficiency, her efforts were consistently undermined.[48] The dissent thus draws attention to the tension between the role Rabidue was supposed to perform as an employee and the sexualized role Osceola and the majority cast her in as a woman. After Rabidue left Osceola, the company reconciled this tension by replacing her with a man, one whose sex would measure up to the demands of performance.

In contrast, in *Ellison v. Brady* the majority begins with an understanding of the plaintiff, Kerry Ellison, as performing the role of employee.[49] Instead of casting her as a sexualized woman, the majority focuses on her status as a worker. The defendant, Sterling Gray, is situated in the home, as a parent—the court tells us that the one time Ellison agreed to have lunch with Gray, they stopped by his house to pick up his son's forgotten lunch. Having cast both plaintiff and defendant, the court sees Gray's actions as efforts (whether intentional or not) at sexualization, as attempts to encode an identity onto the plaintiff apart from her position as employee. The opinion describes how, despite Ellison's attempts to avoid Gray, and her requests that he leave her alone, Gray persisted in sending her bizarre love letters in which he described watching and experiencing her from afar. Adopting the perspective of the reasonable woman, the *Ellison* court concludes that such behavior is harassing.

Although most commentators have emphasized this use of the reasonable woman standard, what is striking to me about the *Ellison* decision is not that it depicts Gray's conduct as "sufficiently pervasive and severe," but that it acknowledges how Gray's behavior alters the conditions of employment. His performance is viewed as masculine; he is sexualized. By pursuing Ellison, Gray attempted to bring modes of behavior perhaps acceptable in a restrictively sexualized private sphere into a more diverse public sphere. The majority writes: "Analyzing the facts from the alleged harasser's viewpoint, Gray could be portrayed as a modern-day Cyrano de Bergerac wishing no more than to woo Ellison with his words. There is no evidence that Gray harbored ill will toward Ellison. He even offered in his 'love letter' to leave her alone if she wished."[50] Although Gray's conduct was not violent and abusive, it altered the workplace, changing it from a site of work into a site for his pursuit of his own pleasure. That this behavior is construed as harassing suggests that, far from relying on a conception of reasonableness, the court is no longer basing its decision on a gendered conception of public and private spheres, and is instead using privacy as the boundary for admissible performances.

Implicitly employing the notion of privacy as a boundary, the *Ellison* decision suggests the importance of respecting the feelings of another even when they may be different from our own. The court explains that even well-intentioned compliments can provide the basis for a cause of action if a reasonable victim viewed them as sufficiently severe to alter the conditions of employment and create an abusive working environment. The very oddness of this remark — for why would a reasonable victim take offense at well-intentioned compliments? — displaces reasonableness and calls our attention to the changed working conditions. Moreover, the court concludes, "When employers and employees internalize the standard of workplace conduct we establish today, the current gray in perception between the sexes will be bridged."[51] Yet the court did not articulate a standard of workplace conduct. It simply stressed the importance of the victim's, or reasonable woman's, perspective in determining when working conditions are altered. This unstated standard points toward an ideal workplace in which sexualized and sexualizing performances are prevented from playing an influential role. Such performances are inappropriate when they violate the boundary of another, when they encroach upon her privacy.

My reading of *Ellison* suggests that the impetus behind the court's decision lay less in the notion of a reasonable woman than in a shift in the understanding of privacy. The Supreme Court's unanimous holding in *Harris v. Forklift* in 1993 supports this reading.[52] Like the *Ellison* court, the Supreme Court begins with Theresa Harris's occupational status as manager, thereby viewing her first as an employee rather than as a woman whose proper place is at home. Similarly, it describes the actions of Forklift's president, Charles Hardy, in sexual terms. The opinion notes an instance when Harris was arranging a deal, only to have Hardy ask her in front of other employees, "What did you do, promise the guy . . . some [sex] Saturday night?"[53] Thus, despite Justice O'Connor's rhetoric of "objectively hostile environment" and "reasonableness," and despite the "middle path" that the Court sought to take between conduct that is "merely offensive" and conduct that causes "tangible psychological injury," the Court's decision had little to do with mediating between diversity and conformity, freedom and protection. In fact, the Court refrained from articulating determinate standards of abusiveness, projecting instead the possibility of an ideal altered through harassment.[54]

The failure of reasonableness in sexual harassment cases stems from its connection to a traditional domestic and sexual conception of the private. The notion of the private in sexual harassment law creates a bounded space. When it carries with it gendered assumptions of masculine activity aided by feminine support, this traditional private sphere remains beyond the scope of public norms of reciprocal equality and mutual respect. Indeed, the archetype of sexual harassment disputes, the Clarence Thomas–Anita Hill exchange, illustrates the inability of a woman so ostensibly reasonable as Hill to escape the private sphere. Her attackers repeatedly entrapped her in the private, constructing her as that other of the reasonable woman, the rare, hypersensitive hysteric, as they referred to her as psychotic, as a spurned lover, as Thomas's discarded helpmate and subordinate. Once a woman is encased in the private sphere, reasonableness cannot protect her. She has to be crazy, since no reasonable woman would choose to endure what goes on in the public sphere.

Yet when the private is no longer a sphere, and when women are seen as participants in the workplace, the idea of a boundary protecting personal and sexual concerns helps to secure women's equality. Their harassers are the ones performing sexually, seeking to privatize an already public interaction. Relying on the boundary of privacy enables the court to refrain from articulating a determinate standard of workplace conduct, to avoid responding to one set of determinations with still another set, and suggest an as-yet-unrealized ideal of mutual accountability and respect.

I claimed above that Ehrenreich fails to distinguish between a valid and a merely existing consensus. This failure is linked to her (mis)reading of the public/private distinction at work in sexual harassment cases. As we have seen, she does not separate the domestic sphere from the arena of paid employment; instead, she blends them together within a voluntaristic notion of the private. Yet sexual harassment law separates these two worlds. To be sure, by reading the law in terms of such a

separation, I have displaced the element of public exchange present in a
strategic form in Ehrenreich's account. What my reading of differentiated spheres suggests, however, is not the elimination of this exchange
but its reconceptualization in terms of the public as public discourse.
The unstated standard of workplace interaction in *Ellison* and *Harris*
leads us to this conclusion as well. As unstated, it suggests an ideal of
interaction in terms of mutual respect and responsibility rather than
offering a simple description of already existing interactions. Were the
Ellison court to remain content with a factual account of conditions in
the workplace, it would have endorsed the *Rabidue* decision. Instead, it
relies on the notion of an ideal workplace altered by harassment, not
an empirical workplace in which harassing behavior may be subject to
regulation on the basis of a societal consensus. And although the Court
in *Harris* suggests that a hostile environment is one that detracts from
employees' job performance, discourages employees from remaining on
the job, and keeps them from advancing their careers, the Court states
that even "without regard to these tangible effects" discriminatory conduct "offends Title VII's broad rule of workplace equality."[55]

Ehrenreich writes:

In equating "reasonableness" with societal consensus (that is, in defining
discrimination as deviation from the status quo), the *Rabidue* court (like all
courts using this definition of reasonableness) necessarily assumes that the
status quo itself is egalitarian, pluralistic, and nondiscriminatory. This in
turn shifts the focus to the individual, obscuring the possibility of structural
inequalities and creating the impression that only a small number of deviant
people fail to conform to society's pluralistic norms (that is, engage in discrimination).[56]

My argument is that *despite* the *Ellison* court's use of the reasonable
woman standard and the *Harris* Court's appeal to the reasonable person, both escape from a reliance on the status quo, suggesting instead
an *ideal* of equality, pluralism, and nondiscrimination. The decision in
each case rests not on reasonableness, but on the conception of privacy
as a boundary that protects women from sexualizing performances in
the workplace. Paradoxically, this boundary enables women to be seen
as employees in a relatively public sphere. Protected privacy enables
them to perform a public role. In contrast, as they attempt to violate
women's privacy in public, the harassers themselves are privatized and
sexualized, but not protected. By allowing the boundary of privacy to
shift, the courts suggest the possibility of an ideal of mutual respect and
responsibility in the workplace, an ideal informed by a focus on our

shared accountability for each other's privacy. Far from the "merely existing" consensus of the status quo, this ideal represents the potential outcome of a valid consensus.

In focusing on the reasonableness standard, feminist critics have followed a false line, failing to see either the impact of a domestic and sexual conception of the private sphere or the potential of the boundary of privacy in sexual harassment law. Reasonableness obscures the interplay of assumptions of privacy in the public world of the workplace. It remains tainted by its traditional connotations of the "man in his shirt-sleeves who takes the magazines at home." In *Ellison* and *Harris,* the notion of privacy, although still sexual, is no longer gendered: male harassers are depicted as attempting to privatize the interactions of women in public. Here, privacy becomes the boundary determining acceptable workplace interaction. As my analysis of *Ellison* shows, the plaintiff was able to recover because she, although in public, was being privatized. Her harasser, through his effort to privatize her, was transgressing the boundaries of the public. "Reasonableness," "objectivity," and a "middle path," then, had nothing to do with the decisions in *Ellison* and *Harris.* Both began by situating the plaintiffs as employees and then projected standards for governing an ideal, hypothetical workplace. Further, these standards implicitly evoke respect for the privacy of employees, emphasizing the importance of boundaries for participation in public.

Having examined the potential of privacy as a boundary protecting personal and sexual concerns in public, I now turn to the concept of privacy as it appears in debates over abortion and the rights of lesbians and gay men. I continue my account of the shift in privacy, focusing on the way this shift has led to a connection between privacy and identity that prevents us from understanding that publicity is always part of identity. By stressing the public recognition already present in the notion of a right to privacy, I buttress the boundary conception of privacy. To this end, I interpret this boundary as the recognition by legal persons that they are each and all more than legal persons, that they are individuals with projects and concerns extending beyond the purview of law.

Privacy and the Problem of Identity

When the Supreme Court held in 1965 in *Griswold v. Connecticut*[57] that restrictions on birth control violated married persons' right to privacy, it seemed to be signaling a willingness to reconsider the potential of substantial due process after the *Lochner* era.[58] The Court appeared ready to establish a terrain of individual difference and autonomy safe from community eyes and expectations. Indeed, the 1972 and 1973 decisions in *Eisenstadt v. Baird*[59] and *Roe v. Wade*[60] gave the impression that choices regarding sexuality and procreation would be protected from unnecessary state intervention. After the Court upheld Georgia sodomy laws in *Bowers v. Hardwick* (1986), however, the actual freedoms secured by a right to privacy came to rest on ever more shaky ground. Further, the Court's willingness to chip away at the rights embodied in *Roe* have placed even abortion rights in doubt.

Some commentators and critics think that the backlash against privacy indicates the need for a different legal defense of abortion rights and the rights of lesbians and gay men.[61] Others, however, have reacted by reendorsing privacy.[62] They have called for a new understanding of the concept of privacy, and have launched an effort designed to shore up privacy through the careful articulation of the rights deemed to be at stake. Concerned with the role of law in securing and transmitting solidarity, I look at this new work on privacy to see whether it can protect difference in contemporary pluralistic societies. I argue that identity-based arguments for privacy fail either to address the concerns of privacy's defenders or to protect difference.

CHOICE AND DIFFERENCE

The debate around privacy tends to get entangled in issues of choice and difference. Choice issues are constructed in terms of an opposition between freedom and connection. Difference is itself set up against a notion of sameness. Pro-choice feminists often conceive privacy as protecting choice or decisional autonomy. Privacy, they claim, secures the possibility of making choices necessary to maintain one's identity. Implicitly, these pro-choice feminists are also relying on an idea of sameness: Like men, women too are and should be legally recognized as self-determining. What they do with this argument, however, is construct the pro-life position in a particular way. By claiming that privacy protects decisional autonomy, pro-choice feminists construct their pro-life opponents as those who do not view privacy as protecting choice, but instead see the private sphere in terms of traditionalistic understandings of women's roles and duties. Pro-life opponents are placed on the side of difference, where women's capacity for pregnancy renders them fundamentally different from men. For defenders of the right to abor-

tion, then, privacy involves freedom and sameness. Many of these defenders see their opponents as committed to the view that privacy involves relationships of intimacy and belonging in which women differ
from men. Finally, the defenders of privacy understand their opponents
as wanting to secure these relationships with recourse to the traditional
values of the patriarchal family.

For example, Rhonda Copelon's privacy justification for abortion involves a defense of women's freedom against traditional feminine duties
within the patriarchal family. Juxtaposing choice and independence
against duty and servitude, her argument relies on an opposition between sameness and difference, a sexually encoded opposition. Copelon
claims that "at least in principle, [Roe] acknowledged the power of
women to be self-determining, to refuse to be the object of someone
else's desire for procreation, whether that desire is that of the state, the
husband, the progenitor, or the self-styled guardians of embryonic
life."[63] Elsewhere she states that "when pregnancy is viewed as a *voluntary* gift of life to another rather than a *woman's duty,* the abortion debate
will cease to turn on conception or viability."[64]

But the views of pro-life advocates are often more complex than
those of the "opponents" evoked in some pro-choice writing.[65] Pro-
life feminists accept the idea of privacy, but read it in terms of the separation between a masculine public and a feminine private sphere. They
criticize what they see as a masculine encoding of autonomy and independence that seeks at best to deny and at worst to exploit and com-
mercialize human dependency. Pro-life feminists do not set up duties
and roles against self-determination. Instead, they view the goal of self-
determination as itself subverting a collective need for nurturance. For
pro-life feminists, then, the interdependency of identities means that we
cannot simply choose who we are and want to be in the absence of a
consideration for those around us.

As they have adapted to post-*Roe* society, pro-life advocates have re-
defined the problems involved in sexual relationships, pregnancy, and
motherhood as tests of female identity. Faye Ginsburg explains that
"pregnancy is now understood simultaneously as a decision not to
abort, a kind of heroic passage in which [women's] capacity for nurturance has been tested."[66] Confronted with images, stories, and "scientific
facts" that portray the fetus as an innocent child, the pregnant woman
in the pro-life narrative faces the challenge of "saving" (with its connotations of redemption) an innocent life and realizing her role as mother.
Invested with religious metaphors of salvation, redemption, birth, and

rebirth, her role becomes glorified (sanctified) as a choice to suffer for the good, for the life, of innocents. Pregnancy is thus seen as a voluntary gift, *and* the discussion still centers around viability and conception as they set the stage for the struggle between life and death. Again, duties and roles are not the other of self-determination. They are the *result* of self-determination, an achievement that gives meaning to female identity. Women who choose to nurture have not only passed the test of female identity but also engaged in a profoundly feminist act of rejecting the masculine exploitation of dependency and vulnerability. Although women remain different from men because of the choices available only to women, the act of choosing takes on the character of an affirmation, an endorsement of an identity that values care and connection.

Although the discussion of privacy for lesbians and gay men involves a different configuration of autonomy and connection, sameness and difference, the association between privacy and identity operates in a way similar to the abortion debate. When proponents of the rights of lesbians and gay men defend a right to privacy, they stress a notion of the private drawn in terms of intimacy and security. Their opponents are thus positioned as viewing the private in terms of choice (which explains the continued appeal of essentialist arguments for homosexual identity as a counter to these opponents). But, unlike in the abortion debate, notions of sameness and difference are more free-floating. At times the defense of privacy is a defense of difference, an argument for the protection of gay men and lesbians as an oppressed minority. When this is the case, opponents take the position that only individuals and relationships to be found within the traditional heterosexual family are protected under the right to privacy. Only choices that are "natural," that involve heterosexual practices of marriage and procreation, count as choices. Here, both the meaning and the restricted domain of choice involve a decision whether or not to engage in conduct described as criminal, unnatural, or immoral. Yet when the defense of privacy is constructed as a defense of sameness, as an argument showing how homosexuals are "just like everybody else," opponents urge us to think of homosexuals as radically different, as "others" beyond or undeserving of the protection of privacy. So, as the right to privacy sometimes appears in the debate surrounding the rights of lesbians and gay men, the issue boils down to the proper placement and meaning of identity: Is identity a matter of intimacy or choice and is it the same as or different from heterosexual identity?[67]

This aspect of the conflict of privacy stands out in the majority and dissenting opinions in *Bowers v. Hardwick*. Writing for the majority, Justice White presented the issue as "whether the Federal Constitution confers a fundamental right to homosexuals to engage in sodomy."[68] Since the Georgia law applied to homosexuals and heterosexuals alike, White's framing tactic inscribed a strict marker of difference on Michael Hardwick. For Hardwick to prevail, either his difference would have to be protected or his choice would have to be shown to be the same as other choices protected as private. White's interpretation of the history of sodomy laws and moral prohibitions against homosexual behavior blocked off the first possibility. And, rereading the privacy cases in terms of marriage and procreation, the Court found no connection between sodomy and the protected rights grounded in traditional notions of the family. From the majority's position, then, Hardwick had no choice worthy of protection. He could only choose whether or not to behave immorally or illegally.[69]

Writing for the dissent, Justice Blackmun first rejects the majority's limited view of the Georgia statute. His reading of the Georgia law addresses its inclusion of heterosexuals: "Unlike the Court, the Georgia Legislature has not proceeded on the assumption that homosexuals are so different from other citizens that their lives may be controlled in a way that would not be tolerated if it limited the choices of those other citizens."[70] Viewed as the same as heterosexuals, the privacy needs of homosexuals deserve protection. Indeed, with this view of sameness, Blackmun need not concern himself with the relationship between identity and choice: Human personality and existence in general require associations of intimacy and belonging. Thus, this line of his dissent appeals to those central parts of an individual's life — emotional enrichment and sexual relationships — that privacy is supposed to protect.

Aware of the importance of protecting difference, Blackmun weaves a second conception of identity into his dissent, this time one construed in terms of choice. He urges that involved in the recognition of the freedom to choose is an acceptance of difference. Relying on *Wisconsin v. Yoder*, he makes an implicit analogy between the difference of homosexuals and the difference of the Amish: "A way of life that is odd or even erratic but interferes in no rights or interests of others is not to be condemned because it is different."[71] In this second line of argument, Blackmun suggests an understanding of privacy that protects the choices constitutive of identity, the choices that render an identity different.[72]

Comparing the pro-choice feminist stress on the right to privacy to that of proponents of the rights of gay men and lesbians leads us to a rather odd, contradictory conclusion: Privacy is important because it protects choice and because it protects something we do not and cannot choose. Similarly, privacy is said to be dangerous because it breaks intimate connections and because it conceals our free choices. Now, this contradiction is not accidental but rather intrinsic to the very idea of privacy as it has emerged in the American legal context — privacy has been interpreted as a protection of individual self-determination and as a protection of interpersonal relationships.[73] And both self-determination and intimacy play important roles in the emergence of individual identities.

Not surprisingly, then, defenders and opponents of the rights privacy is evoked to protect are united by the view that privacy is deeply connected with personal identity, whether that identity is essential, chosen, or constructed. The defenders' arguments suggest that the mere association of identity and privacy should be enough to secure the identity-constituting practice, association, or choice at issue. The position of the opponents, however, boils down to the fear that certain sorts of identities serve to disrupt community, endangering already fragile intimate ties. Opponents focus on guiding and regulating private activity to prevent the legitimation of those particular identities or practices that they find detrimental to a moral and well-ordered society.

Opponents of abortion and the rights of lesbians and gay men have been able to use identity politics to their advantage. Committed to the view that the personal is political, they actively campaign against abortion and homosexual rights on behalf of those "family values" that they deem vital to the development of personal identity. For example, on 24 February 1994, the *Wall Street Journal* ran a statement by the Ramsey Colloquium, a group of Christian and Jewish scholars affiliated with the Institute on Religion and Public Life. Entitled "Morality and Homosexuality," this attack on lesbian and gay rights characterized the current historical moment in terms of the appearance of "permissive abortion, widespread adultery, easy divorce, radical feminism, and the gay and lesbian movement." For the writers, "the vulnerability of the young" underlying "public anxiety about homosexuality" demonstrates that homosexuality "is a matter of legitimate and urgent public concern." But rather than emphasizing the "naturalness" of heterosexuality, the Ramsey Colloquium accepts it as an historical construction and development: "The social norms by which sexual behavior is inculcated and controlled are of urgent importance for families and for society as a whole." The concerns of opponents of abortion and lesbian and gay rights, then, reflect their awareness that what is at stake in the battle over privacy is the shape of American public life. Both sides in the battle seem to agree that their fight is to be waged on the terrain of privacy; in so doing, however, the point of disagreement between the two sides — namely, what constitutes community — is concealed.

CONCEALMENT AND EXPOSURE

This concealment is enacted by a set of interpretive constraints that overly determine both the decisional and relational aspects of privacy. Both are gendered so that choice takes on a particularly masculine connotation of independent and unattached agency and relation becomes associated with heterosexual understandings of marriage and family. Accordingly, when birth control and abortion are defended as private choices for women, the masculine encoding of privacy remains intact. Building on these assumptions of a stable masculinity, the inclusion of women's reproductive choices takes on a particular form — "Choice X is essential to my identity" — and displaces an inquiry into the presumptions of masculinity upon which privacy rests. Paradoxically, this displacement stabilizes masculinity so that masculinity becomes what is private, while femininity is publicly exposed. Finally, although homosexuality has been denied the protection of privacy, insofar as it must be publicly revealed to be denied its very exposure ends up securing the privacy of heterosexual relationships. Thus, the disagreement over what constitutes community is concealed through the privacy debate itself; the terms of the debate work to protect traditional notions of masculinity and heterosexuality, the ostensible objects of discussion.

Birth control has long been viewed as a woman's issue. When faced with an unwanted pregnancy, a woman encounters an opposition between autonomy and role: Will she make a choice based on her own understanding of her needs or will she follow the dictates of society and sacrifice herself for the good of her unborn child? Located at the intersection of this opposition, the body of the pregnant woman becomes a contested and contestable site. Conversely, men, although they may choose to take responsibility for fathering a child, are rarely understood as defining their identities with regard to reproductive choices. Their choices, like their identities and their bodies, remain purely private matters, outside the scope of law and within their control. This "outsideness" for men is one of the ways law empowers them, assuring their authority.[74] Yet for a woman, the decision to carry a child to term is seen as determining who she is and wants to be. Her identity is at stake. Privacy, for her, can become a protection only after it is rendered public, only after a public claim is raised on behalf of an action or choice that exposes the female body and reveals the femininity of her identity.[75]

In the public debate about the privacy of abortion, the discussion of women's roles and bodies helps to anchor a set of assumptions regarding the meanings of masculinity and femininity. Jeb Rubenfeld explains that "the claim that an abortion is a fundamental act of self-definition is nothing other than a corollary to the insistence that motherhood, or at least the desire to be a mother, is the fundamental, inescapable, natural backdrop of womanhood against which every woman is defined."[76] Put somewhat differently, in the context of abortion, privacy protects men as it places their sexuality outside of a public discussion of the meaning of reproduction. In contrast, women are inside the debate, marked by privacy as the other of men. The privacy defense of abortion has thus failed to challenge the masculine encoding of privacy because the former rests on the latter. Men's sexual right, their personal autonomy so certain as to need little guidance and less attention, is taken as a given. The Court's ruling in *Planned Parenthood v. Casey* in 1992 suggests as much, as it allows for women's "autonomy" to be "guided" through informational requirements and a twenty-four-hour waiting period.[77]

The articulation of women's right to choose as an identity need is a response to this encoding. It is a construction occasioned by interpretive constraints that prohibit inquiry into straight male sexuality. Indeed, such an identity-based defense of privacy assumes that because this sexuality is given, part of the "nature of things," we can only build on it and from it, continuing to determine our notions of privacy by "adding in" a stunted notion of female sexuality construed as a choice for or against maternity. Privacy for women has rested on the "X-is-essential-to-identity" argument because the masculine presuppositions of privacy exclude women. "X" marks women's difference. Thus, the context of meaning in which privacy as choice remains embedded inscribes a specific practice of feminine identity on the female body. Women's identity needs are at stake in abortion. Women determine who they are through such a choice. To this extent, the language of privacy constructs feminine identity as the outcome of an existential choice, thus mirroring the attitude of pro-life feminists.

Consequently, the inscription of a limited account of femininity on masculinist presumptions has led to an exclusively heterosexual interpretation of privacy. In *Bowers v. Hardwick* the Court viewed the issue presented as one concerning a right to homosexual sodomy. Beginning with background assumptions regarding traditional notions of family and gender, the Court could not construct Michael Hardwick as making a choice about his identity. His identity was beyond or outside the range of choice. If privacy protects choices necessary for identity and intimate, familial concerns, identities that cannot be chosen remain at the margins — secret, but not private and worthy of protection. The way Justice White's majority opinion (mis)interpreted the Georgia statute shows precisely how "that which cannot be chosen" — homosexuality — is beyond the scope of privacy. Although the Georgia sodomy law outlawed sodomy in general, the Court denied standing to the heterosexual couple seeking to challenge the law. As Janet Halley explains, this move "generates a class of homosexuals *within,* even as it excludes that class *from,* an unmarked class of human persons all subject to the Georgia sodomy law. . . . Potentially felonious under the actual statute before the Court in *Hardwick,* the class of heterosexuals is allowed to drop silently out of the picture. Indeed, 'dropping out of the picture' becomes a, perhaps *the,* salient characteristic of the class."[78] Because the behavior of the heterosexual couple did not appear before the Court, it could remain private and protected. So, by creating and revealing Michael Hardwick as a homosexual, by assigning him an identity rather than allowing him even the option of a choice (for the very possibility of choosing would dissolve the majority's fragile distinction between homosexuality and heterosexuality), the Court was able to reaffirm the association of relationship and intimacy with heterosexuality.

The assumption that choice, action, or practice "X" must be articulated as an identity need to be protected by privacy results from the continued impact of masculinely encoded interpretive constraints. As long as privacy relies on a backdrop of expectations that constitute the meaning of reproductive choices for *women,* as long as privacy requires definitional anchoring in the link between such decisions and identity, it will fail to secure either the ideals of self-determination or the hope for intimacy on which it purports to rest. The masculine presuppositions of privacy construct feminine identity as the outcome of a choice. Similarly, an identity-based conception of privacy cannot do justice to the scope of concerns confronting lesbians and gay men. The heterosexual presuppositions of privacy construct homosexuality as "that which cannot be chosen." Both femininity and homosexuality become public, but while choice enables privacy to protect women (even as it constrains possible understandings of feminine identity), the construction of homosexuality inserts gay men and lesbians into the public as the vulnerable and exposed others of safely privatized heterosexuals.[79]

The restrictiveness of traditional determinations of privacy becomes clearer when we realize the different meaning of privacy for lesbians and gay men. As Kendall Thomas notes, for them "the claim of privacy always structurally implies a claim to secrecy."[80] Victims of violence and discrimination in domains recognized as public, they are neither protected nor respected when their rights to love and intimacy are justified in terms of a concept of privacy that both exposes them further and relies on a restrictive concept of identity. The masculine and heterosexual determination of privacy reveals why opponents of abortion and gay and lesbian rights often fight their battles on the terrain of privacy: the determinations already constraining the debate are reiterated and secured through the debate over privacy itself.

THE PUBLICITY OF PRIVACY

This suggests the need for a defense of privacy that meets its opponents head-on. It challenges us to stop offering up laundry lists of contingent identity needs and assert the public and political importance of privacy.[81] Of course, the Court has implicitly rejected using a right to privacy as a vehicle for recognizing an equal right to difference. By upholding Georgia sodomy laws and chipping away at the right to an abortion, the Court has refrained from employing privacy as a means for reconstituting the public sphere, continuing to use it instead to inscribe particular definitions of personal identity. But if privacy itself is seen as public, as the mutual recognition by legal persons of their inalienable difference and fundamental concreteness, at least the terms of the debate are altered. Rather than being a means for reconstructing the public sphere, privacy is already part of it.

Understanding the publicity of privacy requires that we shift our focus from the choices, characteristics, and actions deemed essential for identity and stress instead the public recognition of the right to have an identity already present in the notion of a right to privacy. We have to reject the assumption that privacy protects the patriarchal family and reinforces an atomistic conception of the rights-bearing individual; instead, we must view privacy as the public recognition of a boundary. Building from Jean Cohen's reconstruction of the right to privacy, my idea of privacy as a boundary holds that privacy secures decisional autonomy, inviolate personality, and bodily integrity "when matters central to one's personal identity are at stake."[82] The difference between privacy as a boundary and identity-based defenses of privacy is that these "matters" remain indeterminate in the former conception. Rather than fixed upon some unitary conception of identity, these "matters" depend on "shifting cultural self-understandings and shifting perceptions of threats to individual integrity which must be articulated and resolved in the public spheres of civil and political society."[83] What is central to personal identity is a public concern. It is constructed in and through the discourses and debates already part of civil society. The boundary designated by privacy thus shifts as legal persons recognize different "matters" as necessary for having an identity.

By emphasizing decisional autonomy, inviolate personality, and bodily integrity, the boundary conception of privacy sees privacy as providing a set of protections necessary for self-realization and self-determination. Privacy secures our capacity to develop and change as concrete persons already connected with others. To this extent, privacy depends on a notion of equality, on the idea that each individual is equally enabled by the protections of privacy. As Kenneth Karst explains, from the constitutional standpoint, personal sexual and procreative issues are entitled to special consideration because the values at stake therein involve respect and participation.[84] He argues that the right to reproductive choice rests most securely on an interest in status and dignity, on a public commitment to equality: "The choice to be a spouse or a parent is, among other things, a choice of social role and self-concept. For the state to deny such a choice is for the organized society to deny the individual so incapacitated of the presumptive right to be treated as a person, one of equal worth among citizens."[85] The stress on equality reminds us, then, of the right "to be" in public that the right to privacy already signifies. Privacy rights enable persons to move among the variety of discursive spheres in civil society.[86] By focusing on equality, the boundary conception does not conceal the public dimension of privacy but rather moves it to the fore as part of legal persons' recognition of the right to have an identity.

The boundary conception of privacy thus takes seriously the continued importance of privacy in political struggle. Appeals to privacy are responses to perceived threats to individual integrity. Indeed, this is what motivates the effort to construe privacy in terms of identity. But rather than simply resorting to a rigid notion of identity, the boundary conception allows us to acknowledge the potentially destabilizing effects of privacy claims by stressing the way privacy rights are often exercised in public spaces. The body of the pregnant woman is visible. Decisions about abortion are already situated in various publics — from the doctor's office, to the significant others brought into the decision, to the various political and ethical discourses informing a woman's decision. Lesbian and gay identities are not simply sets of private sexual practices but are public ways of acknowledging self, others, and communities. Far from reinforcing some ideological divide between pregiven public and private spheres, privacy rights, properly conceived, destabilize it, calling into question the very privileges and categories that have rendered the needs and concerns of women and homosexuals invisible.

Because privacy rights are exercised in public, moreover, masculinity is opened up for discussion and critique. For just as those hidden "others" acquire visibility, so too are the heretofore concealed assumptions of masculinity and heterosexuality revealed as already publicly exercised privileges. The open exercise of the right to privacy tells us how its indeterminacy enables it to disrupt the very interpretive constraints on which it has been based.

This disruptive potential appears more strongly when we recognize that the conflict over privacy has revolved around decisional autonomy and personal integrity in "'the zone of intimacy' — marriage, divorce, sexual relations, procreation, child-rearing, abortion, etc."[87] The "etc." reminds us that the domain of the private is indeterminate and up for renegotiation in our discourse about democracy. What is private is not revealed or guaranteed by law; what is private is formed and constructed by law. Precisely because the right to privacy can no longer be justified with recourse to an already given domain, precisely because it remains open to the interpretive efforts of those who raise claims in its name, privacy serves an important critical function. It provides a means for challenging a variety of intrusions and violations of our personal boundaries and efforts at self-formation. I have already discussed the potential of this dimension of privacy — recent rulings in *Ellison* and *Harris* rely on the critical juxtaposition of public and private. Similarly, Patricia Williams defends privacy from the standpoint of African Americans, arguing that privacy secures a boundary of distance and respect, a remedy against the intrusive familiarity of their treatment by white society.[88] Finally, in his defense of privacy, Morris Kaplan observes that "lesbian and gay marriage, domestic partnerships, the reconceiving of family life as a mode of intimate association among free and equal citizens, all are efforts to appropriate and transform the available possibilities."[89]

In addition to its critical role in political struggle, the boundary conception of privacy is important symbolically. Prior to the New Deal, property symbolized the limits of U.S. governmental authority, establishing a boundary to the exercise of public political power and providing an anchor for individual liberty.[90] But since the fall of the property paradigm, the values property embodied — individual freedom and personal inviolability — have come under increasing threat from the incursions of a regulatory state. "Without a symbolic core for personal liberties," writes Jean Cohen, "without a way to render the discrete list of personal liberties coherent, the activist regulatory state will encounter few principled limits to its reach into the most intimate details and most important decisions of all individuals."[91] For Cohen, privacy, because of its continued connection with the principles and values at the heart of property, presents itself as a new symbolic core.

I agree with Cohen's analogy between privacy and property, for property has always symbolized the right to a public presence within the civil community.[92] I would urge, however, that we replace the rhetoric of "core" with that of "boundary." Constructing it as a "core" prevents privacy from doing justice to the very principles it is supposed to symbolize — decisional autonomy, bodily integrity, and intimacy in a variety of open and fluid domains. Conceived as the boundary protecting individuals and relations throughout civil society, privacy is better able to shed its old patriarchal connotations, its traditional interpretive constraints, and integrate multiple discursive processes as it provides a medium for a particular sort of legal recognition. Furthermore, it helps avoid a misplaced oppositional reading of a regulatory state over and against a somehow nonregulated and preexisting private sphere.

The advantages of the boundary conception of privacy become clear when we recall that the link between property and individual liberty was an outgrowth of the philosophy of the subject — once power moved from the body of the sovereign to the sovereignty of the body politic, the latter had to be sustained. Whether designating who counted as a member of a collectively acting citizenry (the republican model) or delimiting those individual agents whose marketlike interactions and private preferences would be protected and maintained (the liberal model), property *as a symbolic core* served as the locus for the shift of power from one center to another.[93] In other words, property buttressed the idea of a political power centered in the state, whether that state was monarchical, republican, or administrative. If we take seriously the notion of a decentered state, we have no need for a symbolic core, for our understanding of political power itself shifts to the various intersubjective discursive processes flowing throughout civil society and the institutions and administration of law. There is no symbolic transference of power and right because neither the state nor the citizenry exist as a conceptual center. Instead, a variety of rights secure the discursive liberties and forms of association necessary for democratic participation and the maintenance of solidarity—necessary, that is, for both self-determination and self-realization. We should read the right to privacy, then, as the boundary protecting and integrating these liberties and forms of associations.

The boundary conception of privacy points to the important limiting role of privacy rights. Situated in and among a multiplicity of groups, our opportunities for self-realization and self-presentation require protection. As Cohen argues, privacy is crucial here because it provides to the individual "a sense of control over her self-definitions."[94] By "control" Cohen seems to mean a right not to have to give publicly acceptable reasons for one's choices: "A privacy right entitles one to choose with whom one will attempt to examine one's need interpretations and to whom one will choose to justify one's existential choices."[95] The limiting role of privacy thus refers to the way people raise different sorts of claims in different fora. As members of a variety of types of associations, our communicative interactions involve us with different sorts of audiences, with whom we engage for different intents and purposes. Privacy establishes a boundary that allows us to determine when and under what conditions we will enter a particular sort of discourse.

The limiting argument for privacy helps to secure the discursive ideal of open and unrestricted communication important to a democratic civil society by allowing for nondiscourse. One of the problems raised by critics of Habermasian discourse ethics is that it seems to require that we "discursivize" everything. They worry that the ideal of consensus is coercive in that it requires some sort of final consensus on all public matters. Not only does this worry conflate the real with the ideal, misinterpreting the historic and open-ended debate about democracy as one conversation, but also it neglects the explicit limits of discourse ethics. Discourse ethics takes seriously the postmodern insight that meaning depends on nonmeaning in that it allows for the possibility of nondiscourse.[96] This is one of the areas in which privacy rights come into play. By securing those spaces where we may not all want, need, or even be able to achieve a consensus, privacy rights buttress democratic participation, reinforcing those instances of consensus we do, however momentarily, achieve. They provide the boundary to permissible probes and inquiries into our psychic and physical spaces.

Of course, this boundary is neither fixed nor one-dimensional; the concept of discourse in discourse ethics includes a variety of pragmatic, political, moral, ethical, aesthetic, and therapeutic discourses. Once we acknowledge the variety of types of discourse, we come to understand that the meaning of any appeal or claim to a right to privacy depends on the context within which it is raised. For example, privacy might protect the therapeutic interactions between patient and analyst. Yet the right to psychic integrity that privacy protects could entail that these very interactions be opened up to public and legal scrutiny—as we have seen in the 1990s in the rash of cases involving "recovered memories" of abuse. Taking seriously the variety of discourses already part of civil society, we need not and cannot draw a line demarcating once and for all one particular sort of communicative interaction as a limit. In fact, the effort at line drawing tends to undermine an emphasis on privacy insofar as it seeks to render the concept more determinate. Always part of public discourse, any line will remain provisional, the contingent result of prevailing practices and attitudes.

The boundary conception of privacy corresponds to Habermas's distinction between public and private autonomy.[97] Public autonomy refers to our role as participants in a discursive process of self-legislation. Engaged in a communicative effort to come to a consensus on a matter of common concern, participants are legal persons who accept the reciprocal rights and obligations necessary for discourse. Private autonomy designates our activity as subjects of the law. It is the acknowledgment by legal persons of their freedom to withdraw from public debate, to refrain from accepting discursive obligations, to choose not to give others reasons for our decisions, actions, and plans.

This conception of private autonomy does not rely on a preconceived domain of intimacy nor on a determined set of needs and capacities deemed essential to identity. Instead, it acknowledges that, as multiply situated and constituted persons, any activity can be seen as constitutive of our identity. Further, the idea of private autonomy does not require that the choice to refrain from public discourse itself be called into account, for any attempt to compel discursive participation undermines the meaning of a discursive community. Private autonomy allows for a variety of different privacies, each emerging as a right to limit one's discursive interaction in a particular context, each pointing to the notion of privacy as a boundary.

Entailing the recognition by legal persons that each individual is more than a legal person, the boundary conception of privacy thus helps secure the different solidarities of intimacy, ethnicity, and interest crucial to our self-realization. In so doing, the boundary conception strengthens our civic and universal solidarity by providing a means of critique, a legally encoded form of recognition, and a forum for the recognition and protection of vulnerable relationships and identities.

Legal Accountability: The Solidarity of Law

The pluralities and differences that are part of contemporary multicultural societies create the need for ever greater abstraction in law. In the modern period social norms sustained and underpinned abstract notions of legal personality, reasonableness, publicity, property, and privacy. Once these norms came under the gaze of the hypothetical attitude characteristic of postmodernity, the legal concepts they supported have themselves been rendered indeterminate. Law itself has become and must continue to become reflective to mediate among the disparate groups and relationships that make up a complex society. The reflective potential of law enables it to secure solidarity.

This reflective potential rests on the principles of a democratic constitution. As rights of publicity and participation secure the capacity of each individual to take part in decisions regarding the concerns of all, they promote processes of collective reflection on the histories, practices, and values already part of the community. To the extent that such reflection is both guaranteed by and embodied in a constitution, public discussion of histories and practices becomes itself a debate over the very meaning of the constitution. Part of law's capacity to generate solidarity thus stems from its embodiment in a constitution. A constitution provides a framework of contested and contestable meanings. As we argue over these meanings, we reassert ourselves as citizens, as consociates within a shared life practice. We affirm our commitment to a common life through our argument over the meaning of this life.

The indeterminacy of the rights and principles within various laws is also crucial to the reflective potential of law. Law functions as system of action and of knowledge. To secure solidarity in both these dimensions—participatory action and textual interpretation—law must remain open enough to include the differences among and within us. Frank Michelman views this openness as the "generative indeterminancies" produced through the actions of "those who enter the conversation—or, as we may sometimes feel, seek to disrupt it—from its margins, rather than by those presiding at the center."[98] He suggests that "the pursuit of political freedom through law depends on 'our' constant reach for inclusion of the other, of the hitherto excluded — which in practice means bringing to legal-doctrinal presence the hitherto absent voices of emergently self-conscious social groups."[99] This tells us that the solidarity of law requires that we take into account those at the margins, those situated, hypothetical thirds who break through the boundaries of determined legal concepts, generating new possibilities for inclusion. "We critics" and "we who are already included" must strive to see from their perspective, aware of the risks of exclusion accompanying the effort to see from a position other than our own. Moreover, we must create new possibilities for their perspectives to emerge. We must ourselves attempt to break through concepts and interpretations that, though they may seem plausible to "us," remain too determined to allow for the inclusion of "them."

I have tried to show how an identity-based defense of privacy fails to include the differences at the margins because it is structured to reiterate the assumptions of masculinity and heterosexuality that many defenders of privacy want to contest. Recognition and respect in public fora were long part of the meaning of the right to property white men enjoyed as property owners and heads of families. This public recognition and respect also have a long association with the meaning of the traditional family in community. Including lesbians, straight women, and gay men within the rubric of privacy requires that we break through the masculine and heterosexual determinations of privacy by exposing these presumptions of publicity. Just as reflective solidarity reminds us that inclusion does not simply entail numerical extension but always brings with it a change in the meaning of "inside" and "outside," so do the claims of those at the margins for recognition and respect ultimately challenge our interpretations of the very rights and principles through which these claims are raised.

Ultimately, the reflective potential of law stems from its ability to stabilize and generalize the expectations that social members have of each other. Once we acknowledge that these expectations ultimately rest on our sharing a responsible orientation to relationship, we grasp yet again why they can never be fully determined. Responsibility requires that we respect the right of each individual to make decisions regarding her future, decisions that are regulated and controlled at the cost of denying that person membership of the community. By guaranteeing that each is worthy of respect, law fosters the solidarity of participants secure in their discursive rights (public autonomy) and the inviolateness of their bodies and personality (private autonomy). What changes in the shift from one notion of autonomy to the other, then, is not the number of persons or the "degree" of identity involved, but the conditions of communication, the audience whom we address when raising claims and concerns. To be sure, once conceived as characteristic of a decentered society made up of a network of discursive spheres, these rights overlap. The solidarity of our intimate associations, our involvement in groups organized in terms of identity and interest, our civic engagements, and our participation in the universal community of discourse depends on principles that guarantee both our rights to place ourselves in these various spheres and to look upon them with a hypothetical gaze.

In this chapter, my concern has been with those overly determined concepts that tend to block this gaze, that hinder the emergence of the perspective of the situated, hypothetical third. I have endeavored to expose the determinations concealed by the concept of reasonableness in sexual harassment law. Although the extension of sex discrimination to sexual harassment has contributed to women's ability to move out of the rigid confines of the domestic sphere and into the sphere of paid employment, traditional interpretations of the private prevent the law from serving as a transmitter of reflective solidarity. Instead, they reinforce conventional solidarities based on already given understandings of reasonableness. Once the old oppositions are revealed, we can move beyond them, suggesting the ideal workplace altered by harassment. Indeed, as I have shown, this ideal relies on the protections offered by the boundary of privacy.

Recent rulings point toward an indeterminate and forward-looking ideal of reason, one informed by our mutual accountability for and concern with the difference of each other. Because of its indeterminacy, this ideal creates a space that can accommodate the hypothetical third: We have seen how it is no longer necessary to depict a woman who is sexually harassed as typically reasonable or to dismiss her as an hysteric. The boundary concept of privacy allows her to emerge as a situated person who has been harmed.

We must resist the urge to defend privacy on the grounds that it protects practices, choices, or relationships essential to our identity. Since both defenders and opponents of the rights privacy is evoked to protect agree that privacy is connected to identity, we cannot do justice to suppressed identities by continuing to argue in these terms. When we do, we fail to acknowledge the inextricable elements of publicity already part of claims to privacy and protections of it. Further, we risk reaffirming and reifying precisely the most questionable dimensions of traditional interpretations of privacy. In effect, we fall into the trap of thinking that the rights at stake are not aspects of our public life as consociates within a community of those who respect the difference of each other.

The boundary concept of privacy I have defended is formal; I have not provided it with a content, instead viewing it as a legal form of mutual recognition important to law's capacity to secure and transmit solidarity. This notion of privacy, moreover, shifts and changes depending on its context. I have sought to address the meaning of privacy for citizens in a democracy, hoping to render the concept more fluid and to use this fluidity as part of the justification for privacy. Once we conceptualize privacy as the mutual recognition by legal persons that each is more than a legal person and grasp the contestability of the domain of privacy, we break through traditional interpretive constraints. Replacing these constraints with others would undermine the very idea of privacy as a boundary. The boundary privacy establishes — the protections of bodily integrity, decisional autonomy, and inviolate personality it offers — must be viewed as the product of democracy in order for this boundary to change and shift as it extends throughout our various discursive spheres and practices. Such a conception of privacy allows for the emergence of different and differing solidarities, of a wide variety of responsible and responsive identities.

Legal persons come to terms with identity by respecting it through overcoming it, asking not whether a particular identity is sufficiently guaranteed by any given law or legal concept, but whether that law or concept is indeterminate enough to permit the formation of that identity, to allow it to emerge as a personal project or source of solidarity. The challenge is to open up laws to the multiplicity of voices constituting the unity of reason, encouraging dialogues and discussions that break the boundaries of given expectations and allow for the emergence of those hypothetical thirds who remain excluded and unheard. The solidarity that law transmits thus remains partial and unstable, aware of its risks and failures yet drawing strength from the contexts and contests sustaining it.

CHAPTER 5

Feminism and Universalism

*Women and the Universal! Very interesting; one kind of giggles
because women have always been confined to the realm of the
Personal.*

Trinh T. Minh-Ha[1]

In her film *Naked Spaces* Trinh T. Minh-Ha explores the
connections between women and the universal. As the camera weaves
together images of the ancient, rounded dwellings of elder women
found in Senegal, Mauritania, Togo, Mali, Burkina Faso, and Benin,
three women speak. One voice quotes the sayings of villagers and the
words of African writers. A second voice cites European and American
thinkers and represents Western modes of logic. Finally, a third speaks
from her own position, relating personal experiences. All the while,
shadows and light interconnect the inside and outside of the houses,
blurring the boundaries marking what is within from what without.
Discussing her film, Trinh explains: "In working with a notion of
difference that is not synonymous with opposition or segregation, the
apartheid notion of difference, I focus on the relationship between
women and living spaces . . . as the very site of difference on which
the Universal and the Particular (historical, cultural, political) are at
play."[2]

Trinh's evocation of the universal, especially as conjoined with race,
culture, and sex, with difference and domesticity, departs from current
trends in feminist theory. Yet, in evoking the universal, Trinh summons

ideals long part of a discursive tradition embedded in struggles for inclusion and accountability. Whether they have questioned cultural interpretations that depict the rights-bearing subject as masculine, exposed the
presumption of Woman's absence or lack in symbolic forms of representation, or illuminated the interlocking systems of domination that construct women in terms of their place in the hierarchies of sex, race, and
class, feminist theories have shared and continue to share a concern with
including and recognizing the different voices of women. First-wave
feminists were explicit in their commitment to the universalist ideals
championed in the Enlightenment as they claimed the rights and opportunities previously reserved to men. Liberal and marxist feminists
sought to include women in the universal spheres of public discussion
and labor by emphasizing the similarities between men and women as
rational, creative, laboring beings. With their critique of the limited and
masculine character of discourse and labor, second-wave feminists
seemed to reject the association of women and Enlightenment universalism. Nonetheless, their exploration of women's experiences implicitly
reinstated universality in the particularist guise of the feminine. The very
engagement with sex and the body, with intimacy and maternity, universalized the physical and emotional experiences of women and articulated a demand for accountability in the face of women's difference. Although they explicitly reject universal categories, feminists of the third
wave — who focus on the microprocesses of power, on the implication
of power in language, and on the illusory and constructed nature of the
subject — rely on notions of universality. Investigations into the connections between power and language call upon our responsibility toward
the nonidentical, the other who is viewed as outside of or suppressed
by language. Indeed, the critique of systematic exclusion relies implicitly
on the normative force of the ideal of inclusion.

But perhaps I proceed too quickly. Perhaps in my effort to shore up
the universalism within feminism, I have neglected the problems that
have arisen as we have sought to find the feminism within universalism,
problems that for many theorists indicate that universality itself is coercive and totalizing. Although I have appealed to the Enlightenment,
I have not defined my terms: "Universalism" in my narrative shifts as
"universal" is juxtaposed with unmentioned particulars and contexts.
Yet this shift is deliberate, for the issue is not whether feminism raises
universal claims — it does. Indeed, if we are to take seriously feminist
critiques of binary, oppositional structures, we have to extend this critique to the very opposition between particularity and universality. We

have to reject those masculinist assumptions that presume that women always embody the particular.

As the debate over identity politics attests, feminists today have run up against the limits of the particular: Experience cannot ground the category "women" because someone will always be excluded. Emphases on particularity blind us to the multiplicity of our interconnections. But just investigating our connections and particularities is not enough. We have to be willing to claim, and justify our claim, that many of the ways in which we have been connected and particularized are wrong because they are coercive and exclusionary. The issue is which conception of universalism best accords with feminist calls for inclusion and accountability.

Throughout this book I have offered reflective solidarity as just this conception. Rooted in a communicative "we," reflective solidarity projects a universalist ideal urging the inclusion of our concrete differences. As it connects this communicative we with the shared expectations organized in the concept of the generalized other, reflective solidarity opens up the concept to provide a dynamic account of the perspective of relationship. We take the perspective of relationship, but we take it reflectively, always aware of the variety of interpretations and expectations organized therein. Reflective solidarity thus involves those interconnections that reach beyond our given ties and communities to encompass the plurality of the voices of the past, present, and future. Attuned to our limits and failures, it thematizes further the perspective of the situated, hypothetical third, creating a space for our accountability for exclusion. Precisely this space for difference enables us to avoid consolidating the generalized other into a fixed and limited perspective.

As an alternative approach to political action in complex, multicultural societies, reflective solidarity retains identity politics' commitment to connection and community, but reconceives these connections as those created through our questioning and dissent. It provides a post–identity politics capable of acknowledging the myriad differences within any identity category. As an alternative approach to the site of political action, reflective solidarity situates democratic participation within the multiple, interconnecting discursive spheres of civil society. Rather than relying on a split between the public and private spheres that prevents us from taking account of a variety of abuses and exclusions, this multiple-spheres conception allows us to strengthen and redefine notions of social solidarity. Now we can understand the myriad debates and conflicts extending throughout civil society as themselves new forms of engagement and solidarity. As an alternative approach to the role of law in contemporary democratic societies, reflective solidarity sees in the indeterminacy of law the potential for collective and communicative efforts at generating legal meaning. The abstract character of law enables it to transmit opportunities for interpretation and reinterpretation, opportunities that allow us to find new forms of inclusion, as my account of the shift in privacy from sphere to boundary demonstrates. In each discussion — identity politics, civil society, and law — I have sought to find spaces for openness and questioning that can prevent us from rigidifying identities, spheres of action, and legal interpretations and allow the perspective of situated, hypothetical thirds to appear.

The combination of openness and accountability in reflective solidarity arises from its communicative underpinnings. It is able to view questioning and dissent as ways of bringing us together rather than as tearing us apart because it rests on a discursive universalism. Developed by Habermas, discursive universalism or discourse ethics is a procedural theory of justice designed to account for the claim to universality already present in the very concept of a valid norm. If the validity of a norm stems from its acceptability to all who could forseeably be affected by its general observance, then this acceptability suggests the need for a discourse or discussion among the affected. Discourse ethics provides an idealized and provisional description of this discussion. It tells us the conditions that would have to be met for a norm to be valid. In his discussion of discourse ethics, Habermas stresses justice — that is, he is interested in the conditions under which a norm can be said to be just. In contrast, I stress solidarity, the relations among the participants in a discourse that have to apply in the course of their discussion. I argue that what is crucial to discursive universalism is its presupposition of solidarity. Those very conditions that enable discourse to result in the justification of a norm provide the combination of openness and connection necessary for a universalist, reflective solidarity.

To be sure, feminists have raised important criticisms of procedural theories. Defending and even using a procedural, universalist theory like Habermas's may thus seem a rather risky, if not suspect, enterprise. But I argue that discourse ethics, properly interpreted, responds to the feminist critique of proceduralism by incorporating and extending feminist concerns. Once we understand discourse ethics as the fallible, situated, and open-ended conversation of humanity, we gain a concept of universality that enables us to move beyond the opposition between universal and particular to account for the diversity that is always part of universality. We gain the concept of universality within reflective solidarity.

Feminism and Procedural Universalism

Arising in the Enlightenment, procedural theories are peculiarly modern approaches to politics and ethics. Unlike classical and traditional approaches, which anchored political and ethical questions in the substantive concerns of community and religion, procedural theories are based on the idea that the proper formulation of a set of basic rules and requirements, often understood in terms of initial conditions, will yield an outcome that is impartial and therefore just. If the rules are drawn up correctly, following the rules is supposed to generate or constitute a fair result (as opposed to discovering something that was already there). For example, a contract is a sort of procedure designed to generate a fair agreement. To be fair, the contract must be made freely and voluntarily. In this example, the fairness of the contract depends on adherence to an impartial rule of noncoerced consent.

Generally speaking, procedural theories make universalist and cognitivist claims. The universalist claim is that the rules and conditions constituting the procedure are formal and abstract enough to be valid for everyone everywhere. The cognitivist claim is that the procedures are not simply reasonable, but establish conditions or rules that give free reign to reason, that prevent anything but good reasons from entering the procedure. In many cases, the cognitivist and the universalist claims overlap. Rules are designed to give free reign to reason because reason is presumed to extend beyond particular feelings and desires, which could sway the outcome of the procedure in a particular direction. These rules are usually requirements of reversibility — the outcome must be acceptable to everyone involved — and reciprocal equality — everyone treats everyone in the same manner. With these sorts of rules in place, in principle the outcome of the procedure will be impartial in that it will not be influenced by special interests or plays of power.

A key component of the feminist critique of universalism is the rejection of procedural theories in both their political and ethical forms. A number of feminists claim that procedural theories privilege the special interests of men and are constructed to legitimize masculine power.[3] The political critique focuses on contract theories, stressing their origins in patriarchy, their division of the world into public and private spheres, and their exclusively masculine conception of the participant in the contract. The ethical critique addresses the masculinity of the concepts of moral maturity — autonomy, impartiality, self-control, strength of will, and rationality. Ultimately, both critiques come to focus on the failure of procedural theories to include the concerns of women. Further, both critiques understand this failure or exclusion in the same way, as a blindness to context and a blindness to persons.

The accusation of blindness to context is as an overarching critique of procedural theories' claim to present an impartial, universal perspective and a general account of moral reasoning. Feminists argue that such a claim presupposes a unified notion of morality and requires all moral judgments to take a particular form, a form determined by male interactions in the public sphere. Familial, domestic, sexual, and bodily concerns cannot be expressed in terms of autonomy, equality, and reciprocity and hence are excluded from the moral domain. Further, when these principles are brought to bear upon such familial or bodily concerns, they abstract from the particularities of the actual relationships involved, obscuring the embeddedness of moral judgment in the fabric of everyday life. In place of our interpersonal relationships, procedural theories offer an impartial judge, who weighs and calculates in accordance with the abstract logic of universal principles. Consequently, such neutral principles are neither neutral nor "principled." Instead, they serve to reinstate the patterns of inequality and domination of the status quo by treating those who are dependent as if they were free, those who are different as if they were the same. Put somewhat differently, universal principles exclude difference.

The accusation of blindness to persons is used to show the gendered nature of the cognitivist presumptions of universalism. People are not only rational agents. They are also physical and emotional agents. They have desires and concerns intimately connected with their relationships to others. Further, people differ with respect to sex and gender, class and ethnicity. Feminists argue that theories that ground a notion of justice by abstracting from these differences present a fractured, if not incoherent, version of the person. They present a version of the person that in its assertion of neutrality simultaneously presupposes sexual difference and denies it. Indeed, sexual difference itself is generated as that which must be denied in order for the abstract, "abstract-ed" person to emerge as primary, in order for masculinity to function as the norm. On a simpler level, *someone* has to do the dirty work of physical and emotional sustenance for the abstract exchange of the contract to be possible. Thus, the cognitivist presumptions of universalism lead to a moral theory built around a male subject, thereby excluding the emotions long associated with femininity as well as women themselves. Once again, universalism excludes difference.

Feminist critique implies that for a procedural theory to claim a universal status, to yield a result that is valid for women as well as for men, it cannot be based on an abstract notion of the person that excludes individual differences. Rather, those carrying out the procedure have to be understood as real people; participants have to be conceived as those who would actually follow and apply the norms and principles that the procedure is designed to justify. Accordingly, such a theory must take into account the circumstances and relationships in which our identities are formed and our reality as feeling, embodied, differently sexed agents. Further, it must recognize the differences among persons and the ways in which these differences can enhance as well as diminish our perceptions, understandings, and interpretations of moral phenomena. So, the contents that are brought into the procedure must include the concerns and contexts of our everyday moral experiences. Finally, a procedural description of universality that sees women and their experiences as part of the moral domain must also be able to see the complexities and interconnections always involved in particular moral situations. Only such an account can be said to be impartial in the sense that it does not privilege one point of view over others. Only such an account could include spaces for difference.

But why should feminists want a procedural theory with explicit claims to universality at all? Wouldn't any such effort somehow reinstate precisely those abstractions and exclusions already implicated in the Enlightenment project? Further, would we not again be blinding ourselves to ways in which power is already present in the very assertion of universality? Judith Butler challenges us to take up precisely these questions.

Contingency and Universalisms

In her article "Contingent Foundations," Judith Butler examines what is authorized and what is excluded in the effort to establish theoretical foundations.[4] The two types of foundations, of premises functioning as authorizing grounds, that she interrogates are the ideas of normative universality and of subjectivity. Unfortunately, in the course of her interrogation, Butler needlessly totalizes these concepts and, consequently, dismisses them too soon.

Looking at what is authorized in a claim to universality, Butler employs a repressive, concealing conception of power: "To establish a set of norms that are beyond power or force is itself a powerful and forceful conceptual practice that sublimates, disguises and extends its own power play through recourse to tropes of normative universality."[5] We can break this argument down into four claims: first, establishing norms is a powerful practice; second, it is a practice that needs to be disguised; third, it is a practice that needs to be disguised because it is a power play; and, fourth, tropes of normative universality serve as this disguise.

We might think that with these claims Butler is echoing the feminist critique of proceduralism. She could be be arguing that setting up values such as equal treatment and autonomy as general norms instates a hierarchy of masculinity over femininity, of public over private. Accordingly, since this move to establish a hierarchy and exclude is not beyond power but enacts a play of power, it has to be concealed for the masculine norms to be able to sublimate the feminine values. Calling the masculine "universal" effects this concealment. But this is not Butler's argument, although her argument works in a similar fashion. Rather than simply repeating the feminist critique, Butler broadens it to find an "insidious cultural imperialism" attempting to legislate itself under the sign of the universal.[6] Thus, she extends the criticism of the masculinity of norms to account for their ethnocentric biases. These biases set themselves up as universal, repressing cultural difference as they seek to extend themselves beyond their original domain. Imperialism wraps itself in the cloak of the universal to hide the will to power that infuses its claims.

Butler uses the Gulf War of 1990–91 as a metaphor and example of the cultural imperialism at work in the deployment of tropes of normative universality. Viewing the war as the only possible resolution to the clash of intransigent "universalities," she writes:

We have, I think, witnessed the conceptual and material violence of this practice in the United States's war against Iraq, in which the Arab "other" is understood to be radically "outside" the universal structures of reason and democracy and, hence, calls to be forcibly within. Significantly, the US had to abrogate the democratic principles of political sovereignty and free speech, among others, to effect this forcible return of Iraq to the "democratic" fold, and this violent move reveals, among other things, that such notions of universality are installed through the abrogation of the very principles to be implemented.[7]

The claim to universality, then, authorizes war and violence, the oppression of the "other" and its forcible assimilation into a unified social field. But this line of argument cannot tell us why an appeal to universality has authority, why it is necessary for the will to power to conceal itself under the guise of the universal. Because Butler fuses the power at play in a claim to universality with the validity of that claim, she is unable to explain how it is possible for the ideal to serve as a cloak or a disguise. She neglects the way *valid* norms deserve recognition because they reflect the interests of all concerned.

This leads to what a procedural or substantive notion of the universal excludes. For Butler, what is at risk is the exclusion of questioning: "Even when we claim that there is some implied universal basis for a given foundation, that implication and that universality simply constitute a new dimension of unquestionability."[8] Her point is that any conception of universality is totalizing and can thus only be achieved at the cost of producing further exclusions. Accordingly, she argues that the term "universality" must remain "permanently open, permanently contested, permanently contingent, in order not to foreclose in advance future claims for inclusion."[9]

I agree with Butler's argument for the necessity of keeping the concept of universality open, but she overstates her case. It is one thing to assert the importance of revision. It is something else entirely to claim that *any* appeal to normative universality must produce further exclusions. With such an argument, Butler herself employs a totalizing logic that cannot account for inclusion. This becomes clear when we move to her interrogation of the idea of the subject.

Butler rejects the notion of the autonomous, self-created subject as a masculine fantasy. Such a notion of the subject is said to be the product of power relations that conceal the practices constituting the subject as a subject and that, in psychoanalytic terms, repress the subject's dependency on the maternal. Autonomy, then, is an effect of power; it is "the logical consequence of a disavowed dependency, which is to say that the autonomous subject can maintain the illusion of autonomy insofar as it covers over the break out of which it is constituted."[10] Again, the metaphor through which to grasp the effects of this subject is the Gulf War. For Butler, the affirmations that accompanied the apparent successes of U.S. operations championed "a masculinized Western subject whose will immediately translates into a deed, whose utterance or order materializes in an action which would destroy the very possibility of a reverse strike, and whose obliterating power at once confirms the impenetrable contours of its own subjecthood."[11] From the notion of the subject, she shifts to an idea of the Western masculinized subject; from the intentional subject, she moves to the instrumental, the imperialist, and the phantasmic subject. In her words: "The effects of the instrumental action always have the power to proliferate beyond the subject's control, indeed, to challenge the rational transparency of that subject's intentionality, and so to subvert the very definition of the subject itself."[12]

We see again what is authorized in the move to assert the primacy of the subject: war, violence, death, and annihilation. Butler is explicit on this last point as she links the juridical idea of "ordinance" with the military view of sending missiles as "the delivery of an ordnance." This expression regards an attack as a sort of self-enforcing speech-act, a demand for obedience accompanied by the threat of death. "Of course, this is a message that can never be received, for it kills its addressee, and so it is not an ordinance at all, but the failure of all ordinances, the refusal of a communication."[13]

What, then, are the exclusions effected by the notion of the subject? The masculinized subject depends on the exclusion or repression of its dependency on the maternal. The idea of an intentional subject excludes the contexts and relations that constitute agency. The instrumental subject is premised on the exclusion of contingency, of the unanticipated effects proliferating beyond its control. The imperialist subject emerges as that subject who excludes nonviolent possibilities for resolving conflicts, the one who refuses to communicate. Consequently, the phantasmic subject becomes the one who excludes life, and hence subjectivity, itself. As Butler asserts, "It is important to remember that subjects are constituted through exclusion, that is, through the creation of a domain of deauthorized subjects, presubjects, figures of abjection, populations erased from view."[14] Ultimately, Butler criticizes the notion of the subject because she takes it to require the denial, repression, and sacrifice of difference, both of an internal and an external other.

Of course, all these exclusionary effects are predicated on Butler's conflation of subjectivity with the notion of a masculine subject, which ultimately leads to a totalized conception of the phantasmic subject. But why should we accept this conflation and elision? What does *this* move authorize, and what does it foreclose?

In its most extreme version, such a move authorizes an irresponsible psychology of fear: If theorists insist on using the category of the subject, the result will be violence and erasure, abjection and death. In a much weaker form, the same move can be seen as warning — as a reminder of the ever present potential for exclusion operating when we unreflectively use the concept of the subject, and as an indication of our accountability toward those others who may not yet be visible. Unfortunately, precisely this weaker form is foreclosed. What Butler's account excludes is the potential for a revised conception of subjectivity that could allow for the inclusion of deauthorized subjects, figures of abjection, and populations erased from view. By presuming that subjectivity must be predicated on the denial of maternal dependency and constitutive contexts, that it *means* instrumentality, violence, and death, Butler renders the very possibility of inclusion meaningless. What would be included? Into what metaphorical space is this something to be included? What as? And who or what would attempt to control these definitions? For example, would we want a clinical definition of our sexual orientation to be included as relevant characteristics in a list of prerequisites for adopting children? Butler is clearly right in arguing that notions of subjectivity entail exclusions, but that does not have to mean that other *persons* are excluded.[15] She thus overstates her case in concluding that the presence of exclusion means that we must abandon the idea of the subject. A better approach would be to question the concept of subjectivity and develop a way of normatively determining which exclusions we can accept, which we should reject, and in which contexts. Yet Butler's rejection of universalism, her inability to allow for a notion of universality premised on difference and plurality, rules out a possibility whereby we could become accountable for exclusion.

By employing a notion of power as concealment and repression, the Gulf War as a metaphor, and an underdeveloped idea of exclusion, Butler totalizes the notions of universality and subjectivity. Not only does she conflate procedural and substantive universalisms, but also she presumes that all notions of universality signify a foundationalist project. On the contrary, the Habermasian conception of discursive universality (which Butler includes in her critique via references to a "counterfactual" position and a "speech situation") is explicitly nonfoundationalist.[16] Habermas rejects the notion that philosophy can demonstrate once and for all the absolute and universal validity of our concepts of the person and of society, not to mention our categories of knowledge and morality. He supports a more limited and fallibilist notion of philosophy that "rationally reconstructs" the know-how of social participants.[17]

Furthermore, Butler confuses the foundationalist quest for normative criteria with particular political practices operating *in name only* of one culturally determined version of universalism. She fails to consider a universalism that takes seriously the importance of permanent contestability and the ever present reality of exclusion. To be sure, Butler implicitly employs such a notion with her appeals to an ideal of democratic contestation and her critique of U.S. abrogation of free speech and political sovereignty during the Gulf War. Indeed, her very critique would not be possible were she not able to intuit the difference between the United States's use of power and the *validity* of that use. Nonetheless, it remains unclear what democratic contestation without normative standards would entail, for such standards — despite their flaws in given times and places — help to guarantee plurality and include the previously excluded (as the continuing struggle for rights in the United States shows). Finally, Butler presumes that universality must be understood as permanently in opposition to particularity, contextuality, and difference. A discursive conception of universalism, by contrast, relies on the insight that communication makes possible the recognition of difference, that it is a medium for plurality for those who put aside the use of force and seek to coordinate their actions consensually.

Butler's account of subjectivity relies on a repressive model in which difference must be sacrificed for the sake of identity. Her argument boils down to the claim that the release or emancipation of difference can only be conceived by rejecting the subject. Consequently, by presuming that the subject must be a masculine, instrumental subject, Butler forecloses the possibility of a communicative account of subjectivity premised on intersubjective recognition. Thus, it comes as no surprise that her subject refuses to communicate with or take accountability for the other and cannot but deny and destroy her.

A more promising conception of the subject, or self, comes from bell hooks. Describing what she learned from "unschooled southern black folks," hooks writes:

We learned that the self existed in relation, was dependent for its very being on the lives and experiences of everyone, the self not as signifier of one "I" but the coming together of many "I"s, the self as embodying collective reality past and present, family and community. Social construction of the self in relation would mean, then, that we would know the voices that speak in and to us from the past, that we would be in touch with . . . our history. Yet it is precisely these voices that are silenced, suppressed, when we are dominated. It is this collective voice we struggle to recover.[18]

hooks's communicative notion of subjectivity incorporates the same concern for silenced, suppressed, and erased differences that underlies Butler's argument. Whereas Butler ultimately forfeits the ability to conceive of inclusion, hooks's intersubjective account allows us to include that part of the self that does not "belong" to it but in fact comes from others within our notion of the subject. Further, it enables us to acknowledge the heretofore marginalized as subjects worthy of recognition and respect: "As subjects, people have the right to define their own reality, establish their own identities, name their history. As objects, one's reality is defined by others, one's identity created by others, one's history named only in ways that define one's relationship to those who are subject."[19]

Actually, Butler's interrogation of the subject works best as a critique of objectification. A brief comparison of her characterization of the speaking or theorizing "I" with the 1993 debacle surrounding President Clinton's nomination and withdrawal of Lani Guinier for assistant attorney general illustrates this point. Butler asks: "What speaks when "I" speak to you? What are the institutional histories of subjection and subjectivation that "position" me here now? If there is something called "Butler's position," is this one that I devise, publish, and defend, that belongs to me as a kind of academic property? Or is there a grammar of the subject that merely encourages us to position me as the proprietor of those theories?"[20] During the monthlong media massacre in which Guinier's law review articles were twisted and distorted to the point of contradiction, the "I" of Guinier's writing was precisely the voice that was silenced. Against race-conscious quotas, she was positioned as "the quota queen"; a proponent of proportional representation, she was depicted as calling for the end of majority rule. What "spoke" was the constructed fantasy of the far right. Further, institutional histories of racism and sexism functioned to deprive Guinier of her own words. The fear of difference was explicit: "You can't even pronounce her name," remarked Linda Chavez on the *MacNeil-Lehrer News Hour;* an article on Guinier in *U.S. News and World Report* opened with "Strange name, strange hair, strange writing — she's history."[21]

Forcibly occupying the space of her "I," the press reconstructed Lani Guinier as a "type," the crazy, untrustworthy, black woman of the lunatic fringe, and this "type" emerged as the proprietor of theories antithetical to Guinier's. As the "type" took on a life of her own, Guinier's public efforts to reclaim her "I" served merely as more fodder for the "type." Patricia Williams explains: "Throughout, Guinier's own insistence on retaining *her* meaning of *her* words was thrown back at her as 'denial' or as evidence of opportunism, shiftiness, lying, or insanity."[22] The experience of Lani Guinier echoes the implications of Butler's interrogation: What spoke was not Guinier; Guinier was deprived of the opportunity even to defend her position. The strength of Butler's argument

lies in its critical potential. By exposing those plays of power that subvert the "I," Butler challenges us to establish and strengthen the rights
of speaking subjects.

Although Butler's arguments against the "foundational" notions of
the universal and the subject ultimately prevent her from developing a
concept of inclusion capable of remedying those exclusions to which
she draws our attention, her insistence on the pervasiveness of power
continues to unsettle and disturb. I have not shown that we can escape
this power, nor can I. Power *is* implicated in the positioning and structuring of the "theorizing subject," of critics and critiques. Yet just as we
cannot work and write exclusively under the assumption that we are
simply the effects, the constructs, of relations of power (for we often
hear explanations such as "My article was rejected purely because of politics" as excuses), neither can we presume that our efforts for inclusion,
our struggles against oppression and invisibility, are always only recon-
figurations of a repressive, concealing, exclusionary power. Critique depends on our ability to separate through reflection the always intertwined plays of power and claims of validity.[23] And, as Butler shows
us, crucial to this ability is a commitment to openness, contestation,
and inclusion.

At the heart of the feminist critiques of proceduralism and Butler's
interrogation of universalism lie an appreciation of difference and a concern with exclusion. At work in both accounts is the presumption of
an opposition between the universal and the particular. Universality is
thought to exclude the difference of the other. If feminism is committed
to the rejection of oppositional categories, to that mode of binary thinking that requires we elevate one side of a duality above the other, we
have to extend this critique to challenge the opposition between the
universal and the particular. We must reject the claim, long a tenet of
traditional, masculine theories, that women are confined to, represent,
and indeed embody the particular. We are all already particular.

Discourse and Universalism

Discourse ethics is rooted in the notion that humane
ways of living together require the free and equal communication of all
concerned. It is a fundamentally democratic ideal. Where it differs from
those procedural theories criticized by feminists is in its justification

strategy. Rather than based on abstract persons in a hypothetical contract, discourse ethics holds that only those norms are valid that would be agreed upon by real people in a real process of argumentation.[24] As it distinguishes between valid and merely given norms, then, discourse ethics tries to clarify our everyday intuition that there is an important difference between trying to coerce or influence another person and attempting to come to an understanding with another person. To this end, it outlines *provisionally* those ideal conditions that would have to be met if the outcome of a real process of argumentation were to be valid.

These ideal conditions are expressed as the rules of practical discourse. A practical discourse is one in which participants distance themselves from the pressure to act and consider a norm from a hypothetical perspective, asking themselves whether it should exist. Through argumentation they test the worthiness of a norm to be recognized. If a norm can meet with the agreement of all concerned, if it embodies an interest shared by everyone affected by it, then it deserves recognition.[25] But this agreement cannot itself be coerced. To be rational, it has to be reached under the following conditions:

(1) Every subject with the competence to speak and act is allowed to take part in a discourse.

(2) a. Everyone is allowed to question any assertion whatsoever;
b. Everyone is allowed to introduce any assertion whatsoever into the discourse;
c. Everyone is allowed to express his attitudes, desires and needs.

(3) No speaker may be prevented, by internal or external coercion, from exercising his rights as laid down in (1) and (2).[26]

Of course, these rules are ideal and rarely realized in practice. Nonetheless, we intuitively adopt versions of them whenever we try to come to an understanding with another person. And, when we engage in democratic debate, we have to presuppose them.

The presuppositions of argumentation are not hard-and-fast rules per se. Rather, they express formally our appreciation of the difference between persuading another by monopolizing the conversation, interrupting, belittling or ignoring the other's experience (conversational tactics familiar to many women and members of oppressed groups) and coming to a shared understanding by really listening and considering the views expressed by the other. When these rules of argumentation hold, in principle the participants will be able to reach a consensus on the validity of a norm on the basis of good reasons — that is, because the norm is in everyone's interest rather than reflecting the dominance of a few. The idea, then, is that only through hearing the interests of each individual can we reach an agreement regarding the general concerns of all of us.

The universalist component of discourse ethics is expressed as a rule of argumentation that makes it possible to reach agreement in practical discourses. Habermas formulates it as the principle that "every valid norm must satisfy the condition that the consequences and side effects that would foreseeably follow from its general observance for the satisfaction of the interests of each individual could be freely accepted by all concerned."[27] This principle tells us that although consensus itself is an ideal, we have to presuppose it whenever we argue. If we did not assume that we could, in principle, reach an agreement on the basis of good reasons, we would be left only with influence and plays of power. The universalization principle compels participants in argumentation to engage in "ideal role taking"; it requires each participant to take the position of the other in the search for a consensus.[28]

The universalization principle is designed to capture our everyday intuitions regarding fair decisions in moral conflicts. For example, we would usually think that there is something deeply wrong with, say, telling the truth to men and lying to women. Such a flagrant violation of our feelings regarding fairness and impartiality is the sort of intuition that the universalization principle seeks to reconstruct — clearly, women would not agree to a norm that held that they must never be told the truth. So, by stipulating that the rightness or validity of a norm stems from its acceptability to those who could be affected by its being followed as a general practice, the principle of universalization serves as a bridging principle in practical discourses. It establishes a link between the reasons offered up in argumentation — the products of ideal role taking — and the conviction on the part of the participants that a given conclusion is warranted because agreement was uncoerced.[29]

How, exactly, does discursive universalism accord with feminist concerns? The feminist critique of procedural universalism focuses, on the one hand, on the importance of openness, contestation, and inclusion, and, on the other, on the necessity of avoiding blindness to contexts and blindness to persons. Acknowledging the importance of openness, inclusion, and critique, I emphasize the admitted fallibility of discourse ethics. Attuned to our contexts and individualities, I interpret discourse ethics as the contextual conversation of humanity. What appears in the course of each aspect of my reinterpretation of discourse ethics is an emphasis on the way in which discursive universalism presupposes solidarity.

The fallibilism of discourse ethics appears at three different levels. At the initial level is the move away from First Philosophy to rational reconstructions. This involves the claims for discourse ethics itself. Here, Habermas appeals to the idea of procedural rationality in modern accounts of science and morality: Once rationality is no longer seen as a totality, as the revealed whole of the nature or the manifestation of a world-constituting transcendental subject, what counts as rational comes to depend on a set of formal procedures.[30] At the second level are the formulations of the rules of discourse. The contingent products of a particular Western history, these formulations can always be brought up for questioning and critique. Finally, the third level concerns the outcome of any given practical discourse. Even after a norm has met with the agreement of all concerned, there are no guarantees that it remains right or valid for all time.

In his exchange with Richard Rorty, Habermas agrees that philosophy can no longer play the roles of "usher" and "judge" associated with Kantian foundationalism. It cannot presume to be the "highest arbiter in matters of science and culture."[31] Nonetheless, philosophy has not been rendered obsolete. On the contrary, those empirical theories that make universalist claims — theories such as Freud's psychoanalysis of development, Mead's discussion of the place of role taking in identity formation, and Durkheim's conception of the emergence of solidarity — stand as paradigmatic for a new conception of philosophy as occupying a place within the reconstructive sciences. As they link empirical research with universal ideas, these contributions to the reconstructive sciences represent a cooperative venture between science and philosophy.[32] They attempt to explain the systems of rules that underlie pre-theoretical knowledge, to provide rational reconstructions of the "know-how" of competent subjects. For example, a rational reconstruction might try to explain how people discern and resolve moral dilemmas (such an attempt can be seen in the work of Lawrence Kohlberg and Carol Gilligan).

Rational reconstructions are not infallible. Those who develop them can make mistakes. Accordingly, like the hypotheses raised in science, rational reconstructions are always subject to testing and retesting. They depend on corroboration. So, the "rationality" of these reconstructions does not lie in their substance or subject matter per se. "Rational" does not refer to some ultimate knowledge attained in a reconstruction, but

rather to the methods and approaches — the procedures — used to generate and test them. Hence, rational reconstructions remain open, always
subject to interpretation and reinterpretation, to further critique or con-
firmation.[33] Itself a rational reconstruction of the moral intuitions of
competent subjects *today,* discourse ethics, too, remains open for corroboration, revision, and critique.

The fallibilism of discourse ethics also appears in the formulation of
the presuppositions of argumentation. Part of discourse ethics' reconstruction of our basic moral intuitions, these rules are tentative and provisional. They are aspects of our contemporary understanding of the
meaning of uncoerced communication.[34] In addition to this "external
fallibility," the rules are also "internally fallible." Not only can the presuppositions be questioned from the perspective of the theoretical observer, but also they can be thematized by the participants in a practical
discourse. Since anything whatsoever can be brought up in argumentation, these rules, too, are not beyond questioning. They themselves can
be held up against the ideal of communication free from violence that
they are designed to realize. For example, the fundamental notions of
intersubjective reciprocity, of concern and respect for others, would be
harmed were not participants in discourse aware of the limits of language. As Thomas McCarthy observes, participants in practical discourse can "call into question the language that frames debate, that is,
the terms in which problems are identified and posed, data selected and
described, reasons formulated and weighed, warrants proposed and as-
sessed and so forth."[35] The moral understanding that discourse ethics is
designed to capture would be a narrow one indeed if the language of
discourse prevented people from expressing themselves, if discourse itself was damaging to the participants' sense of self.

Finally, the fallibilism of discourse ethics emerges from the idea that
any given consensus can always be questioned. By acknowledging the
limits of language and the necessity of calling into question relationships
of exclusion and domination that come into language use itself, this
version of procedural universalism pushes us toward a view of moral
justification as a historically ongoing discussion and critique.[36] Thus,
criticisms such as those raised by Chantal Mouffe are misplaced. Discourse ethics neither insists on "a final rational reconciliation of value
claims" nor envisions "the possibility of a politics from which antago-
nism and division would have disappeared."[37] Not only does Mouffe
fail to grasp the difference between the ideal presuppositions of discourse and the actual practice of discourse, but also she neglects the fact

that there is not just one discourse in which questions are settled "from now on." Issues do not simply appear as items on an agenda to be resolved and then set aside for implementation. Instead, practical discourse is a long, sometimes messy process of continued efforts to include the excluded and confront domination.

The fallibility of any given consensus leads to the insistent contextuality of discursive universalism. This contextuality can be seen in the universalization principle. By focusing on the intersubjectively shared conviction of the rightness of a norm on the part of all affected, this formulation of the principle of universality rules out monological interpretations of the moral point of view.[38] Unlike the accounts of universality offered by Kant and Rawls, Habermas's principle of universalization requires a real process of argumentation because participants can only share the knowledge that collectively they are convinced of the validity of a norm if they have *actually* come to an understanding. Since norms reflect collective interests, one person cannot simply engage in a thought experiment to test whether a norm is worthy of her assent. Rather, by participating in argumentation, each person ensures that her own interests and needs are taken into account. Further, each also subjects her own expression of her needs and interests to examination and criticism from others. This makes it possible to move beyond culturally given need interpretations and toward a fuller awareness of the way in which our needs are constructed through the discursive operation of power. Unlike previous versions of universalism, discourse ethics thus embeds the actuality of our existence as gendered and embodied persons in its conception of the moral point of view by insisting that universalizability requires actual discourse.

Since practical discourses are procedures for testing the validity of norms and do not themselves generate valid norms, they always depend on content brought to them from outside the procedure itself. As Habermas explains:

Without the horizon of the lifeworld of a specific social group and without action conflicts in a specific situation in which those concerned looked upon the consensual resolution of controversial social matters as their task, it would be senseless to want to engage in a practical discourse. The concrete point of departure of a disturbed normative agreement, to which practical discourses are always antecedently tied, determines the objects and problems that come up 'on the agenda.' This procedure, then, is not formal in the sense of an abstraction from content. In its openness, discourse is directly dependent on contingent content being 'fed into' it.[39]

Rather than relying on a conception of universality that entails a blindness to the context in which our moral decisions are situated, discourse ethics provides a procedure for the restoration of a disturbed consensus. This presupposes that the participants are socialized individuals who bring with them into argumentation the concerns, desires, and beliefs arising out of and constituting their own particular experiences. Discourse ethics, then, does not privilege certain contents as proper to the moral domain; instead, inextricably tied to the contexts within which discourses take place, discourse ethics holds that any issue can be brought up or treated in a practical discourse. The reasons offered by participants in practical discourse are not abstract arguments removed from time and place. Instead, they include our particular, situated, and contextual beliefs and concerns.

Such an opening up of the notion of what counts as a good reason allows discourse ethics to avoid a rationalistic rejection of our moral feelings. Discursive universalism both takes seriously our feelings of morality and presupposes the embedded quality of our moral attitudes within the relationships and practices of everyday life. On the one hand, since our experience of moral phenomena arises out of our participation in a social world of relationships and interactions, our moral feelings often appear as emotional responses to ethical violations and conflicts. They form the basis of our perception that something is moral. These feelings of indignation, guilt, and obligation point beyond our initial situation to suprapersonal standards for judging moral conflicts. On the other hand, given that it is often irrational to deny our feelings and emotions, the procedural stipulations of discourse ethics guarantee the inclusion of those sentiments that we as participants feel to be relevant for the justification of a norm. So while it remains cognitivist in its assertion of the primacy of good reasons, by construing rationality from the standpoint of what participants understand as convincing or persuasive, discourse ethics reasserts its context dependency.

Finally, the contextuality of discursive universalism appears in the importance placed on our intersubjective ties and relationships. Our relationships with others serve as significant features of discourse ethics on two basic levels: the notion of the self or person in discourse ethics, and the relationship among participants in argumentation who have put aside the use of force and seek to reach an agreement on matters of common concern. First, discourse ethics relies on a communicative account of subjectivity: We acquire distinct identities through our interaction with others. We become individuals to the extent that we become involved in ever-increasing relationships of mutual responsibility and recognition.[40] Since individuation and socialization are two aspects of the same process, our capacity to participate in practical discourse grows out of our immediate experience with others to whom we are intimately connected. When we meet to discuss matters of concern in a practical discourse, then, we do not shed our earlier memberships. Instead, we meet already as members of a variety of differing groups and associations—for example, as members of a family, community, ethnic group, class, or sex. Consequently, we bear a responsibility for the outcome of argumentation in ways that must include these prior memberships.[41] A norm would not warrant our acceptance if its general observance required us to deny those relationships that give meaning and a sense of validity to our lives.

Second, discourse ethics presupposes a particular sort of relationship among participants in moral argumentation, a relationship of solidarity. Those who have put aside the use of force or coercion and meet with a shared interest in reaching agreement are bound together through reciprocal expectations and responsibilities. If I am expected to be sincere and to give good reasons for the beliefs and claims I offer up in argumentation, then I expect that others will allow me to do so, that they will give me the opportunity to state my position and will listen respectfully to my views. Further, I am expected to allow others to do the same and to heed their concerns. Thus, participants in practical discourse are mutually interconnected through the reciprocal rights and obligations that structure the presuppositions of argumentation. Indeed, the idea that we share an orientation toward reaching understanding corresponds with our mutual expectation that we will not agree or disagree on various points and positions trivially or arbitrarily. Rather, we will understand ourselves as solidarily bound members of a moral community. The willingness to put aside violence and enter into discourse itself expresses this ideal of solidarity.

Rather than viewing solidarity as a precondition for practical discourses, Habermas limits himself to the claim that justice and solidarity are two aspects of the same thing.[42] If by this assertion Habermas means to say that inclusion, reciprocity, equal respect, and mutual recognition are not only requirements for the justification of normative claims to validity but also standards by which we can evaluate solidarity, then I fully agree. While his discussion often suggests as much, it nonetheless remains somewhat vague, often seeming to underestimate the extent to which practical discourses require solidarity.

A brief review of Habermas's discussion of solidarity bears this out. Habermas introduces solidarity as the flip side of justice in the context of the universalism-communitarian debate (Rawls vs. Sandel) and the justice-care debate (Kohlberg vs. Gilligan).[43] He stresses that the primacy of rights need not be viewed as antagonistic to an appeal to community since moral norms cannot protect one without the other: "They cannot protect the equal rights and freedoms of the individual without protecting the welfare of one's fellow man and of the community to which the individual belongs."[44] Rather than remaining caught in the traditional opposition, then, discourse ethics stresses both freedom and community, both justice and solidarity. Yet, as Habermas seeks to show how the presuppositions of argumentation entail solidarity as well as justice, he inadvertently asserts the very primacy of solidarity — ideal role taking requires overcoming an egocentric perspective. Furthermore, he points out that empathetic sensitivity from each to all is necessary for practical discourse to result in an agreement worthy of consent.[45] What this means is that taking the role of the other is a capacity required not simply of rational, accountable subjects who orient their action to validity claims, but more fundamentally of accountable subjects endeavoring to sustain and renew their intersubjective ties.

Understanding solidarity as the prerequisite for practical discourses fits more readily with Habermas's project in *The Theory of Communicative Action*. There he argues that "the 'ought-quality' of moral norms implicitly invokes the danger that any harm to the social bond means for all members of a collectivity — the danger of anomie, of group identity breaking down, of the members common life-contexts disintegrating."[46] Indeed, precisely these disturbances are measured against a normative ideal of solidarity.[47] Furthermore, his overall colonization thesis — the problem of the penetration of the systems of power and money into the lifeworld — relies on the notion of solidarity, both for the maintenance of the processes of reaching understanding that are threatened and as a bulwark against further encroachments.[48]

I argue that the fallibility and contextuality of practical discourses make such discourses dependent on solidarity. As we abstract from the requirements of action and assume the attitude of participants in discourse, we have to take responsibility for our utterances and for the other participants. Our questions and claims cannot be raised vindictively or arbitrarily. Not only would this violate the presupposition of mutual respect, but also it would presume a degree of infallible self-assertion that would instrumentalize the very process of coming to a consensus. Consequently, because anything whatsoever can be brought up in a practical discourse, we have to remain attuned to the vulnerability of each participant. We have to share an awareness of our mutual interdependence. Moreover, since discourses remain embedded in the relationships and practices of our everyday life, maintaining the bonds of social integration is a prerequisite for argumentation itself. Indeed, the universalist model of discourse ethics always relies on the ethical achievements of concrete forms of life. Yet, unlike the models offered by classical republicans and communitarians, discursive will-formation does not rest on a substantive ethical consensus. Instead, the myriad solidary relationships within which we construct our identities and among which we move give us an insight into ideals of accountability and inclusion capable of being extended to all potential members of the community of discourse. The concept of reflective solidarity builds from this idea.

Both the fallibilism and contextuality of discourse ethics lead to an open-ended understanding of discursive universalism as the never-ending conversation of humanity. Previous conceptions of the moral point of view, such as Rawls's original position or the contract theories of the Enlightenment, were profoundly outcome oriented. In contrast, discursive universalism is oriented toward *processes* of reaching understanding.[49] Discourses are not like miniaturized and contextualized original compacts. They are the actual discussions and debates always part of the learning process of democracy. While their rules and presuppositions are to a certain extent abstract, discourses themselves remain embedded in the conversations, associations, and institutions of civil society.[50] Analogies better than the original compact are the century-long debate over slavery in the United States, the current struggle for lesbian and gay rights, and the abortion controversy. In each instance, when contemporary social members refuse to acknowledge the legitimacy of the claims raised by and on behalf of the excluded, those struggling toward greater inclusion nevertheless project ideal communication communities in which they argue their cases.

Once we see that discourses embody the never-ending debate within and about democracies, we can grasp the critical component of discursive universalism. The idealizing presuppositions of practical discourse reflect our contemporary understanding of what it means to include another, to recognize her difference, and treat her with respect. Because those intuitions are in practice counterfactual, the critical component of democratic debate comes into focus as the ongoing exposure of our failure to recognize, include, and respect.

Finally, with the realization that discourses embody an actual process of rational will-formation among socialized subjects comes the rearticulation of the requirement of solidarity, for without it the very procedure of universalization would be meaningless. "Every requirement of universalization," remarks Habermas, "must remain powerless unless there also arises, from membership in an ideal communication community, a consciousness of irrevocable solidarity, the certainty of intimate relatedness in a shared life context."[51]

By interpreting discourse ethics in terms of the conversation of humanity and emphasizing the way in which this conversation presupposes solidary relations among participants in communication, we can grasp that this account of universality is not conceived in opposition to particularity and contextuality, but instead relies on and guarantees them. Habermas writes:

My reflections point toward the thesis that the unity of reason only remains perceptible in the plurality of its voices — as the possibility in principle of passing from one language to another — a passage that, no matter how occasional, is still comprehensible. This possibility of mutual understanding, which is now guaranteed only procedurally and is realized only transitorily, forms the background for the existing diversity of those who encounter one another — even when they fail to understand one another.[52]

I read Habermas as making three points in this passage. The first involves his procedural conception of rationality. Claims to validity such as truth, rightness, and sincerity install idealizations necessary for communication — "they lend unity and organization to the situation interpretations that participants negotiate with one another."[53] Negotiating requires that participants understand one another, that they can translate their own particular experiences and understandings into a comprehensible language. The unity of reason, be it in the form of a particular claim, category, or concept, or understood in terms of the rationality inherent in action oriented toward reaching understanding, thus cannot be grasped in the absence of the diverse particularities on which it depends. The second point concerns diversity. In the absence of a communicative engagement with the other, difference disappears, assimilated or dominated by the logic of identity characteristic of instrumental reason. However, by seeking to come to an understanding with another, we are able to encounter her as a participant in discourse, to meet her in an attitude of solidarity that respects her difference. The goal of understanding, then, provides the background against which we strive to include those others who have remained excluded. In Habermas's words:

"More discourse means more contradiction and difference. The more abstract the agreements become, the more diverse the disagreements with which we can *nonviolently* live."[54] The third point in this passage returns us to the contextualism and fallibalism of discourse ethics. In any given context, we may fail to understand the other. We may not be able to grasp her meaning, to translate her experience into our language without violence. Yet recognizing her demands that we continue to try, that we alter our language in accordance with what she teaches us.

By stressing an interpretation of discourse ethics as the fallible and contextual conversation of humanity, I have sought to suggest an account of universalism that embodies the ideals and insights fundamental to feminism. Rooted in the presupposition of solidarity, discourse ethics is blind neither to contexts nor to persons. It urges real discourses among real persons, taking into account the relationships in which we develop as particular individuals and the place for this particularity as it appears in the reasons we proffer in argumentation.[55] As it makes the questioning of need interpretations a project of solidarily bound members, discourse ethics does not present a reified account of difference. Instead, the construction of difference is a collective enterprise whereby participants emphasize and develop those differences they construe as meaningful for their sense of self. This more fluid conception of difference as a component of lives in the process of formation breaks away from the apartheid notion of difference, a conception of difference that lies at the heart of the identity politics debate and that infuses Butler's critique of universality and subjectivity. Finally, with its admitted fallibalism, discursive universalism remains permanently open. It thus embodies Butler's insight into the importance of questioning and contestability without denying the necessity of normative criteria. For inclusion to serve as a coherent ideal, we need to have norms for determining how, when, in what, and as what we are to be included. Discursive universalism provides procedures for the justification of these norms.

To be sure, feminists such as Seyla Benhabib, Jean Cohen, and Nancy Fraser have questioned the limits of discourse ethics on precisely this point. They are skeptical regarding the ability of discourse ethics to include women and their concerns within the public sphere—or, to use my phrasing, to include women as part of the conversation of humanity. Their concerns center on the separation Habermas makes between justice and the good life. Given the influence of this criticism, it is necessary to consider it in some detail.

Discourse ethics sets out strict criteria for justifying the validity of norms — the free agreement of all concerned in a practical discourse. Yet with such a strict conception of validity, a number of important ethical issues seem to slip out of the moral domain. For Habermas, this is the difference between justice or morality and ethics or the good life. Norms or values incapable of meeting with general consensus cannot claim universal validity. They remain a concern for the individual and the community and relationships of which she is a part. Morality, then, is just a small portion of our ethical life.

Benhabib and Cohen argue that with this separation of issues of morality from issues of the good life Habermas repeats the distinction between the public and private spheres.[56] But their association of justice with the public and the good life with the private confuses the levels of the discussion: Those norms and values traditionally linked with one realm or the other provide *contents* for practical discourse; the public and private realms themselves do not provide a formal structure according to which one could redeem or classify claim to validity. Benhabib acknowledges these different levels but nonetheless asserts that insofar as discourse ethics is "indebted" to the liberal tradition, the ambiguity forcing the private sphere outside of the realm of justice is also at work in Habermas's theory.[57]

Frankly, I do not find such a guilt-by-association argument convincing. The discourse ethics model is based on a hypothetical attitude in which we question oppressive and exclusionary norms and traditional roles and understandings. Furthermore, ethical questions of the good life are neither strictly private nor confined to the aesthetic-expressive realm. The ethical question concerning "Who I am and who I want to be" is always embedded within the horizon of a given way of life. This question, too, remains part of an intersubjective praxis and can thus be considered in ethical-existential discourses.[58] Questions regarding the good life also appear in plural: Who are we and who do we want to be?" To call these questions private, then, does not make sense — they are already the questions people in a variety of communities ask themselves about the meanings and expectations of their shared ways of life. Both moral-practical and ethical-existential discourses are always part of the ongoing debate within and about democracy.

In fact, the distinction between justice and the good life incorporates a number of concerns at the heart of feminism. It embodies the insistence on a critical approach to norms with claims to universality. Discourse ethics' strict requirements enable us to withdraw legitimacy from expressions of particular interests that represent themselves as general. At the same time, with our recognition that these particular interests do not present expectations that are necessarily binding for us all comes an appreciation of their roles as essential components of the life plans of others. In this way, specialized concerns of ethnicity and sexuality, though nongeneralizable, nonetheless present constant challenges to normative validity claims and remain integral components of personality and culture. What was claimed as a universal or fundamental norm may simply be an attempt to secure the good life for the rich, heterosexual, white male.

The distinction between justice and the good life also provides a way to conceptualize a variety of issues while avoiding the distinction between the public and private realms. Those practical questions decided with reasons, those conflicts of action that can be resolved through consensus, are understood as issues of justice.[59] Justice, then, while always a public matter, is not confined to those questions traditionally part of the public sphere. This ability to cut across boundaries traditionally used to bar women's concerns from the public or moral domain allows discourse ethics to address feminist issues in a way that other procedural theories cannot. As my discussion of civil society attests, this understanding of justice as cutting across boundaries makes it possible to argue for an end to the public/private distinction.

The discourse ethics approach takes seriously the feminist insight into the limits of justice. Only those norms that meet with the agreement of all concerned in a practical discourse are just and worthy of recognition. Those values we hold as essential to our self-realization, as particular to our needs and concerns, we understand as aspects of the good life. We choose to act on norms that are nongeneralizable insofar as they hold meaning and value for us. We can, and do, attempt to defend them. We may try to convince others that our values are universalizable and should be embodied in norms. But without a real discourse, we cannot say for sure. The distinction between justice and the good life thus recognizes that there may never be a consensus on a large number of important issues. This implies that the conception of justice in discourse ethics presupposes a space in which people can construct their own life plans. With a formal notion of justice and the moral, then, we are not put in the position of privileging one particular point of view or conception of the good life.

The idea of universality in discourse ethics, like the universality evoked by Trinh, conjoins difference and domesticity as it envisions the process of justification as an open-ended conversation that breaks through an oppositional way of thinking about the public and the private, about what is universal and what is particular and contextual. Further, because this conversation is one in which we all participate, it does not require us to separate issues of race, culture, and sex as particularities always already segregated from some preconceived homogeneity. Instead, universality simultaneously arises out of and helps to guarantee diversity and plurality. Engaging another in discourse, we are required to recognize her difference and irreplaceability, even as she recognizes our own.

The Perspective of the Third

The universal ideal articulated in discourse ethics rests on the presuppositions competent speakers must make when engaging in argumentation. Participants in practical discourse have to be able to engage in ideal role taking. Habermas argues that this capacity is anchored in language in the communicative roles connected with the system of personal pronouns: "The structure of linguistic intersubjectivity that lays down the communicative roles of the person speaking, the person spoken to and the person who is present but uninvolved, forces the participants, insofar as they want to come to an understanding with one another, to act under the presupposition of responsibility [or accountability: *Zurechnungsfähigkeit*]."[60]

In practical discourse, participants raise claims with a communicative intent. As speakers they utter statements to a particular hearer, aware that the hearer has the option of responding either yes or no. Taking the perspective of the hearer, they must be prepared to back up their claims if necessary. Additionally, participants have to understand that their interaction is not an immediate interaction concerning the interests of a particular speaker and hearer. Rather, they are testing normative validity claims, claims that extend beyond the situation at hand. Understanding that norms involve generalized behavioral expectations, speakers have to objectify their interaction with the hearer, looking at it from the perspective of an observing bystander.

With the introduction of the observer perspective, "ego can split up the communicative role of alter into the communicative roles of an *alter ego*, a participating counterpart, and a *neuter*, a member of the group present as an onlooker."[61] Alterity is thus split into two moments. The other appears not simply in opposition to the speaking "I," but emerges as a third space in the interaction. By looking from this third space, speakers separate the "I-you" participant perspectives from the situation at hand, realizing that in principle they are interchangeable. These perspectives are not merely aspects of *this* situation; anyone could adopt them. Taking the perspective of the observer forces participants in practical discourse to move beyond the particular situation and adopt a general, hypothetical attitude.

Another way to understand these shifting perspectives is through a comparison with David Wiggins' discussion of universalization from the perspectives of the actor, the victim, and the observer. Wiggins envisions a "public scene"

in which moral agents are at once actors and spectators, and in which the way actors act informs the way they see things, and the way in which they see things informs the way they act. Actors here are persons doing things and persons having things done to them. Spectators are not strangers to these roles. Nor are actors strangers to the role of spectator. For everyone plays each of these three roles at some point, and his direct and indirect knowledge of the other roles constantly informs his playing of each.[62]

What for Wiggins is the role of the actor is the "I" or first-person perspective for Habermas. Again, this role focuses on the individual agent in his performative capacity—on who speaks and who listens in moral argumentation. The second-person hearer or "you" perspective is found in Wiggins' "victim" or "person-having-things-done-to-him" role. This perspective highlights the way in which we consider the effects of norms on our actions—how we would feel when others acted toward us in accordance with the given norm. Additionally, as we have seen, the Habermasian version of the second-person perspective draws attention to the other with whom we are communicating, the hearer who can always respond to our assertions with a yes or a no. Finally, the third-person or spectator position, sometimes called the "neutral third," refers to the objectifying capacity required of participants in moral argumentation. They must be able to see both their own subjective point of view and the other's view from a "neutral" perspective. The third-person perspective, then, refers to our capacity to distance ourselves from the immediacy of argumentation, to generalize from and assess impartially the situated claims and responses we make as speakers and hearers within the dialogic context.

All of these roles are mutually interconnecting; there is no perspective outside of the moral dialogue or "public scene." Habermas's use of the observer perspective as a perspective within a moral dialogue thus should not be confused with a "view from nowhere" or with the equation of the moral point of view with the privileged standpoint of an ideal spectator. In fact, Habermas stresses that ego, alter, and neuter all belong to a community in which their interpersonal relations and actions are norm governed and thus can be judged in accordance with these norms.[63] Again, it is the capacity of each participant to take each of the three positions that creates the potential for agreement in a practical discourse.

Looking at the third-person perspective as a neutral third — a spectator, as someone present but uninvolved — obscures two ways in which this perspective is not neutral at all. Before I discuss these ways, I want to distinguish between two possible interpretations of the term "neutral" in the notions of moral dialogue and public scene. Habermas and Wiggins could understand "neutral" as meaning "not having a stake in the outcome." This interpretation highlights the spectator's "uninvolved" status. But "neutral" might also mean "not affecting the outcome." This would emphasize the distance between the observer and the actors. In fact, however, the neutral third fails to be neutral in either of these senses. And this leads to the first way in which the observer perspective is not neutral at all.

From the observer position, one is supposed to evaluate the arguments or actions of the participants. This means that the observer is a judge. Now, the matter at hand is morality, presumably a topic in regard to which our sense of self, deep-seated beliefs, and interests and desires influence our understanding in complicated ways. It is difficult to see how the observer could be neutral with regard to a judgment with potentially far-reaching effects on his life plans. The fact that the observer is a judge also disrupts the second interpretation of "neutral." Interpretation is always context-bound. The very idea that this perspective involves generalization and assessment implicitly appeals to the context that makes such processes meaningful. The partiality of interpretation, by highlighting one set of elements as opposed to another set, affects the character of the outcome (regardless of the judge's personal interest in the outcome). Thus, the term "neutral" conceals the fact that the observer is a context-bound judge.

The second way in which "neutral" obscures our vision lies in its denial of difference. The third person is embodied, positioned in terms of sex and race. This action-capable, norm-following member of a community who occupies the observer position is either male or female, and has experiences of inclusion and exclusion directly linked to ethnicity. By thematizing sexual difference specifically, I want to draw out the difficulties with the observer in Habermas's and Wiggins' examples. To accentuate the importance of the sex of the third person, whose perspective we are supposed to be able to take, I first suggest a "Dumb View" and then offer a more promising "Critical View."

If Habermas's uninvolved third person is a female, why isn't she involved in the conversation? Does her absence prevent the participants from taking her judgment seriously? If his third person is a male, then the masculine perspective (especially when it reflects the dominant structure of society) defines the norms of the conversation. Similarly, if Wiggins' spectators are female, they seem cut off from the action in this public scene. If the spectators are men, then women are objectified, caught within a masculine gaze. They are "victims," those-having-things-done-to-them. It is as if women's absence from the moral conversation, their presence as victims and objects of judgment, makes possible the objectifying evaluative stance that renders men moral subjects. While the Dumb View thus distorts the intent of ideal role taking or the change in perspective required of participants in moral argumentation, it nonetheless exposes the tensions that arise when we replace the seemingly neutral third with the nonneutral "he" or "she."[64] The detachment of the neutral observer and the distance of an uninvolved spectator seem to reflect an objectifying way of looking at relationships that distorts the very notion of intersubjectivity that moral discourse is designed to reflect.

The more interesting Critical View arises when we take seriously the requirement of moral perspective taking and emphasize that, in the context of a language that gives a gender to the third-person-singular perspective, we must always be attuned to the difference signified by the third person. If we subsume the third-person perspective into the standpoint of a neutral third, we undermine the morality of the judgment or agreement that is supposed to arise from ideal role taking. We risk repeating and furthering the exclusion and domination of those designated by the feminine. In societies where women are subordinated and the dominant point of view is masculine, this point of view becomes doubly strengthened when we attempt a "neutral" perspective. What is neutral is associated with what is conventionally acceptable; but what is conventionally acceptable has been constructed from a masculine standpoint to support men's power over women. The "neutral" standpoint is not neutral at all; it is simply another way of designating the third person masculine. A consensus that mirrors this standpoint cannot determine the validity of a norm because such a consensus ignores interests that must be taken into account if a norm is to be universalizable. Further, if we are not aware of the difference of the third person, we forfeit the opportunity to expose the unnoticed biases that often creep into both our moral argumentation and our everyday communicative action. Thus, I argue that moral responsibility requires more than taking the perspective of a neutral observer. It entails that we take the perspective of differently sexed, embodied third persons. The Critical View, then, uses the perspective of difference built into the system of personal pronouns to draw attention to the presence of women and demand that their position be taken into account.

By focusing on the sexual difference present in the system of personal pronouns, both the Dumb View and the Critical View expose how the assertion of neutrality denies the situatedness and particularity of the third-person perspective. By articulating this situatedness we can reinterpret the third-person perspective as that of a situated, hypothetical third. "Language, of course, is never neutral," argues Trinh. "It is a site where power relationships are most complex and pernicious; yet it is also a place of liberation. Whether it frees or enslaves depends on how it is used, and it is pernicious only when its workings are invisible."[65] Replacing neutrality with situatedness, the concept of the hypothetical third enables us to increase the liberatory potential of practical discourse by making visible perspectives that have been hidden. The stress on "situatedness" reminds us that the third-person perspective is precisely that — the perspective of a concrete person whose assessment of the action in practical discourse remains unique and irreplaceable. To this extent, stressing the situatedness of the third prevents us from falling prey to the misconception that the third signifies an absolute "other," a misconception that would both reify difference and make agreement impossible. Instead, we strive to see from the perspective of myriad others. The term "hypothetical" reminds us of the limits of our perspective and entreats us to an awareness of what always remains excluded. Thus, the hypothetical status of the third refers to a space that must remain permanently open.

My reinterpretation of the observer perspective as that of a hypothetical third relies on the idea of split alterity. When the other is not only a hearer in opposition to a speaker but also a third person, we increase our awareness of the limits of discourse. On the one hand, the language used by speakers and hearers may prevent them from reaching an agreement. Here, the perspective of the third prevents them from speaking past each other; it thereby provides an interpretive standpoint necessary for facilitating consensus by instantiating the necessity of patience and creativity in the effort to reconstruct and develop adequate vocabularies. On the other hand, the specificity of the observing other serves as a reminder that the discussion between speaker and hearer risks overlooking needs that have not yet found expression. The hypothetical third signifies the space occupied by the excluded other, the perspective that would be included *if* the voices of the marginalized could be heard. In moving from our roles as speaker and hearer to the role of observer, we are not moving away or standing apart from the action of discourse. We are instead trying to grasp and understand the implications of this action from a different place. One of our goals, then, should be to keep this place always free and empty, clearing it so that others can stand there.

Split alterity also comes into play when we realize that the other is not just a hearer, but a seer too. Here, thematizing the perspective from which the seer "sees" enables us to move away from the oppositional structure of participant roles. The difference between speaker and hearer is not the apartheid notion of difference but a particular set of differences that can be understood as sharing some similarities when seen from another perspective. Just as Trinh's use of three voices enables her to avoid setting up dialogues in which voices express their difference through conflict, so does an emphasis on the hypothetical third remind us that in the conversation of humanity what is important is that the voices meet.

Ultimately, the perspective of a hypothetical third strengthens the presupposition of accountability on the part of participants in discourse. In contrast to a "neutral third," which repeats the point of view dominant at any given time, the hypothetical third understands moral accountability as requiring competent subjects to see from the perspective of the dominated and excluded. Because taking a hypothetical attitude entails looking at norms in light of potential harms and violations, it must be anchored in the situated perspectives of those who have been harmed and violated. Admittedly, it could seem that the requirements of inclusion already part of discourse ethics make such a perspective redundant. But my claim is that once we take seriously the fallibilism and contextuality of discourse, the ideal of the conversation of humanity entails that we anchor our accountability toward unseen instances of neglect, denigration, and exclusion in our conception of ideal role taking. Our solidarity toward all demands no less.

Indeed, our ability to take the role of hypothetical, situated thirds also serves as the bridging principle in moral argumentation, for it is only after judging the dialogue from a variety of perspectives that we can be sure to have reached an agreement freely acceptable to *all* concerned. Patricia Williams writes: "A part of ourselves is beyond the control of pure physical will and resides in the sanctuary of those around us; a fundamental part of ourselves and of our dignity depends on the uncontrollable, powerful, external observers who make up society. Surely a part of socialization ought to include a sense of caring responsibility for the images of others that are reposited within us."[66] When these observers are understood not as neutral but as embodied members of the community, our responsibility toward the excluded other appears as a constitutive component of moral perspective taking. We are required to see that the images of the others we carry with us may be the results of ignorance or bias, representations or expectations generalized without regard to the needs and identities of those who occupy these roles. Not to be accountable is thus to participate in the perpetuation of bias. As a capacity presupposed of participants in moral argumentation, the ability to stand back from an interaction and look at it from the perspective of another need not be seen as distancing us from the reality of our moral experience. Rather, by taking the perspective of the hypothetical third, we help prevent moral indignation and outrage from solidifying into languages that distort the needs and pains of the dispossessed through concepts and vocabularies not their own. We assert and reestablish our solidarity in that act of moral perspective taking whereby we acknowledge that the other's perception of our experience may not be the same as our own but is nonetheless one deserving of our attention and respect.

I have argued that discursive universalism best accords with the calls for inclusion and accountability at the heart of feminist concerns. It carries on feminism's critique of binary oppositions by refusing to construct universality in opposition to particularity and presume that women signify the latter. Furthermore, rather than falling prey to the presumptions of masculinity, identity, and exclusion that feminists have pointed out in traditional procedural theories, discursive universalism presupposes plurality and difference. As the fallible, contextual conversation of humanity, this procedural understanding of morality conceives universalism as arising out of and guaranteeing the irreplaceable specificity of each.

But even more importantly, discursive universalism does not remain content simply with the recognition of difference. It asserts the importance of coming to an agreement about those aspects of our lives affecting us all, of working within our differences to find norms and practices worthy of the consent of each individual. The recognition of difference remains meaningless so long as it is not included as an element of our common life context and incorporated into the struggle to end exclusion and oppression. Racist and patriarchal norms recognize difference. What they do not do is allow difference to be a valued aspect of our lives or include it as a component of equal respect. Moreover, they explicitly deny our accountability toward others who are not like us, disrupting the solidarity of our interrelationship.

I have sought to strengthen the ideal of discursive universalism by stressing the way in which it presupposes solidarity and by replacing Habermas's idea of a neutral observer with the notion of the situated, hypothetical third. The claim to "neutrality" blinds us to the perspective from which the observer assesses the action of practical discourse—when we generalize the claims raised and heard in the first- and second-person positions, we do this from a particular standpoint, from what we regard as our shared needs and concerns. Yet by accentuating the particularity of this perspective we are reminded of the necessity of leaving it open. The perspective of a situated, hypothetical third thus enables us to take accountability for others whom we risk excluding. It transforms taking the attitude of the other into seeing from *their* perspective, questioning norms in light of the risk of harm to those whom we have not yet fully included.

Identity has been presumed to oppose universality. Reconceived in terms of reflective solidarity, identity can be understood as depending on universality.

Epilogue
The Risky Business of Reflective Solidarity

Many people who "write" identity politics begin with definitions, introducing themselves with a string of identifications: "I am" a race, sex, class, sexual orientation, age, and ability. These identifications somehow "authorize" the author, establishing the legitimacy of the words, experiences, and theories that follow. In connecting the author with those beyond the self, with those other members of the author's identity categories who as a collectivity reinforce the author's authority, these identifications construct the author as a self. Yet even as they are raised triumphantly, defying both the presumption of universality and neutrality of the authorial voice and its implicit whiteness, maleness, and heterosexuality, these identifications often take on the character of an excuse: "I" cannot (will not?) be accountable for that or those beyond my experience or outside my identity. As an excuse, identifications establish boundaries, effectively ending discussion and setting up barriers to accountability: When "I" raise a claim on the basis of my identity, what is left for "you" to say? At best, you can give voice to your experience, telling me your side of the story. But why should you take any responsibility for me or what has happened to me in the absence of an overlap of identity categories? Is contestation simply a matter of who is speaking or writing? Or is it perhaps more often a question of what is written or spoken? Identity politics often displaces our attention from the claims to the claimants, in effect disrespecting their right or worthiness to write and speak at all.

I want to claim that I have not written from my identity, not because "my" words are somehow not "mine," not because they try to insinuate a contextless authority, but because the contexts and discursive practices informing and determining the words "I" use (as well as the "I" who uses them) are multiple, overlapping, and contradictory. Were I to assert my identity, listing the appropriate categories, I would risk installing a foreclosure that ends discussion, that establishes my authority to speak or write for those who share these categories with me. I would be excusing myself for what I have excluded, suggesting my inability even to imagine the possibility of another perspective. Instead of taking responsibility for my silences and omissions, I would conceal them behind proclamations of who "I" am—all the while knowing that "I" am, of course, more than that, that this "I" is no defense.

But, of course, I have written from my identity. In engaging in the risky business of claiming that I have not, I have subverted my intent, making my identity part of the matter of contestation. How, then, can I acknowledge my situatedness without losing my "self" in a string of always incomplete identifications, the explicit articulation of which leads me into precisely the sort of discursive practice that I have argued we should avoid? Perhaps, I can appeal to how I have asserted my identity. Instead of seeking authority or pardon in a string of significations, I have intentionally presented myself in conversation and connection with those around me, be they my family, friends, colleagues, or fellow citizens. Although there is always the risk that mentioning these conversations and connections may evoke responses I neither intend nor foresee, I have sought to suggest the potential of the "I" of discourse; that is, I have attempted to replace the identified "I" with the "I" of reflective solidarity, the "I" who raises claims to a hearer (to a "you") and who remains aware of the situated, hypothetical thirds witnessing the interaction, attempting to see from their perspective. To this extent, the authority of the discursive "I" rests less on its identity than on its accountability. And even if I have not done justice to or given voice to such an "I," I have sought to suggest that insofar as it attempts to open up dialogue, rather than end it, insofar as it relies on connection with and the recognition of differing "you's," such a discursive "I" points us beyond identity politics and toward reflective solidarity.

But just as articulating a discursive "I" capable of embracing its identifications without raising them to the status of authorizing and pardoning claims is a risky business, so too is reflective solidarity. Reflective solidarity substitutes for the confident (if nonetheless concealing) security of identity politics the fragility of ties that rest on the respect for difference. It seeks to claim as part of solidarity the potential for the disruption of that solidarity, acknowledging that the extension of accountability to and for the excluded brings with it a change in our already given expectations and understandings. On the one hand, the critique of identity politics has taught us that we can neither solve the problems of social and legal exclusion nor do justice to the complexity of multiple, shifting, and situated identities so long as we continue to struggle on the terrain of identity politics. Many of us have diverse and conflicting identifications that escape categorization yet remain in need of articulation. On the other hand, we cannot ignore the promise of identity politics, its ideals of security, belonging, and self-respect.

Reflective solidarity seeks to redeem this promise by reconstructing it in the categories of discursive universalism. Rather than basing the strength of our association on our common experiences of pain and oppression, or tradition and affection, it anchors it in our ability to recognize each other as mysterious, inviolate, and worthy of respect, a recognition that allows us to assert and contest the claims each raises as we attempt to come to understanding.

As we have seen, this recognition requires the "query," an attitude of questioning that corresponds to our capacity to adopt the perspective of situated, hypothetical thirds. This hypothetical attitude instantiates a degree of distance, an abstraction, from the web of traditions, performances, and beliefs constructing us as selves. Nonetheless, it presupposes neither a context-free realm of questioning nor an essential or "core" notion of the self as questioner. Questioning is always situated, a contribution to a discussion already in process. Although the scope and terrain of this discussion remain in flux, not everything is questioned at the same time. Indeed, the possibility of even temporary, transient answers suggests a store of taken-for-granted meanings. Moreover, if constructed selves are not determined selves but selves formed through a variety of intersecting discursive practices and relationships of mutual recognition, adopting a hypothetical attitude is one response (though often a necessary one) to the barriers and conflicts such practices and relationships present. Simply put, constructed selves are nonetheless differentiated selves, and this individuation both requires recognition from others and establishes the potential for disagreement that engenders questioning. Constructed selves, then, are connected selves never certain about the character of their interconnection.

The risks of reflective solidarity seem to erupt most destructively at the levels of interest, ethnicity, and identity and of universality. Most people, I think, would agree that despite the ever present reality of destructive friendships and relationships, at the heart of our intimate ties lie an attunement to vulnerability, a desire for care and connection, and a concern with the well-being and self-realization of those close to us. Additionally, many people would probably accept the idea that contemporary, pluralist democracies should aim toward including the excluded and enabling persons and communities to develop their differing life plans and express their cultural values, provided that these plans and values incorporate a respect for those who do not share them. In this regard, some might say that reflective solidarity seems like another term for liberal tolerance. However, although reflective solidarity and liberal toleration are clearly on the same side of the fence, both rejecting positions that seek to establish one particular notion of the good as valid for everyone, reflective solidarity resists claiming neutrality, arguing instead for accountability. For instance, liberals might urge us to tolerate abortion and sodomy. But this "us" is predetermined. It explicitly positions those who perform or require abortion and those who practice "sodomy" outside the boundaries of "our" community. Moreover, such an appeal to toleration denies "our" accountability toward those others outside our boundaries. It suggests that so long as we do not deny the right of women to have an abortion or the right of homosexuals to engage in particular acts, we have fulfilled our obligations as citizens. Finally, liberal tolerance seems to adopt a just-add-it-on perspective toward inclusion. In other words, by denying our responsibility to displace those crystallizations of meaning constructing women and homosexuals as "other," it fails to examine the oppositional and exclusionary interpretations of rights as they have become embedded in our legal system. The difference between reflective solidarity and liberal toleration, then, is essentially one of attitude — reflective solidarity replaces complacency with critique and engagement.

Turning to the level of interest, ethnicity, and identity, one might say that eschewing traditional identity categories could result in constant bickering and fighting that would impede actual political struggle and disrupt community cohesion. Moreover, it might be argued that reflective solidarity is so hopelessly idealistic that it leads to self-satisfaction and apathy, again displacing attention from the battles left to be fought. Finally, those skeptical about the very possibility of reflective solidarity might claim that solidarity itself requires a connection stronger than recognition through discourse, that what I have offered is not solidarity at all but a weak formalist abstraction.

The first criticism overlooks the fact that the presence of identity categories has not prevented debate from emerging. On the contrary, the very effort to suppress debate and claim unity in the face of plurality has been a major problem for a variety of groups and movements, including those of feminists, people of color, and lesbians and gay men. Reflective solidarity urges that we replace ascribed identities with achieved ones and substitute an enforced commonality of oppression with communities of those who have chosen to work and fight together. The second criticism is correct in pointing out the idealism of reflective solidarity but wrong in concluding that idealism leads to apathy. What else if not some form of idealism motivates any struggle for change? Reflective solidarity seeks to conceive of struggle as both an aspect of community and a vehicle for changing communities without recourse to violence. While this conception, of course, limits the value of *reflective* solidarity in situations where civil war and aggression have replaced efforts toward communicative and peaceful conflict resolution, it nonetheless urges those outside the conflict to respond responsibly and those within the conflict to see beyond the oppositions dividing them. Reflective solidarity requires that we be willing to take a stand, that we open ourselves up to risk and realize that only insofar as we make claims and take stands can we connect with those with whom we might disagree. Finally, the third criticism neglects the contextual basis of reflective solidarity. Although the concept itself is abstract, urging us to take a hypothetical attitude toward already given interpretations of the expectations of members and offering a formal account of the necessary conditions for solidarity in postmodern, pluralist societies, the very nature of these expectations always refers us back to the values, traditions, and practices informing our shared commitments. Reflective solidarity, then, provides a way of moving beyond those expectations incapable of withstanding investigation without breaking the bonds of community.

Far from denying the importance of our intersubjective ties in motivating and instilling solidarity, the concept I offer seeks to create a space for difference through which we can come to terms with the meaning of these ties for each and all of us. If solidarity is to move beyond the demand of unquestioning conformity, if it is to escape an "us/them" mentality that predetermines the content of membership and character of our contribution, and if it is to take responsibility for those others always beyond our reach, it will have to be based on the communicative efforts of those who respect one another in their difference. Ultimately, reflective solidarity brings us together in a way analogous to the mutually beneficial exchange involved in the giving and receiving of a gift: In recognizing the difference of the other, we strengthen her self-trust and esteem; as she is valued for her own unique and irreplaceable contribution to us, she renews our bonds with one another by validating those relationships that protect the integrity of all.

At the universal level, the problem of reflective solidarity appears in a weaker and stronger version. The weaker version would argue that reflective solidarity denies the incommensurability of language games. The stronger version would hold that in so doing, reflective solidarity seeks to impose a totalizing logic that terroristically denies the difference of the other by establishing unity. To the extent that reflective solidarity draws from insights developed in Habermas's theory of communicative action, the weaker critique is right. Reflective solidarity builds from the premise that it is possible, although it may be rare and transitory, to pass from one language to another. Yet as it does so, reflective solidarity acknowledges the fallibility of its own vocabulary, fully aware that translation will necessarily transform the terms in which reflective solidarity has been laid out. Thus, the stronger critique is misplaced. For, in urging the contextuality, fallibility, and openness of discourse, I have offered an interpretation of discourse based on the diversity of the voices of those who enter and change it. This discourse, far from tending toward unity, allows for a nonviolent plurality — open spaces for differences in which we can strive for recognition and understanding. Indeed, by denying the possibility of translation and understanding, the stronger critique prevents difference from making a difference; positing barriers to our communication, it allows us to remain complacent before those whom we have excluded, effectively silencing them.

On 3 July 1994, the *New York Times Magazine* ran a story describing the stand against hate crimes taken by the people of Billings, Montana. Faced with the increasingly vocal presence of the Ku Klux Klan and a rise in acts of racism, homophobia, and anti-Semitism, the town rallied together in a "dramatic act of solidarity and community will." After a cinder block had smashed a child's menorah-decorated window, thousands of non-Jewish families, in an act recalling the story of the King of Denmark's response to the Nazis, decorated their own homes with menorahs. Moreover, they organized a candlelight vigil across the street from a synagogue while services were being held.

Although the story thus far demonstrates reflective solidarity — a solidarity extending beyond already given identity categories — what makes it all the more exemplary was the citywide debate that followed. Rather than resting content with their response to violence, the people of Billings began looking within themselves and their history for "the deep-seated prejudice that prepared the ground for the hate groups in the first place." They recognized that the powerful symbolism of the menorah movement could easily cloak complex and contradictory thoughts and feelings. They discussed the differences between opposing bigotry and encouraging diversity. They grappled with the town's own history of violence against Native Americans, Chinese miners, and Hispanic migrant workers. Having acted out of solidarity, the people of Billings took the risk of further reflection. As the author of the article concludes: "What appeared at first to be a test of moral courage has evolved into an examination of moral nature, which undoubtedly will be challenged frequently in the coming months. The victory seems rather easy compared with the self-respect the people of Billings now seek to win, and that, many of them realize, will require the kind of courage that sees moral strife as a condition rather than a circumstance."

Reflective solidarity is a risky business. It can always fail, collapsing under the weight of those who deny their responsibility for the other, coming up against intransigent vocabularies and languages, and prematurely offering closure. It remains burdened by its very contextuality. Old habits are hard to break; we often resist inquiry into those practices that have given meaning to our lives. And openness itself can at times suggest a vacuum, a lack of centeredness incapable of providing us with direction. Nonetheless, as it draws from our already given experiences as members of families, groups, and communities, reflective solidarity reminds us of the need to take responsibility for those around us, the richness of our shared practices of communicative investigation and discovery, and the continued need for recognition. Perhaps it is a risk we have to take.

Notes

Introduction

1. María Lugones, "Playfulness, World-Traveling, and Loving Perception," in *Women, Knowledge, and Reality,* ed. Ann Garry and Marilyn Pearsall (Boston: Unwin Hyman, 1989), 275–290; Trinh T. Minh-ha, *Framer Framed* (New York: Routledge, 1992); and Gloria Anzaldúa, *Borderlands, La Frontera: The New Mestiza* (San Francisco: Aunt Lute Books, 1987).

2. See Judith Butler's response to Seyla Benhabib in "Contingent Foundations: Feminism and the Question of 'Postmodernism,'" *Praxis International* 11, no. 2 (July 1991), 150–165.

3. See the contributions to the following: *At the Boundaries of Law: Feminism and Legal Theory,* ed. Martha Albertson Fineman and Nancy Sweet Thomadsen (New York: Routledge, 1991); *Feminist Jurisprudence,* ed. Patricia Smith (New York: Oxford University Press, 1993); and *Feminist Legal Theory: Foundations,* ed. D. Kelly Weisberg (Philadelphia: Temple University Press, 1993).

4. See Shane Phelan, *Identity Politics: Lesbian Feminism and the Limits of Community* (Philadelphia: Temple University Press, 1989).

5. See the essays collected in *Home Girls: A Black Feminist Anthology,* ed. Barbara Smith (New York: Women of Color Press, Kitchen Table, 1983); and *This Bridge Called My Back: Writings by Radical Women of Color,* ed. Cherríe Moraga and Gloria Anzaldúa (New York: Women of Color Press, Kitchen Table, 1981).

6. Todd Gitlin, "The Rise of Identity Politics," *Dissent* (spring 1993), 172.

7. See the critical assessment of identity politics within feminism from Mary Louise Adams, "There's No Place Like Home: On the Place of Identity in Feminist Politics," *Feminist Review* 31 (spring 1989), 22–33.

8. Nancy Fraser, "Rethinking the Public Sphere: A Contribution to the Critique of Actually Existing Democracy," in *Habermas and the Public Sphere,* ed. Craig Calhoun (Cambridge: MIT Press, 1992), 123.

9. See Martha Minow, *Making All the Difference* (Ithaca: Cornell University Press, 1990), 36.

10. Ed Cohen, "Who are 'We'? Gay Identity as Political (E)motion," in *Inside/Out: Lesbian Theories, Gay Theories,* ed. Diana Fuss (New York: Routledge, 1991), 172.

11. Ibid., 73. See also Diana Fuss, *Essentially Speaking: Feminism, Nature, and Difference* (New York: Routledge, 1989), 104; Judith Butler, "Imitation and Gender Insubordination," in *Inside/Out* 13–31; and Bonnie Honig, "Toward an Agonistic Feminism: Hannah Arendt and the Politics of Identity," in *Feminists Theorize the Political,* ed. Judith Butler and Joan W. Scott (New York: Routledge, 1992), 215–235.

12. Combahee River Collective, "A Black Feminist Statement," in *This Bridge Called My Back,* ed. Moraga and Anzaldúa, 212.

13. Fuss, *Essentially Speaking,* 101.

14. See Nancy Fraser, "Toward a Discourse Ethic of Solidarity," *Praxis International* 5, no. 4 (January 1986), 425–429; and Richard Rorty, *Contingency, Irony, and Solidarity* (Cambridge: Cambridge University Press, 1989).

15. See Axel Honneth, "Integrität und Missachtung. Grundmotive einer Moral der Anerkennung," *Merkur* 12 (December 1990), 1043–1053; Jürgen Habermas, "Justice and Solidarity: On the Discussion Concerning Stage 6," *Philosophical Forum* 21, nos. 1–2 (fall–winter 1989–90), 32–52; and Sharon Welch, "An Ethic of Solidarity and Difference," in *Postmodernism, Feminism, and Cultural Politics,* ed. Henry A. Giroux (Albany: State University of New York Press, 1991), 83–99.

16. Kathleen B. Jones, *Compassionate Authority: Democracy and the Representation of Women* (New York: Routledge, 1993), 228–229.

17. Chandra Mohanty, "Cartographies of Struggle," introduction to *Third World Women and the Politics of Feminism,* ed. Chandra Talpade Mohanty, Ann Russo, and Lourdes Torres (Bloomington: Indiana University Press, 1991), 2.

18. See Nancy Fraser's interesting and important account of the possibility of alliances between poststructuralism and critical theory, "False Antitheses: A Response to Seyla Benhabib and Judith Butler," *Praxis International* 11, no. 2 (July 1991), 166–167. Pointing out the convergence between her arguments and various others often thought to represent "opposing camps," Bonnie Honig makes a similar point; see her *Political Theory and the Displacement of Politics* (Ithaca: Cornell University Press, 1993), 14.

19. See Richard J. Bernstein, *The New Constellation: The Ethical-Political Horizons of Modernity/Postmodernity* (Cambridge: MIT Press, 1992); Axel Honneth, "Das Andere der Gerechtigkeit: Habermas und die ethische Herausforderung der Postmoderne," *Deutsche Zeitschrift für Philosophie* 2 (1994), 195–220; Emilia Steuerman, "Habermas vs. Lyotard: Modernity vs. Postmodernity," in *Judging Lyotard,* ed. Andrew Benjamin (London: Routledge, 1992), 99–118; and Stephen White, *Political Theory and Postmodernism* (Cambridge: Cambridge University Press, 1991). Habermas himself has also acknowledged the importance of a Foucaultian approach, finding it "useful for revealing hidden asymmetries and power structures. . . . It's a good guess to suppose that most discourses are of that kind, that they do imply power structures that are not only hidden but systematically latent, that is, structurally concealed from their participants." See Jürgen Habermas, "Concluding Remarks," in *Habermas and the Public Sphere,* ed. Calhoun, 478.

1. Reflective Solidarity

1. I take this formulation, in part, from Ronald Dworkin, "A Year Later, the Debate Goes On," *New York Times Book Review*, 25 October 1992, 39. See also the essays on the Thomas hearings in *Race-ing Justice, En-gendering Power*, ed. Toni Morrison (New York: Pantheon Books, 1992).

2. bell hooks, *Feminist Theory: From Margin to Center* (Boston: South End Press, 1984), 43–65.

3. Judith Butler, *Gender Trouble: Feminism and the Subversion of Identity* (New York: Routledge, 1990), 14–15.

4. See Seyla Benhabib, "The Generalized and the Concrete Other," in *Feminism as Critique*, ed. Seyla Benhabib and Drucilla Cornell (Minneapolis: University of Minnesota Press, 1987), 87.

5. Ibid.

6. This expression comes from Elizabeth V. Spelman's "On Treating Persons as Persons," *Ethics* 88 (1977–78), 150–161. She writes, "I treat you as the person you are just insofar as I recognize and respond to those features of you which, in your view, are necessary to who you are" (151).

7. See also Axel Honneth's discussion of intimate relationships of mutual recognition in "Integrity and Disrespect," *Political Theory* 20, no. 2 (May 1992), 192–193.

8. Nel Noddings writes, "The caring attitude, that attitude which expresses our earliest store of memories of both caring and being cared for, is universally accessible." Nel Noddings, *Caring* (Berkeley: University of California Press, 1984), 5. See also Gilligan's contention that "an ethic of care rests on the premise of non-violence — that no one should be hurt." Carol Gilligan, *In a Different Voice* (Cambridge: Harvard University Press, 1982), 174.

9. See Noddings, *Caring*, 84.

10. Rorty, *Contingency, Irony, and Solidarity*, 192.

11. Ibid., 190.

12. Ibid.

13. This seems to be what Nancy Fraser has in mind with her concept of the standpoint of the collective concrete other: "This standpoint would require one to relate to people as members of collectivities or social groups with specific cultures, histories, social practices, values, habits, forms of life, vocabularies of self-interpretation and narrative traditions." Fraser, "Toward a Discourse Ethic of Solidarity," 428.

14. bell hooks, *Yearning: Race, Gender, and Cultural Politics* (Boston: South End Press, 1990), 37.

15. Dworkin, "A Year Later," 38.

16. Manning Marable, "Clarence Thomas and the Crisis of Black Political Culture," in *Race-ing Justice*, ed. Morrison, 74–75.

17. Dworkin, "A Year Later," 38.

18. Kimberlé Crenshaw, "Whose Story Is It, Anyway?" in *Race-ing Justice*, ed. Morrison, 417.

19. "The deification of Thomas and the vilification of Anita Hill were prefigured by practices within the black community that have long subordinated gender domination to the struggle against racism. In the process, the particular

experiences of black men have often come to represent the racial domination of the entire community, as is demonstrated by the symbolic currency of the lynching metaphor and the marginalization of representations of black female domination." Crenshaw, "Whose Story Is It, Anyway?" 417.

20. Kendall Thomas, "Strange Fruit," in *Race-ing Justice,* ed. Morrison, 370.

21. Crenshaw, "Whose Story Is It, Anyway?" 420.

22. Ibid., 435.

23. Compare Michael Walzer, "It is not difficult to imagine a community whose members have no honor to defend: their solidarity would be extraordinary, beyond all doubt, beyond testing." Michael Walzer, *Obligations: Essays on Disobedience, War and Citizenship* (Cambridge: Harvard University Press, 1970), 201.

24. See hooks's account of the way in which the expectation that one's "sisters" would provide unqualified approval at any point, that "sisters" were always to avoid conflict and mutual criticism, clashed with the confrontations and disagreements that were always part of the women's movement. hooks, *Feminist Theory,* 43–65.

25. For example, see Michael Sandel, *Liberalism and the Limits of Justice* (New York: Cambridge University Press, 1982).

26. Lynet Uttal, "Nods That Silence," in *Making Face, Making Soul: Haciendo Caras,* ed. Gloria Anzaldúa (San Francisco: Aunt Lute Books, 1990), 317–331.

27. Ibid., 318.

28. Ibid., 319.

29. My analysis of these two different ways of using the term "we" relies heavily on Jürgen Habermas's discussion of the asymmetry between speech acts in the first-person singular and first-person plural. He writes: "The expression "we" is used not only in collective speech actions vis-à-vis an addressee who assumes the communicative role of *you,* under the reciprocity condition that *we* in turn are *you* for them. In individual speech actions, *we* can also be used in such a way that a corresponding sentence presupposes not the complementary relation to another group but that to other individuals of one's own group." Jürgen Habermas, "The Development of Normative Structures," in *Communication and the Evolution of Society,* trans. Thomas McCarthy (Boston: Beacon Press, 1979), 107–108.

30. Uttal, "Nods That Silence," 319.

31. See also Charles Taylor's "Theories of Meaning," in *Human Agency and Language: Philosophical Papers,* vol. 1 (Cambridge: Cambridge University Press, 1985). He writes: "What the expression has done here is to create a rapport between us. . . . Language creates what one might call a public space, or a common vantage point from which we survey the world together" (259).

32. Uttal, "Nods That Silence," 319.

33. My discussion here draws from Jürgen Habermas, *The Theory of Communicative Action, vol. 1, Reason and the Rationalization of Society,* trans. Thomas McCarthy (Boston: Beacon Press, 1984), 302. Habermas argues that the binding effect of a speaker's utterance, its ability rationally to motivate a hearer's acceptance, stems not from the validity of the utterance itself, but from the *warranty* that the speaker can redeem the claim to validity. He thus distinguishes between

three components of action oriented toward reaching understanding: the *validity* of the action or underlying norm; the *claim* that the conditions for its validity are satisfied; and the *redemption* of the validity claim, in other words, grounding the claim that the conditions for the validity of the action or norm are satisfied.

34. Trinh T. Minh-ha, "Not You/Like You: Postcolonial Women and the Interlocking Questions of Identity and Difference," in *Making Face, Making Soul*, ed. Anzaldúa, 375.

35. Uttal, "Nods That Silence," 317.

36. George Herbert Mead, *Mind, Self, and Society* (1934, reprint, Chicago: The University of Chicago Press, 1962), 261.

37. See Linda Alcoff "Cultural Feminism versus Postmodernism: The Identity Crisis in Feminist Theory," *Signs* 13, no. 3 (1988), 405-436; Kimberlé Crenshaw, "Demarginalizing the Intersection of Race and Sex: A Black Feminist Critique of Antidiscrimination Doctrine, Feminist Theory and Antiracist Politics," in *Feminist Legal Theory: Foundations*, ed. Weisberg, 383-395; and Norma Alarcón, "The Theoretical Subject(s) of *This Bridge Called My Back* and Anglo-American Feminism," in *Making Face, Making Soul*, ed. Anzaldúa, 365-366.

38. Anzaldúa, *Borderlands*, 79.

39. Mead, *Mind, Self, and Society*, 168.

40. Benhabib, "The Generalized and the Concrete Other," 87.

41. Ibid.

42. Ibid.

43. Mead, *Mind, Self, and Society*, 154.

44. To be sure, respect for the difference of the other does *not* mean that one must blindly accept the other's claims. Depending on the context, the other, when questioned, may be obliged to offer good reasons for the assertion that her difference is relevant in the context at hand.

45. hooks, *Yearning*, 8.

46. Cornel West, "Black Leadership and the Pitfalls of Racial Reasoning," in *Race-ing Justice*, ed. Morrison, 397.

47. Iris Marion Young, *Justice and the Politics of Difference* (Princeton: Princeton University Press, 1990), 167.

48. I am indebted to Lutz Wingert for this point. See also Jürgen Habermas, *Faktizität und Geltung* (Frankfurt: Suhrkamp Verlag, 1992), 374.

49. Julia Kristeva, *Nations without Nationalism*, trans. Leon S. Roudiez (New York: Columbia University Press, 1993), 29.

50. Chantal Mouffe, "Democratic Citizenship and the Political Community," in *Dimensions of Radical Democracy*, ed. Chantal Mouffe (London: Verso, 1992), 234-235.

51. Elizabeth Mensch and Alan Freeman, *The Politics of Virtue* (Durham: Duke University Press, 1993).

52. See also Jürgen Habermas, "Nachholende Revolution und linker Revisionsbedarf: Was heisst Sozialismus heute?" in *Die Moderne — ein unvollendetes Projekt* (Leipzig: Reclam-Verlag, 1990). Habermas writes: "In the setting of a politically extensive integrated society, indeed one in the horizon of a worldwide communication net, the idea of a solidary social existence is itself only to be had in an abstract form, namely in the shape of a justifiable intersubjectively shared expectation. All would have to be able to expect from the institutionalized pro-

cedure of inclusive and democratic opinion and will-formation that these processes of public communication have for them a justifiable supposition of reasonableness and effectiveness" (232). (My translation).

53. Nancy Fraser explodes the ambiguities involved in the general assumption that people need shelter to live: "Do homeless people need forbearance, so
that they may sleep undisturbed next to a hot-air vent on a street corner? A
space in a subway tunnel or a bus terminal? A bed in a temporary shelter? A
permanent home? Suppose we say the latter. What kind of permanent housing
do homeless people need? Rental units in high-rises in central city areas remote
from good schools, discount shopping and job opportunities? Single-family
homes designed for single-earner, two-parent families? And what else do homeless people need in order to have permanent homes? Rent subsidies? Income
supports? Jobs? Job training and education? Day care?" Nancy Fraser, *Unruly
Practices: Power, Discourse and Gender in Contemporary Social Theory* (Minneapolis:
University of Minnesota Press, 1989), 163.

54. Rorty divides "the human race into the people to whom one must justify
one's beliefs and the others. The first group—one's *ethnos*—comprises those
who share enough of one's beliefs to make fruitful conversation possible." Richard Rorty, "Solidarity or Objectivity?" in *Objectivity, Relativism and Truth: Philosophical Papers, vol. 1* (Cambridge: Cambridge University Press, 1991), 30.

55. See Lutz Wingert, "Haben wir moralische Verpflichtungen gegenüber
früheren Generationen? Moralischer Universalismus und erinnernde Solidarität," *Babylon* 9 (November 1991), 78–93.

56. I owe this example to Carolin Emke.

57. Habermas, "Justice and Solidarity," 47.

2.   Struggling for Recognition

1. Henry A. Giroux, "Living Dangerously: Identity Politics and the New
Cultural Racism: Towards a Critical Pedagogy of Representation," *Cultural
Studies* 7, no. 1 (January 1993), 6.

2. See Wendy Brown, "Wounded Attachments," *Political Theory* 21, no. 3
(August 1993), 390–410; and Kirstie McClure, "On the Subject of Rights: Plu-
ralism, Plurality, and Political Identity," in *Dimensions of Radical Democracy,* ed.
Mouffe, 108–127.

3. For a brief yet comprehensive overview, see Steven Seidman, "Identity
and Politics in a 'Postmodern' Gay Culture: Some Historical and Conceptual
Notes," in *Fear of a Queer Planet: Queer Politics and Social Theory,* ed. Michael
Warner (Minneapolis: University of Minnesota Press, 1993), 105–142. For a
comparative and historical discussion of the lesbian and gay movement, see
Barry D. Adams, *The Rise of a Gay and Lesbian Movement* (Boston: G. K. Hall
and Company, 1987).

4. Seidman, "Identity and Politics," 111.

5. Adams, *The Rise of a Gay and Lesbian Movement,* 64.

6. Vera Whisman, "Identity Crises: Who Is a Lesbian, Anyway?" in *Sisters,*

Sexperts, Queers: Beyond the Lesbian Nation, ed. Arlene Stein (New York: Plume, 1993), 51.

7. See Phelan, *Identity Politics,* 37–45; and Radicalesbians, "The Woman-Identified Woman," in *Out of the Closets: Voices of Gay Liberation,* ed. Karla Jay and Allen Young (New York: New York University Press, 1972), 172.

8. Adrienne Rich, "Compulsory Heterosexuality and Lesbian Existence," in *The Lesbian and Gay Studies Reader,* ed. Henry Abelove, Michèle Aina Barale, and David M. Halperin (New York: Routledge, 1993), 239.

9. Thus, in *Lesbian Nation: The Feminist Solution* (New York: Simon and Schuster, 1977), Jill Johnson writes: "The lesbian/feminist is the woman who defines herself independently of a man" (153).

10. Cheryl Clarke, "Lesbianism: An Act of Resistance," in *This Bridge Called My Back,* ed. Moraga and Anzaldúa, 128.

11. Seidman, "Identity and Politics," 114. See also Allen Young, "Out of the Closets, Into the Streets," in *Out of the Closets,* ed. Jay and Young, 6–31.

12. Adams, *The Rise of a Gay and Lesbian Movement,* 78.

13. Douglas Crimp writes: "All queers have extensive experience with the closet, no matter how much of a sissy or tomboy we were as children, no matter how early we declared our sexual preferences, no matter how determined we are to be openly gay or lesbian. The closet is not a function of homosexuality in our culture, but of compulsory and presumptive heterosexuality." Douglas Crimp, "Right On, Girlfriend!" in *Fear of a Queer Planet,* ed. Warner, 305.

14. Judith Butler, "Imitation and Gender Subordination," in *Inside/Out,* ed. Fuss, 16.

15. Seidman, "Identity and Politics," 125.

16. See also Shane Phelan, "(Be)Coming Out: Lesbian Identity and Politics," *Signs* 18, no. 4 (summer 1993), 765–790.

17. Lisa Kahaleole Chang Hall, "Bitches in Solitude: Identity Politics and Lesbian Community," in *Sisters, Sexperts, Queers,* ed. Stein, 227.

18. See Cindy Patton's discussion of the connections between new-right and queer identity. She writes: "Gay identity comes from spilling the beans, from coming out of the closet to claim the other's derogatory speech as one's inverted reality. New-right identity cloisters self-revelation, reinterprets proud gay speech as confessions to the distinctive perversion that gay liberation's reversal sought to expose as fraud. If coming out says, 'We're queer, we're here, get used to it,' new-right identity appropriates this to say, 'We knew it,' and to society, 'We told you so.' What operates as a performative act of identity assertion for 'queers' is read by the new right as *descriptive,* as not performative at all." Cindy Patton, "Tremble, Hetero Swine!" in *Fear of a Queer Planet,* ed. Warner, 146–147.

19. Of course, the move away from separate strategies for lesbians and gay men and toward a larger alliance was also a result of the AIDS crisis and the increased homophobia of the eighties.

20. Hall, "Bitches in Solitude," 229. See also Biddy Martin, "Lesbian Identity and Autobiographical Difference[s]," in *The Lesbian and Gay Studies Reader,* ed. Abelove, Barale, and Halperin, 274–293.

21. Dan Danielson, "Representing Identities: Legal Treatment of Pregnancy and Homosexuality," *New England Law Review* 26 (summer 1992), 1453–1508.

22. Lauren Berlant and Elizabeth Freeman, "Queer Nationality," in *Fear of a Queer Planet*, ed. Warner, 193–229.

23. David J. Thomas, "Gay Political Visions: The 'Q' Word" (paper presented at the annual meeting of the American Political Science Association, Washington, D.C., September 1993), 21.

24. Ibid., 16.

25. See Janet E. Halley, "The Construction of Heterosexuality," in *Fear of a Queer Planet*, ed. Warner, 82–104; Teresa de Lauretis, "Queer Theory: Lesbian and Gay Studies, *An Introduction*," *differences* 3, no. 2 (1991), iii–xviii; John D'Emilio, "Capitalism and Gay Identity," in *The Lesbian and Gay Studies Reader*, ed. Abelove, Barale, and Halperin, 467–476; and Butler, *Gender Trouble*.

26. Cornell West, *Keeping Faith: Philosophy and Race in America* (New York: Routledge, 1993), 17.

27. Jean Smith, "I Learned to Feel Black," in *The Black Power Revolt*, ed. Floyd B. Barbour (Boston: Porter Sargent Publisher, 1968), 211.

28. West, *Keeping Faith*, 283.

29. Stokely Carmichael, "Power and Racism," in *The Black Power Revolt*, ed. Barbour, 65.

30. West, *Keeping Faith*, 279.

31. Glenn C. Loury, "Free at Last? A Personal Perspective on Race and Identity in America," in *Lure and Loathing: Essays on Race, Identity, and the Ambivalence of Assimilation*, ed. Gerald Early (New York: Penguin Books, 1993), 7–8.

32. For an interesting overview, see Diana Fuss's chapter "Poststructuralist Afro-American Literary Theory" in *Essentially Speaking*, 73–96.

33. hooks, *Yearning*, 37.

34. Ibid., 6.

35. West, *Keeping Faith*, 19–27.

36. A dialogue between bell hooks and Cornel West, "Black Women and Men: Partnership in the 1990s," in hooks, *Yearning*, 213.

37. Michael Eric Dyson, *Reflecting Black: African American Cultural Criticism* (Minneapolis: University of Minnesota Press, 1993), xvii.

38. West, *Keeping Faith*, 238.

39. Patricia Williams, *The Alchemy of Race and Rights* (Cambridge: Harvard University Press, 1991), 11.

40. Ibid., 67.

41. Ibid., 149.

42. Ibid., 234.

43. See Robin West, "Jurisprudence and Gender," in *Feminist Jurisprudence*, ed. Smith, 495–497.

44. Susan Sherwin, "Philosophical Methodology and Feminist Methodology: Are They Compatible?" in *Women, Knowledge and Rationality*, ed. Garry and Pearsall, 27.

45. See Judith Grant, *Fundamental Feminism: Contesting the Core Concepts of Feminist Theory* (New York: Routledge, 1993), 24–31.

46. Catharine A. MacKinnon, *Toward a Feminist Theory of the State* (Cambridge: Harvard University Press, 1989), 87.

47. Catharine A. MacKinnon, *Only Words* (Cambridge: Harvard University Press, 1993), 3.

48. Alarćon, "The Theoretical Subject(s)," 358–359.

49. One of the best critiques of "experience" comes from Joan W. Scott, "Experience," in *Feminists Theorize the Political,* ed. Butler and Scott, 22–40. See also Teresa de Lauretis, *Alice Doesn't* (Bloomington: Indiana University Press, 1984), especially chapter 6.

50. Butler, *Gender Trouble,* 14.

51. Ibid., 15.

52. Describing late-modern postindustrial societies, Wendy Brown writes: "The increased fragmentation, if not disintegration, of all forms of association until recently not organized by the commodities market — communities, churches, families — and the ubiquitousness of the classificatory, individuating schemes of disciplinary society combine to produce an utterly *unrelieved* individual, one without insulation from the inevitable failure entailed by liberalism's individualistic construction. In short, the characteristics of late modern secular society, in which individuals are buffeted and controlled by global configurations of disciplinary and capitalist power of extraordinary proportions, and are at the same time nakedly individuated, stripped of reprieve from relentless exposure and accountability for themselves, together add up to an incitement to ressentiment that might have stunned even the finest philosopher of its occasions and logics." Brown, "Wounded Attachments," 402.

53. See Jürgen Habermas, "Discourse Ethics: Notes on a Program of Philosophical Justification," in *Moral Consciousness and Communicative Action,* trans. Christian Lenhardt and Shierry Weber Nicholsen (Cambridge: MIT Press, 1990), 89.

54. Teresa de Lauretis, "Upping the Anti (Sic) in Feminist Theory," in *Conflicts in Feminism,* ed. Marianne Hirsch and Evelyn Fox Keller (New York: Routledge, 1990), 266.

55. Donna Haraway, *Simians, Cyborgs, and Women: The Reinvention of Nature* (New York: Routledge, 1991), 109.

56. Biddy Martin and Chandra Talpade Mohanty, "Feminist Politics: What's Home Got to Do with It?" in *Feminist Studies, Critical Studies,* ed. Teresa de Lauretis (Bloomington: Indiana University Press, 1986), 192.

57. Ibid., 210.

58. Ibid., 195.

59. Haraway, *Simians, Cyborgs, and Women,* 123.

60. Phelan, *Identity Politics,* 170.

61. Martha Minow shows this beautifully in *Making All the Difference.*

62. Dorothy Allison, *Skin: Talking About Sex, Class, and Literature* (Ithaca: Firebrand Books, 1994), 24–25.

3. Including Women

1. See Chantal Mouffe, "Feminism and Radical Politics," in *Feminists Theorize the Political,* ed. Butler and Scott, especially 373–377.

2. Jean Cohen and Andrew Arato, *Civil Society and Political Theory* (Cambridge: MIT Press, 1992).

3. Carole Pateman, "Feminist Critiques of the Public/Private Dichotomy," in *The Disorder of Women* (Stanford: Stanford University Press, 1989), 118–140.

4. Claude Lefort, "The Question of Democracy," in *Democracy and Political Theory*, trans. David Macey (Minneapolis: University of Minnesota Press, 1988), 17.

5. Claude Lefort, "Permanence of the Theologico-Political?" in *Democracy and Political Theory*, ed. Macey, 226.

6. Lefort, "Permanence of the Theologico-Political," 227; "The Question of Democracy," 18.

7. For example, important discussions have focused both on the notion of a black public sphere and the relevance of the concept of the public sphere to African American political history. This work, although it often draws attention to the position of black women, generally thematizes race and the problem of racial exclusions within the modern conception of the public in a way similar to the feminist focus on gender and sexual difference. See Elsa Barkley Brown, "Negotiating and Transforming the Public Sphere," *Public Culture* 7, no. 1 (fall 1994), 108–112; and, in the same issue, Michael Dawson, "A Black Counterpublic?" 195–223.

8. Early overviews of feminist theory tended to use the categories of liberal feminist, marxist feminist, socialist feminist, and radical feminist. As the complexity of the debate grew during the early eighties, the categories of black feminism, cultural feminism, lesbian feminism, psychoanalytic feminism, and French feminism were added and then supplemented by various subgroups like black lesbian feminism, S/M lesbian feminism, dual structuralist feminism, and so forth. While these distinctions have been useful in pinpointing the diversity of women's experiences and concerns, they often serve to occlude the formal similarities among the various types of feminist argument. For an interesting account of the way some of the similarities emerged out of radical feminism, see Grant, *Fundamental Feminism*.

9. As in, for example, the classic texts by Mary Wollstonecraft, Olympe de Gouges, Harriet Taylor and John Stuart Mill, Elizabeth Cady Stanton, and Susan B. Anthony.

10. The effort to secure an Equal Rights Amendment in the United States is a clear example. See also the Bill of Rights of the National Organization of Women. For a defense of the continuing struggle for rights against the Critical Legal Studies critique, see Elizabeth M. Schneider, "The Dialectics of Rights and Politics: Perspectives from the Women's Movement," in *At the Boundaries of Law*, ed. Fineman and Thomadsen, 301–319. For a thorough account of the successes, failures, and general complexity surrounding women's rights claims, see Deborah L. Rhode, *Justice and Gender* (Cambridge: Harvard University Press, 1989).

11. See Frances Fox Piven, "Women and the State: Ideology, Power and the Welfare State," and Alice Kessler-Harris, "The Debate over Equality for Women in the Workplace: Recognizing Differences," both in *Families and Work*, ed. Naromi Gerstel and Harriet Engel Gross (Philadelphia: Temple University Press, 1987).

12. See Lorenne M. G. Clark, "Women and Locke: Who Owns the Apples

in the Garden of Eden," in *The Sexism of Social and Political Theory,* ed. Lorenne M. G. Clark and Lynda Lange (Toronto: University of Toronto Press, 1979), 16–40; Christine Di Stefano, "Masculinity as Ideology in Political Theory: Hobbesian Man Reconsidered," in *Hypatia Reborn,* ed. Azizah Y. Al-Hibri and Margaret A. Simons (Bloomington: Indiana University Press, 1990), 90–109; Zillah Eisenstein, *The Radical Future of Liberal Feminism* (New York: Longman Press, 1979); Jean Bethke Elshtain, *Public Man, Private Woman* (Princeton: Princeton University Press, 1981); Joan B. Landes, *Women and the Public Sphere in the Age of the French Revolution* (Ithaca: Cornell University Press, 1988); Lynda Lange, "Rousseau on Women," in *The Sexism of Social and Political Theory,* ed. Clark and Lange, 42–52; Linda Nicholson, *Gender and History* (New York: Columbia University Press, 1986); Patricia Jagentowitcz Mills, "Hegel and the Woman Question," in *The Sexism of Social and Political Theory,* ed. Clark and Lange, 74–98; and Susan Moller Okin, *Women in Western Political Thought* (Princeton: Princeton University Press, 1979).

13. See especially Landes's account of the development of a gendered conception of the public sphere as it emerged during the French Revolution. She writes that "while the norms of publicity, authenticity, transparency and universal reason may have affirmed men's participation in the public realm, an emerging code of gender propriety prescribed that women were most in conformity with these norms when their behavior and conduct were least public." Landes, *Women and the Public Sphere,* 147.

14. Rhode, *Justice and Gender,* 94, 96.

15. Rhode writes: "Female flight attendants in hot pants and high boots allegedly were necessary to personify Southwest's [Airlines] 'sexy image' and take passengers 'skyward with love.'" Ibid., 94. Naomi Wolf, *The Beauty Myth* (London: Vintage, 1991), 37–42.

16. See Christine Di Stefano, *Configurations of Masculinity: A Feminist Perspective on Modern Political Theory* (Ithaca: Cornell University Press, 1991).

17. "The civil sphere gains its universal meaning in opposition to the private sphere of natural subjection and womanly capacities. The 'civil individual' is constituted within the sexual division of social life created through the original contract. The civil individual and the public realm appear universal only in relation to and in opposition to the private sphere, the natural foundation of civil life. Similarly, the meaning of civil liberty and equality, secured and distributed impartially to all 'individuals' through the civil law, can be understood only in opposition to natural subjection (of women) in the private sphere. Liberty and equality appear as universal ideals, rather than as the natural attributes of the men (the brothers) who create the social order within which the ideals are given social expression, only because the civil sphere is conventionally considered on its own. Liberty, equality *and* fraternity form the revolutionary trilogy because liberty and equality are the attributes of the fraternity who exercise the law of male sex right." Carole Pateman, *The Sexual Contract* (Stanford: Stanford University Press, 1988), 113–114. See also Pateman's essays in *The Disorder of Women.*

18. "The unbreachable line between public and private values rests on the tacit assumption that women will continue to preserve and protect personal life, the task to which they have been assigned. In this way the political morality can

sustain the fiction of the wholly autonomous individual, whose main concern is a system of rights that protects him from other individuals like himself. The public world is conceived as a place in which direct recognition and care for others' needs is impossible — and that is tolerable as long as the private world 'cooperates.'" Jessica Benjamin, *The Bonds of Love* (New York: Pantheon, 1988), 197.

19. "Feminism does not begin with the premise that it is unpremised. It does not aspire to persuade an unpremised audience, because there is no such audience. Its project is to uncover and claim as valid the experiences of women, the major content of which is the devalidation of women's experience. This defines the task of feminism not only because male dominance is perhaps the most pervasive and tenacious system of power in history, but because it is metaphysically nearly perfect. Its point of view is the standard for point-of-viewlessness, its particularity the meaning of universality. Its force is exercised as consent, its authority as participation, its supremacy as the paradigm of order, its control as the definition of legitimacy. In the face of this, feminism claims the voice of women's silence, the fullness of 'lack,' the centrality of women's marginality and exclusion, the public nature of privacy, the presence of women's absence." Catharine A. MacKinnon, *Toward a Feminist Theory of the State* (Cambridge: Harvard University Press, 1989), 117.

20. Habermas, "Nachholende Revolution und linker Revisionsbedarf," 232. (My translation.)

21. Young, *Justice and the Politics of Difference,* 110–111.

22. Habermas, "Discourse Ethics," 66.

23. Klaus Günther, "Universalistische Normbegründung und Normanwendung in Recht und Moral," in *Generalisierung und Individualisierung im Rechtsdenken,* ed. M. Herberger, U. Neumann, and H. Russmann (Stuttgart: Franz Steiner Verlag, 1992), 6–7. Habermas, "Discourse Ethics," 83–85.

24. Benhabib, "The Generalized and the Concrete Other," 81.

25. Jürgen Habermas, "Morality, Society and Ethics," *Acta Sociologica* 33 (1990), 96–97.

26. See Klaus Günther, *Der Sinn für Angemessenheit: Anwendungsdiskurse in Moral und Recht* (Frankfurt: Suhrkamp Verlag, 1988).

27. See Günther, "Universalistische Normbegründung und Normanwendung."

28. See Susan Moller Okin's discussion of the breakdown of a clear distinction between the domestic and public spheres in *Justice, Gender and the Family* (New York: Basic Books, 1989), 128–133. See also Donna Haraway's rejection of the public/private distinction and her notion of the "integrated circuit," in *Simians, Cyborgs, and Women,* 170 ff.

29. "It has been common forever to speak of the public functions of the family in producing and socializing the 'next generation.' Using this and other rationales the state attempts to determine the content of and then enforce the performance of familial roles, both of parents and children. Modern statutory schemes authorize social welfare agencies backed by the courts to intervene on no more precise grounds than 'the best interests of the child' or the child's 'need for supervision.'" Duncan Kennedy, "The Stages of the Decline of the Public/Private Distinction," *University of Pennsylvania Law Review* 139 (1982), 1356. See

also Frances Olsen, "The Family and the Market: A Study of Ideology and Social Reform," *Harvard Law Review* 96, no. 7 (May 1983), 1497–1578.

30. See Carol B. Stack's discussion of the complexities of household composition in a poor section of an American Midwestern community, "Sex Roles and Survival Strategies in an Urban Black Family," in *Woman, Culture and Society*, eds. Michelle Zimbalist Rosaldo and Louise Lamphere (Stanford: Stanford University Press, 1974), 113–128. Additionally, Frances Olsen's "The Myth of State Intervention in the Family" reveals some of the ways in which the designation of a group as a family tends to empower some members at the expense of others. In *Journal of Law Reform* 18, no. 4 (summer 1985), 835–864.

31. Fraser, "Rethinking the Public Sphere," 109–142.

32. For example, see Elshtain, *Public Man, Private Woman;* and Annette C. Baier, "What Do Women Want in a Moral Theory?" *Nous* 19, no. 1, 53–63.

33. Jürgen Habermas, "Three Normative Models of Democracy," *Constellations* 1, no. 1 (April 1994), 1.

34. Cohen and Arato, *Civil Society and Political Theory*, 346.

35. In their critique of Foucault (and Luhmann), Cohen and Arato refer to the following concepts as the "key categories" of civil society: the juridical subject; the autonomous, self-reflective moral individual; normativity; legality; publicity; democratic control; and plurality. Jean Cohen and Andrew Arato, "Politics and the Reconstruction of the Concept of Civil Society," in *Zwischenbetrachtungen Im Prozess der Aufklärung*, ed. Axel Honneth, Thomas McCarthy, Claus Offe, and Albrecht Wellmer (Frankfurt: Surhkamp Verlag, 1989), 490. I will not address legality and normativity per se insofar as these concepts are intertwined with the notions of the juridical subject and the autonomous, self-reflective moral individual.

36. My alternative to the public/private distinction thus differs from Chantal Mouffe's. Although I agree with her that "every situation is an encounter between 'private' and 'public,'" I disagree with her claim that "wants, choices, and decisions are private" while "performances" are public. As I see it, wants, choices, and decisions have a public dimension in that they are constructed interrelationally and always situated in cultural representations, discourses, and matrixes of power. In other words, we can be called upon to defend and justify our choices and decisions and we are often accountable for the ways in which wants and decisions are constructed and imputed. See Mouffe, "Feminism and Radical Politics," 378.

37. Cohen and Arato conceive of five complexes of rights: those concerning cultural reproduction (freedoms of thought, press, speech, communication); those insuring social integration (freedoms of association, assembly); those securing socialization (protection of privacy, intimacy, inviolability of the person); those mediating between civil society and the capitalist economy (rights of property, contract, labor); and those mediating between civil society and the modern bureaucratic state (electoral rights of citizens, welfare rights of clients). See Cohen and Arato, "Politics and the Reconstruction of the Concept of Civil Society," 441. While a number of these rights would clearly fall under the general category of discursive rights (inviolability of the person, freedom of thought and speech, freedom of association), others would lose their fundamental character and become just one consideration among others within a dilemma or dispute.

38. Rhode, *Justice and Gender*, 3.

39. Cohen and Arato, "Politics and the Reconstruction of the Concept of Civil Society," 490.

40. Dyson, *Reflecting Black*, xxiii.

41. As Cohen and Arato argue: "Both the complexity of and the diversity within contemporary civil societies call for the posing of the issue of democratization in terms of a variety of differential processes, forms, and loci depending on the axis of division considered," Cohen and Arato, "Politics and the Reconstruction of the Concept of Civil Society," 415.

42. Ibid., 417.

4.   Solidarity and Legal Indeterminacy

1. Lefort, "The Question of Democracy," 19.

2. Habermas, *Faktizität und Geltung*, 78. I am indebted to William Rehg for making available to me his translation of this text. Unless otherwise noted, all translations are his.

3. Ibid., 141.

4. Ibid., 144.

5. See Minow, *Making All the Difference*, 292–303.

6. Habermas, *Faktizität und Geltung*, 68.

7. Claude Lefort, "Human Rights and the Welfare State," in *Democracy and Political Theory*, trans. Macey, 39.

8. See Margaret Jane Radin and Frank Michelman, "Pragmatist and Poststructuralist Critical Legal Practice, *University of Pennsylvania Law Review* 139, no. 4 (1982), 1024–1027; Habermas, *Faktizität und Geltung*, 247–248; and Drucilla Cornell, *The Philosophy of the Limit* (New York: Routledge, 1992). Cornell writes: "Legal positivism argues that legal systems are self-enclosed hierarchies that generate their own elements and procedures as part of the mechanism of the self-perpetuation of the system. In Anglo-American jurisprudence, legal positivism has traditionally been based on the writing of H. L. A. Hart. Hart proposed that all legal systems are based on the master rule of recognition, which establishes the initial hierarchies of the elements of the legal system. From out of this master rule of recognition, Hart argued that it would be possible to directly derive two categories of secondary rules: the rules of process by which the law is applied, and then the rules of prescription we think of as doctrine in a common law system" (101).

9. Minow, *Making All the Difference*, 164. For an overview of the Critical Legal Studies (CLS) movement, see Mark Kelman, *A Guide to Critical Legal Studies* (Cambridge: Harvard University Press, 1987). For a collection of CLS writings that includes a number of seminal works from Duncan Kennedy, Clare Dalton, Frances Olsen, Peter Gabel, and Mark Tushnet, see Allan C. Hutchinson, ed., *Critical Legal Studies* (Totowa, N.J.: Rowman and Littlefield Publishers, 1989).

10. Radin and Michelman, "Pragmatist and Poststructuralist Critical Legal Practice," 1036. For an analysis which condenses the various versions of the in-

determinacy thesis in CLS circles into three main variants ("the unruly social-political world," "the unruly legal practice," and "the unruly rule of law"), see Günter Frankenberg, "Down by Law: Irony, Seriousness, and Reason," *Northwestern University Law Review* 83, nos. 1–2 (fall–winter 1988), 391–393.

11. Cornell, *The Philosophy of the Limit,* 101.

12. Drucilla Cornell, *Transformations* (New York: Routledge, 1993), 25.

13. For a discussion of the process of application in communications-theoretic terms (application discourses), see Günther, *Der Sinn für Angemessenheit,* and "Universalistische Normbegründung und Normanwendung."

14. Frank Michelman, "Law's Republic," *Yale Law Journal* 97 (1988), 1513–1514 (citations omitted).

15. Ibid., 1529.

16. See Günther, "Universalistische Normbegründung und Normanwendung," 28–31. Similarly, Duncan Kennedy writes: "It is impossible to think about the legal system without some categorical scheme. We simply cannot grasp the infinite multiplicity of particular instances without abstractions. Further, the edifice of categories is a social construction, carried on over centuries, which makes it possible to know much more than we could know if we had to reinvent our abstractions in each generation. It is therefore a priceless acquisition. On the other hand, all such schemes are lies. They cabin and distort our immediate experience, and they do so systematically rather than randomly." Duncan Kennedy, "The Structure of Blackstone's Commentaries," in *Critical Legal Studies,* ed. Hutchinson, 142.

17. *Bowers v Hardwick,* 478 US 186 (1986) (upholding Georgia sodomy law). Among others see, Richard D. Mohr, *Gays/Justice: A Study of Ethics, Society, and Law* (New York: Columbia University Press, 1988); Phelan, *Identity Politics;* and Vincent J. Samar, *The Right to Privacy: Gays, Lesbians, and the Constitution* (Philadelphia: Temple University Press, 1991).

18. For a good example of a strategic use of the division aimed at reformulating privacy see Elizabeth M. Schneider, "The Violence of Privacy," *Connecticut Law Review* 23 (1991), 973–999.

19. Much of the success in this area can be attributed to the work of Catharine MacKinnon. See her *Feminism Unmodified* (Cambridge: Harvard University Press, 1987), 103–116; and *Sexual Harassment of Working Women* (New Haven: Yale University Press, 1979).

20. *Meritor Savings Bank, FSB v Vinson,* 477 US 57 (1986) (holding that "hostile environment" harassment is a form of sex discrimination in violation of Title VII).

21. *Meritor,* at 65 and 67 (quoting *Henson v Dundee,* 682 F2d 897, 904 [11th Cir 1982]). A number of feminist commentators have pointed out the similarity between the consent standard in rape law and the unwelcome requirement in sexual harassment law. For critical discussions of the unwelcome requirement, see Martha Chamallas, "Consent, Equality, and the Legal Control of Sexual Conduct," *Southern California Law Review* 61 (1988), 777–862; Susan Estrich, "Sex at Work," *Stanford Law Review* 43, no. 4 (1991), 813–861; and "Note: Did She Ask for It?: The 'Unwelcome' Requirement in Sexual Harassment Cases," *Cornell Law Review* 77 (1992), 1558–1592.

22. See Lucinda M. Finley, "A Break in the Silence: Including Women's Issues in a Torts Course," *Yale Journal of Law and Feminism* 1 (1989), 41–73.

23. *Rabidue v Osceola Refining Co.*, 805 F2d 611 (6th Cir 1986), *cert. denied*, 481 US 1041 (1987), at 627 (Keith, J., dissenting).

24. *Rabidue*, at 624 (Keith, J., dissenting).

25. *Ellison v Brady*, 924 F2d 872 (9th Cir 1991).

26. *Ellison*, at 878–880.

27. Eileen M. Blackwood, "The Reasonable Woman in Sexual Harassment Law and the Case for Subjectivity," *Vermont Law Review* 16 (1992), 1021. See also Deborah S. Brenneman, "From a Reasonable Woman's Point of View: The Use of the Reasonable Woman Standard in Sexual Harassment Cases," *Cincinnati Law Review* 60 (1992), 1281–1306.

28. Estrich, "Sex at Work," 846; and Kathryn Abrams, "Gender Discrimination and the Transformation of Workplace Norms," *Vanderbilt Law Review* 42 (1989), 1202.

29. Naomi R. Cahn, "The Looseness of Legal Language: The Reasonable Woman Standard in Theory and in Practice," *Cornell Law Review* 77 (1992), 1416.

30. See Blackwood, "The Reasonable Woman," 1023; Cahn, "The Looseness of Legal Language," 1403.

31. Finley, "A Break in the Silence," 64; Cahn, "The Looseness of Legal Language," 1416.

32. Blackwood, "The Reasonable Woman," 1005.

33. Nancy S. Ehrenreich, "Pluralist Myths and Powerless Men: The Ideology of Reasonableness in Sexual Harassment Law," *Yale Law Journal* 99, no. 6 (1990), 1178. As she makes this argument, Ehrenreich is following Duncan Kennedy's method in "The Structure of Blackstone's Commentaries."

34. Ibid., 1188–1189.

35. Ibid., 1191.

36. Ibid., 1198.

37. Ibid.

38. Ibid., 1206.

39. *Rabidue*, (Keith, J., dissenting) at 624.

40. Ehrenreich, "Pluralist Myths," 1223.

41. Ibid., 1224.

42. I am indebted to Karen Engle for pointing out the potentially radical character of Ehrenreich's formulation.

43. To be sure, the understanding that sex is at the basis of sexual harassment has tended to have been overlooked in the focus on "welcomeness" (*Meritor*) and the reasonableness of the victim's claims (*Rabidue, Ellison*). Nonetheless, I contend that it is precisely the element of sex that operates underneath decisions in sexual harassment cases and that must be brought to the fore.

44. Ehrenreich, "Pluralist Myths," 1210.

45. *Rabidue*, at 623.

46. *Rabidue*, at 623.

47. *Rabidue*, at 624 (Keith, J., dissenting).

48. *Rabidue*, at 624 (Keith, J., dissenting).

49. *Ellison*, at 873.

50. *Ellison,* at 879.

51. *Ellison,* at 880.

52. *Theresa Harris v Forklift Systems, Inc.,* 1993 WL 453611 (US) (holding that to be actionable as "abusive work environment harassment" conduct need not seriously affect an employee's psychological well-being or lead the plaintiff to suffer injury).

53. *Harris,* at 2.

54. Indeed, in his concurring opinion Justice Scalia writes: "'Abusive' (or 'hostile,' which in this context I take to mean the same thing) does not seem to me a very clear standard—and I do not think clarity is at all increased by adding the adverb 'objectively' or by appealing to a 'reasonable person's' notion of what the vague word means. Today's opinion does list a number of factors that contribute to abusiveness . . . but since it neither says how much of each is necessary (an impossible task) nor identifies any single factor as determinative, it thereby adds little certitude. As a practical matter, today's holding lets virtually unguided juries decide whether sex-related conduct engaged in (or permitted by) an employer is egregious enough to warrant an award of damages." *Harris,* at 5.

55. *Harris,* at 3.

56. Ehrenreich, "Pluralist Myths," 1205.

57. *Griswold v Connecticut,* 381 US 479 (1965) (holding that Connecticut birth-control law violates right of marital privacy).

58. The *Lochner* era was characterized by the active intervention of the judiciary. Courts in this period used the Due Process clause to strike down economic regulation. For an overview, see Cass R. Sunstein, *After the Rights Revolution: Reconceiving the Regulatory State* (Cambridge: Harvard University Press, 1990), 11–46.

59. *Eisenstadt v Baird,* 405 US 438 (1972) (striking down Massachusetts law prohibiting the transfer of contraceptives to single persons).

60. *Roe v Wade,* 410 US 113 (1973) (allowing for abortion).

61. See Ruth Colker, *Abortion and Dialogue* (Bloomington: Indiana University Press, 1992); Norman Viera, "*Hardwick* and the Right of Privacy," *The University of Chicago Law Review* 55 (1988), 1181–1191; Rosalind Pollack Petchesky, *Abortion and Woman's Choice* (Boston: Northeastern University Press, 1990); Reva Siegel, "Reasoning from the Body: A Historical Perspective on Abortion Regulation and Questions of Equal Protection," *Stanford Law Review* 44 (January 1992), 261–381; and Kendall Thomas, "Beyond the Privacy Principle" *Columbia Law Review* 92 (1992), 1431–1516.

62. See Jean L. Cohen, "Redescribing Privacy: Identity, Difference, and the Abortion Controversy," *Columbia Journal of Gender and Law* 3, no. 1 (1992), 43–117; Rhonda Copelon, "Losing the Negative Right of Privacy: Building Sexual and Reproductive Freedom," *Review of Law and Social Change* 18 (1990–91), 15–50; Morris B. Kaplan, "Autonomy, Equality, Community: The Question of Lesbian and Gay Rights," *Praxis International* 11, no. 2 (July 1991), 195–213; Michelman, "Law's Republic"; and Jeb Rubenfeld, "The Right of Privacy," *Harvard Law Review* 102, no. 4 (February 1989), 737–807.

63. Copelon, "Losing the Negative Right of Privacy," 41.

64. Ibid., 45 (emphasis added).

65. Faye D. Ginsburg, *Contested Lives: The Abortion Debate in an American Community* (Berkeley: University of California Press, 1989); and Kristin Luker, *Abortion and the Politics of Motherhood* (Berkeley: University of California Press, 1984).

66. Ginsburg, *Contested Lives,* 110.

67. For an interesting discussion of the variety of conceptions of identity in discrimination law, see Dan Danielson, "Representing Identities: Legal Treatment of Pregnancy and Homosexuality," *New England Law Review* 26 (summer 1992), 1453–1508.

68. *Bowers,* at 2843.

69. As Nan Hunter points out, "Opponents of the rights claim [of lesbians and gay men] have focused on the volitional nature of sexual conduct." See Nan Hunter, "Life after *Hardwick,*" *Harvard Civil Rights–Civil Liberties Law Review* 27 (1992), 549 (citations omitted).

70. *Bowers,* at 2847 (Blackmun, J., dissenting).

71. *Bowers,* at 2852 (Blackmun, J., dissenting) (citation omitted).

72. See also the brief amicus curiae for Lesbian Rights Project et al. in support of Michael Hardwick. It provides a privacy argument constructed in terms of choice and sameness. *Review of Law and Social Change* 14 (1986), 953–972.

73. See Thomas, "Beyond the Privacy Principle," 1443–1448. In addition to the relational and decisional models of privacy, Thomas provides an overview of the zonal conception of privacy. This third model, which lies beyond the scope of my discussion, can be summed up by the phrase, "a man's home is his castle." In other words, here privacy protects particular spaces from government intrusion.

74. Karen Engle makes a similar point with regard to the power of the private in international law in "After the Collapse of the Public/Private Distinction: Strategizing Women's Rights," in *Reconceiving Reality: Woman and International Law,* ed. Dorinda G. Dallmeyer (Washington, D.C.: American Society of International Law, 1993), 149–150.

75. As Jeb Rubenfeld argues, "Underlying the idea that a woman is *defining her identity* by determining not to have a child is the very premise of those institutionalized sexual roles through which the subordination of women has so long been maintained." Rubenfeld, "The Right of Privacy," 782.

76. Ibid.

77. *Planned Parenthood of Southeastern Pennsylvania v Robert P. Casey,* 112 Sup. Ct. 2791 (1992).

78. Halley, "The Construction of Heterosexuality," 90.

79. As Cindy Patton writes: "Homosexuals' attempts to gain protection to practice sex as private have produced a legal paradox: to insert privacy in the already accepted package of civil rights (to political participation, equal access, protection from discrimination) requires establishing lesbians and gay men as a publicly inscribed class. In the most immediate sense, a gay person must 'come out' in order to get the right to privacy." Patton, "Tremble, Hetero Swine," 170.

80. Thomas, "Beyond the Privacy Principle," 1455.

81. See Michelman, "Law's Republic," 1534–1535.

82. Cohen, "Redescribing Privacy," 59.

83. Ibid., 113, note 212.

84. Kenneth Karst, "Forward: Equal Citizenship under the Fourteenth Amendment," *Harvard Law Review* 91, no. 1 (November 1977), 32.

85. Ibid.

86. As Jean Cohen points out, "The personal dynamics of shifting involvements among separate spheres, roles, and commitments required by life in a highly differentiated modern society create the need and the possibility for each individual to develop a strong sense of self, along with the ability to form, affirm, and express *her unique identity* as it develops and changes over time in an open multiplicity of contexts." Cohen, "Redescribing Privacy," 99.

87. Ibid., 48.

88. Williams, *The Alchemy of Race and Rights*, 146–165.

89. Morris Kaplan, "Intimacy and Equality: The Question of Lesbian and Gay Marriage," *Philosophical Forum* 25, no. 4 (summer 1994), 354.

90. Cohen, "Redescribing Privacy," 116.

91. Ibid., 112.

92. Michelman makes a similar point: "Just as property rights—rights of having and holding material resources—become, in a republican perspective, a matter of constitutive political concern as underpinning the independence and authenticity of the citizen's contribution to the collective determinations of public life, so is it with the privacies of personal refuge and intimacy." Michelman, "Law's Republic," 1535.

93. See Habermas, "Three Normative Models of Democracy." Habermas writes: "Discourse theory altogether jettisons certain premises of the *philosophy of consciousness*. These premises either invite us to ascribe the praxis of civic self-determination to one encompassing macro-subject or they have us apply the rule of law to many isolated private subjects. The former approach views the citizenry as a collective actor that reflects the whole and acts for it; in the latter, individual actors function as dependent variables in system processes that move along blindly. Discourse theory works instead with the *higher-level intersubjectivity* of communication processes that flow through both the parliamentary bodies and the informal networks of the public sphere" (13).

94. Cohen, "Redescribing Privacy," 100.

95. Ibid., 102–103, note 169.

96. See Mary Joe Frug, *Postmodern Legal Feminism* (New York: Routledge, 1992), 123.

97. Habermas, *Faktizität und Geltung*, 152–154.

98. Michelman, "Law's Republic," 1529.

99. Ibid., 1529.

5.   Feminism and Universalism

1. Trinh, *Framer Framed*, 185.

2. Ibid.

3. See Seyla Benhabib, "The Generalized and the Concrete Other," *Situating the Self: Gender, Community and Postmodernism in Contemporary Ethics* (New York: Routledge, 1992), 148–177; Jessica Benjamin, *The Bonds of Love* (New York: Pantheon Books, 1988); Clark, "Women and Locke," 16–40; Di Stefano, "Mas-

culinity as Ideology in Political Theory," 90–109; Eisenstein, *The Radical Future of Liberal Feminism;* Elshtain, *Public Man, Private Woman;* Alison Jaggar, *Feminist Politics and Human Nature* (Totowa, N.J.: Rowman and Allenheld, 1983); Lange, "Rousseau on Women," 42–52; Genevieve Lloyd, "The Man of Reason," in *Women, Knowledge and Reality,* ed. Garry and Pearsall, 111–128; Nicholson, *Gender and History;* MacKinnon, *Toward a Feminist Theory of the State;* Okin, *Women in Western Political Theory;* Pateman, *The Disorder of Women,* and "'God Hath Ordained to Man a Helper': Hobbes, Patriarchy and Conjugal Right," in *Feminist Interpretations and Political Theory,* ed. Mary Lyndon Shanley and Carole Pateman (University Park, Penn.: University of Pennsylvania Press, 1991), 53–73; and Iris Marion Young, "Impartiality and the Civic Public," in *Feminism as Critique,* ed. Benhabib and Cornell, 56–76.

4. Butler, "Contingent Foundations," 7.

5. Ibid.

6. Ibid., 6.

7. Ibid., 7.

8. Ibid., 7.

9. Ibid., 8.

10. Ibid., 12.

11. Ibid., 9–10.

12. Ibid., 10.

13. Ibid., 11.

14. Ibid., 13.

15. See Fraser's "False Antithesis," 173.

16. See Habermas, *The Theory of Communicative Action,* vol. 1, 2: "All attempts at discovering ultimate foundations, in which the intentions of First Philosophy live one, have broken down."

17. Jürgen Habermas, "Philosophy as Stand-in and Interpreter," and "Reconstruction and Interpretation in the Social Sciences," in *Moral Consciousness and Communicative Action,* trans. Lenhardt and Nicholsen; and Jürgen Habermas, "Erläuterungen zur Diskursethik," in *Erläuterungen zur Diskursethik* (Frankfurt: Suhrkamp Verlag, 1991), 190–196. See also Seyla Benhabib, *Critique, Norm, and Utopia* (New York: Columbia University Press, 1986), 280–282; and Stephen White, *The Recent Work of Jürgen Habermas* (Cambridge: Cambridge University Press, 1988), 128–136.

18. bell hooks, *Talking Back: Thinking Feminist, Thinking Black* (Boston: South End Press, 1989), 31.

19. Ibid., 42–43.

20. Butler, "Contingent Foundations," 8–9.

21. Quoted by Patricia Williams in "Lani, We Hardly Knew Ye: How the Right Created a Monster out of a Civil Rights Advocate and Bill Clinton Ran in Terror," *The Village Voice* 38, no. 24 (15 June 1993), 27.

22. Ibid.

23. See Jürgen Habermas's discussion of Nietzsche, Horkheimer, and Adorno in "The Entwinement of Myth and Enlightenment: Re-Reading *Dialectic of Enlightenment,*" trans. Thomas Y. Levin, *New German Critique* 26 (spring–summer 1982), 13–30.

24. Habermas, "Discourse Ethics," 66.

25. Habermas, *The Theory of Communicative Action*, vol. 1, 19.

26. Habermas, "Discourse Ethics," 89.

27. Jürgen Habermas, "Moralbewusstsein und kommunikatives Handeln," in *Moralbewusstsein und kommunikatives Handeln* (Frankfurt: Suhrkamp Verlag, 1983), 131. (My translation. The English version mistakenly refers to the particular interests of each. See "Moral Consciousness and Communicative Action," in *Moral Consciousness and Communicative Action*, trans. Lenhardt and Nicholsen, 120.)

28. Habermas, "Discourse Ethics," 65.

29. See Günther, "Universalistische Normbegründung und Normanwendung," 6–7; and Habermas, "Discourse Ethics," 66–68.

Habermas justifies the universalization principle with two arguments. First, he grounds it on the presuppositions of argumentation through a "transcendental-pragmatic derivation." Insofar as participants in discourse have to observe the rules outlined above, they implicitly acknowledge the universalization principle. If they do not observe these rules, they permit a "performative contradiction." For example, if I try to claim that certain people should not be allowed to express their views in a discussion regarding the validity of a norm that applies to them, I would first have to convince them that they should be excluded. Yet by including them in *this* discussion, I am already contradicting my previous intention to exclude them. But why, one might ask, do I enter into argumentation at all? Couldn't I simply refrain from talking about norms and go on excluding whomever I please? The answer to this question provides the second justification of the universalization principle. Habermas argues that once we understand argumentation as a reflective, more demanding type of communication, we see that, as members of ethical communities, we have no choice but to enter into practical discourse. Simply put, we are deeply intermeshed within relationships and societies. Our identities, in fact, are dependent upon them. Our personalities, cultures, and societies reproduce and integrate themselves through the communicative interaction of members. Daily we take "yes" or "no" positions on criticizable claims to validity. So, our choice is either argumentation or the termination of our "membership in the community of beings who argue — no more and no less." Habermas reminds us that choosing the latter is only possible if we are ready to flee into suicide or serious mental illness. See Habermas, "Discourse Ethics," 93, 100.

30. Jürgen Habermas, *Postmetaphysical Thinking*, trans. William Mark Hohengarten (Cambridge: MIT Press, 1992), 35–36.

31. Habermas, "Philosophy as Stand-in and Interpreter," 14.

32. "Starting primarily from the intuitive knowledge of competent subjects — competent in terms of judgment, action, and language — and secondarily from systematic knowledge handed down by culture, the reconstructive sciences explain the presumably universal bases of rational experience and judgment, as well as of action and linguistic communication. . . . Fallibilistic in orientation, they reject the dubious faith in philosophy's ability to do things single-handedly, hoping instead that the success that has for so long eluded it might come from an auspicious matching of different theoretical fragments." Ibid., 15–16.

33. As Habermas explains: "To be sure, the intuitive knowledge of rules that subjects capable of speech and action must use if they are to be able to partici-

pate in argumentation is in a certain sense not fallible. But this is not true of *our reconstruction* of this pretheoretical knowledge and the claim to universality that we connect with it. The *certainty* with which we put our knowledge of rules into practice does not extend to the *truth* of proposed reconstructions of presuppositions hypothesized to be general, for we have to put our reconstructions up for discussion in the same way in which the logician or the linguist, for example, presents his theoretical descriptions." Habermas, "Discourse Ethics," 97.

34. Thus, I am puzzled by Shane Phelan's claim that Habermas "has not been able to subvert the charge that his claims are particular to a certain, modern Western, world." Habermas has not been able to subvert this charge because he accepts it. But it does not undercut the ideal of open, uncoerced communication. Nor does it suggest a "retreat" to rationalism as much as a renewed understanding of rationality in communicative terms. Moreover, Habermas meets Phelan's own criteria for serious consideration. She writes: "Those who have been ignored or degraded within the Western tradition may justly retain their skepticism toward those theorists . . . who do not specifically address the question of their inclusion." Habermas has written explicitly about the struggle for inclusion of women, homosexuals, people of color, and the colonized. See Phelan, *Identity Politics,* 148; and Jürgen Habermas, "Anerkennungskämpfe im demokratischen Rechsstaat," in *Multikulturalismus und die Politik der Anerkennung,* trans. Reinhard Kaiser (Frankfurt: S. Fischer Verlag, 1993), 147–196.

35. Thomas McCarthy, "Practical Discourse: On the Relation of Morality to Politics," in *Habermas and the Public Sphere,* ed. Calhoun, 55.

36. Seyla Benhabib, "In the Shadow of Aristotle and Hegel," in *Situating the Self,* 37.

37. Chantal Mouffe, "Democratic Politics Today," in *Dimensions of Radical Democracy,* ed. Mouffe, 13. Mouffe also mistakenly claims that Habermasian universalism is *grounded* on a stagist conception of moral development. As my account of rational reconstruction attests, however, developmental moral theories such as Kohlberg's do not ground discourse ethics; they provide independent corroboration and are themselves open for revision and critique.

38. Habermas, "Discourse Ethics," 66.

39. Jürgen Habermas, "Diskursethik—Notizen zu einem Begründungsprogramm," in *Moralbewusstsein und kommunikatives Handlen,* 113. (My translation.) See "Discourse Ethics," 103.

40. Jürgen Habermas, "Lawrence Kohlberg und der Neoaristotelismus," in *Erläuterungen zur Diskursethik* (Frankfurt: Suhrkamp Verlag, 1991), 97; and Habermas, "Individuierung durch Vergesellschaftung," in *Nachmetaphysisches Denken* (Frankfurt: Surhkamp Verlag, 1988), 191.

41. See Lutz Wingert, "Haben wir moralische Verpflichtungen gegenüber früheren Generationen? Moralischer Universalismus und erinnernde Solidarität," *Babylon* 9 (November 1991), 78–93.

42. Habermas, "Justice and Solidarity," 70.

43. Jürgen Habermas, "Morality and Ethical Life," in *Moral Consciousness and Communicative Action,* trans. Lenhardt and Nicholsen, 213; and "Justice and Solidarity," 45–47.

44. Habermas, "Justice and Solidarity," 47.

45. Habermas, "Morality and Ethical Life," 202.

46. Jürgen Habermas, *The Theory of Communicative Action, vol. 2, Lifeworld and System: The Critique of Functionalist Reason*, trans. Thomas McCarthy (Boston: Beacon Press, 1987), 93.

47. Ibid., 142–143.

48. "The processes of reaching understanding upon which the lifeworld is centered require a cultural tradition across the whole spectrum. In the communicative practice of everyday life, cognitive interpretations, moral expectations, expressions, and valuations have to interpenetrate and form a rational interconnectedness via the transfer of validity that is possible in the performative attitude," Ibid., 327.

49. Benhabib, "In the Shadow of Aristotle and Hegel," 37.

50. See Jürgen Habermas, "Volkssouveränität als Verfahren," in *Die Moderne — ein unvollendetes Projekt* (Leipzig: Reclam Verlag, 1990), 206.

51. Habermas, "Justice and Solidarity," 48.

52. Habermas, *Postmetaphysical Thinking*, 117.

53. Ibid., 143.

54. Ibid., 140.

55. As Habermas writes: "The transitory unity that is generated in the porous and refracted intersubjectivity of a linguistically mediated consensus not only supports but further accelerates the pluralization of forms of life and the individualization of lifestyles." Ibid., 140.

56. Benhabib, "The Generalized and the Concrete Other," note 12, 177, and "Models of Public Space," in *Situating the Self,* 89–93; Cohen and Arato, *Civil Society and Political Theory*, 688, note 27. Nancy Fraser has also accused Habermas of repeating the division between the public and private spheres in his system/ lifeworld distinction; Fraser, "What's Critical about Critical Theory?" in *Feminism as Critique*, ed. Benhabib and Cornell, 31–55. (For a thorough critique of this and other aspects of her argument, see Cohen and Arato, *Civil Society and Political Theory*, 532–548.) What I find strange about all of these arguments is that Habermas never claims to abandon a split between the public and private spheres. This distinction plays a role in his work from *The Structural Transformation of the Public Sphere* through *The Theory of Communicative Action*. Given that he already accepts this distinction, he has no need or reason to introduce it "covertly" via other sets of oppositions.

57. Benhabib, "Models of Public Space," 90–92.

58. Jürgen Habermas, "Vom pragmatischen, ethischen und moralischen Gebrauch der praktischen Vernunft," in *Erläuterungen zur Diskursethik*, 111–112.

59. See Jürgen Habermas, *Autonomy and Solidarity: Interviews*, ed. Peter Dews (London: Verso, 1986), 170.

60. Habermas, *Theory of Communicative Action*, vol. 2, 100.

61. Ibid., 35.

62. David Wiggins, "Universalizability, Impartiality, Truth," in *Needs, Values, Truth* (Oxford: Basil Blackwell, 1987), 82. See also Habermas, "Lawrence Kohlberg und der Neoaristotelismus," 95–96; and Günther, "Universalistische Normbegründung und Normanwendung," 8–9.

63. Habermas, "Erläuterungen zur Diskursethik," 143.

64. For an enlightening and entertaining discussion of the illusory neutrality of the word "man," see Janice Moulton, "The Myth of the Neutral 'Man,'" in *Women, Knowledge and Reality,* ed. Garry and Pearsall, 219–232. One of Moulton's best examples comes from her discussion of Bertrand Russell's paper, "On Denoting." She quotes Russell: "Suppose now we wish to interpret the proposition, 'I met a man.' If this is true, I met some definite man; but that is not what I affirm. What I affirm is, according to the theory I advocate: '"I met x and x is human" is not always false.'" "If Russell were correct," writes Moulton, "then parents familiar with his theory would have no cause for anxiety if their young female child, on arriving home several hours late from kindergarten said, 'I met a man.'" (226–227).

65. Trinh, *Framer Framed,* 169.

66. Williams, *The Alchemy of Race and Rights,* 73.

Index

Jodi Dean is Assistant Professor of Political Science at Hobart–William Smith Colleges. She is on the editorial boards of *Constellations* and *Philosophy and Social Criticism,* and is the editor of an anthology, *Resiting the Political: Feminism and the New Democracy.*

Compositor: Graphic Composition, Inc.
Text: 10/13 Galliard
Display: Galliard
Printer: Book Crafters
Binder: Book Crafters